RELATIONAL PSYCHOTHERAPY

A Primer

Patricia A. DeYoung

Brunner-Routledge
New York and Hove

Published in 2003 by
Brunner-Routledge
29 West 35th Street
New York, NY 10001
www.brunner-routledge.com

Published in Great Britain by
Brunner-Routledge
27 Church Road
Hove, East Sussex
BN3 2FA
www.brunner-routledge.co.uk

Brunner-Routledge is an imprint of the Taylor & Francis Group.
Printed in the United States of America on acid-free paper.

Cover design by Kimberly Glyder

10 9 8 7 6 5 4 3 2 1

Library of Congress Cataloging-in-Publication Data
   DeYoung, Patricia A., 1953–
      Relational psychotherapy : a primer / Patricia A. DeYoung.
         p. cm.
      Includes bibliographical references and index.
      ISBN 0-415-94432-5 — ISBN 0-415-94433-3 (pbk.)
         1. Interpersonal psychotherapy. 2. Interpersonal relations. 3. Psychotherapist
   and patient. I. Title.

RC489.I55 D495 2003
616.89'14–dc21

                                                                2002152051

CONTENTS

To Mary B. Greey

ACKNOWLEDGMENTS

This book wouldn't have seen the light of day without the editors at Brunner-Routledge. Bernadette Capelle was the first to take an interest, George Zimmar guided me toward a format that would work, and Shannon Vargo and Cindy Long suggested useful substantive and stylistic revisions. I'm grateful that the Brunner-Routledge team saw the value in what I had to say and helped me fashion an appropriate vehicle for it.

Graduates and students of the Toronto Institute of Relational Psychotherapy will recognize the book at once because the gist of it is what they have heard from me over the years. I owe them thanks for all the ways they taught me how to translate relational theory into language they could understand and use. I am also grateful to my colleagues, past and present, at TIRP: Louise Gamble, Rozanne Grimard, Mary Greey, Carl Moore, Jim Olthuis, Rita Fridella, and Catherine Comuzzi. Each of them has brought a unique, valuable perspective to the relational synthesis we have worked on together.

I have, of course, been a student of therapy myself. My understanding of self psychology has been deepened in supervision and study groups with Howard Bacal, Ellen Lewinberg, and Alan Kindler. A self psychological psychoanalysis with Sam Izenberg has taught me from the inside out what it's like to benefit from a relationship that's dedicated to the patient, thoughtful reworking of one's own organizing principles. Peer supervision groups have been another rich resource for learning how to put relational theory into practice. Thanks to the members of my current and longstanding group—Pat Archer, Midge Breslin, Judy Lester, Susan Marcus, Sonia Singer, and Lisa Walter—not only for what I've learned from them, but also for their gratifying enthusiasm about my book project.

Thanks, too, to members of another study/supervision group—Diane Johnson, Alisa Hornung, Harriet Tarshis, and Jan Turner—for their supportive, helpful response to an early version of the text.

My clients have taught me as much about relational therapy as anyone, for one by one they teach me how to be with them. I am grateful for all that we have discovered together, for shared journeys and projects completed well, and for permission to use some vignettes of that work. All of the longer case histories given are composites of many stories I've heard over the years—except for Lucy's story. She graciously gave me permission to use her story as I had written it, and I'm thankful for that and for what we accomplished together.

I owe special thanks to those colleagues and friends who read early versions of the manuscript with a critical eye and a willingness to challenge my ideas and agendas: psychotherapist readers Midge Breslin, Pat Archer, Sonia Singer, Susan Marcus, Mary Greey, Betty Kaser, and Cathy Schwartz, and writerly readers Adriel Weaver and Adrian and Johanna Peetoom.

I owe special thanks of another kind to Mary Greey, who has been not only a TIRP colleague and a careful reader of early versions of the text, but also a loving partner who has welcomed the presence of this book in our daily lives. Her unshakable confidence in me helped me keep the faith in difficult times, and her good-natured support made it all so much easier than it might have been.

Pat DeYoung
Toronto
September, 2002

INTRODUCTION

In a small, quiet, simply furnished room, two people sit facing one another. One of them talks as the other listens. The one who is talking looks tense and anxious as she tries to explain the trouble to the one who is listening. When tears spring to her eyes, she dabs at them with a crumpled tissue. The listener puts a box of tissues within the speaker's reach and continues to listen without interrupting her.

These two people will be here together for exactly 50 minutes. Both of them hope that by the end of that time, the listener will have been able to offer meaningful help to the one in distress. They will meet again next week at the same time for another 50 minutes, because the trouble is complicated and the help isn't a quick fix.

You are the one who sits and listens. You are the psychotherapist. One hour at a time, one person at a time, you listen to the trouble people have living their lives. You hear about what goes wrong, and you hear about how anxious, frustrated, and depressed they feel. They confess to you the self-destructive patterns they've fallen into as they've tried to do the best they can. They're stuck. They're at the end of their rope. They're in pain. You listen to them one by one, and every hour you think hard: What meaningful help can I offer this person?

Every time you answer that question, every time you offer a comment, a suggestion, or an intervention, you do so with conscious or subliminal reference to a theory of how psychotherapy works. The theory to which you refer will give you some kind of conceptual filter for understanding what's wrong in the picture, and it will give you a matching set of ideas about what needs to change if this person is to feel better. The theory will also guide you, the therapist, to make certain moves to facilitate those necessary changes.

Some general theories of psychotherapy—psychodynamic, feminist, solution-focused, or cognitive-behavioral therapies, for example—view many kinds of psychological problems through the same lens of assessment and treatment. Other more specific theories of psychotherapy have been developed in response to specific problems, such as phobias or eating disorders. Most experienced therapists work from a general theory of psychotherapy, and then they integrate this general theory with various specific theories that they have found useful with different kinds of client problems. In other words, most therapists identify as a certain kind of therapist (psychodynamic or feminist, for example), and they are also eclectic in the best sense of the word: they choose approaches carefully from diverse sources—because they want the best outcomes for their clients.

This book puts forward a general theory of psychotherapy, a theory I call *relational psychotherapy*. It's not entirely new, for its roots are in psychodynamic and humanist therapies that have been around for many years. It also owes a lot to feminist theories about a fundamentally relational self. But at the same time, relational psychotherapy, understood in its own terms, is a new phenomenon. Over the last 15 years, a relational perspective has opened up new vistas for psychoanalytic theory. And of course analysts aren't the only therapists who read psychoanalytic theory. Through books, journals, and conferences, by way of therapist training institutes and informal supervision and reading groups, relational theory has become a powerful force on the psychotherapy scene in North America.

There are very good reasons for the strength of this new movement: First, relational theory is a powerful and useful general theory of psychotherapy; second, a relational approach provides a strong foundation for responsible, coherent eclecticism; and third, relational psychotherapy is a reasonable and flexible alternative to goal-oriented, authority-driven models of psychotherapy.

Relational psychotherapy is a model driven by the client's experience and the client's needs. It pays close attention to how those needs are understood and addressed within the therapy relationship. The relational therapist tunes in very carefully to all of the client's experience, and especially to the client's ongoing, moment-to-moment, and cumulative experience of the therapy. Since relational psychotherapy is so client-centered and experience-near, I have written this primer of relational psychotherapy in a way that tracks very closely a client's experience of relational psychotherapy. Since a relational therapist is always personally engaged in the process of therapy, I will speak to you, the (would-be) relational therapist, with as much immediacy and personal presence as a written text allows.

THE BOOK: AN OVERVIEW

The chapters of this book are laid out in a sequence that mirrors a client's deepening involvement in the therapy process. Chapter 1 responds to a question a client might ask before beginning therapy with you: What's unique about relational therapy? or, What does it offer that other therapies don't? The chapter is a useful resource when clients come from other kinds of therapies or are "shopping" and asking you questions, hoping to understand where relational therapy fits in the spectrum of treatment possibilities.

Even if clients don't ask about your theoretical orientation—and most don't—they pick up on your confidence in your own way of working. Confidence comes from experience, but it also comes from knowing where you stand and what you think. While this entire book is intended to help you develop your thinking about relational therapy, Chapter 1 will give you a sense of where a relational therapist stands in relation to other therapists. In the chapter, after I sketch the primary themes of relational therapy, I compare and contrast various contemporary theories of psychotherapy from this vantage point, this relational point of view. This point of view, which the book will develop, is not the property of one school of therapy. Relational theory is spoken in many voices. What I present is a working synthesis of several relational theories, a relational eclecticism. In the last part of Chapter 1, therefore, I review the several sources that contribute to the case I make for a dynamic, creative relational therapy.

Chapter 2 begins with the assumption that the client has decided to give you a try. I pursue the question: At the beginning of every course of therapy, what do you, the therapist, need to know and communicate about the structure, boundaries, and ethics of relational therapy? The next question is: What can clients expect will happen when they show up for sessions, and what can they hope for as therapy progresses? To these two basic questions about how the therapy will be done, I propose the basic answer of *empathy*. As a relational therapist, you will not predict any particular course or outcome of therapy, but you will demonstrate your commitment to understanding the client on her own terms. You will stay as close as possible to what she says about her own experience, and you will do whatever you can to enter into the feeling of that experience and to communicate your empathy to her in ways that let her know you *get* it.

Empathy is such an apparently simple medium and method that clients are often nonplussed in its presence, at least at first. Often they want more direct intervention in what they perceive is going wrong for them. They wonder, How can just "being understood" ever help? But your active, inquiring, supportive empathy only seems to be a simple process. And your clients soon begin to feel its effects. In this second chapter, I explore in depth what empathy is, how it works in relational therapy, and how it provides a broad, sturdy base for more specific kinds of interventions.

Chapter 3 addresses the question of assessment. As your client tells you the story of his trouble, how will you pin down the essence of what's wrong for him? This is a critical question, of course, because providing accurate help depends on making an accurate assessment of what's wrong. Here I begin to spell out one of the basic tenets of relational psychotherapy: what's wrong is neither entirely inside the client, in his psychological makeup or dysfunctional patterns, nor entirely outside in the world, in forces that impinge on him. Instead, according to a relational model of psychotherapy, the problem exists in those spaces or activities where outside influences and inside responses interact to create the shape and feel of a "self." I explain how patterns of interaction between self and others become principles that organize a personal psychology, and I show how these patterns very quickly become woven into interactions between therapist and client. Noticing these patterns as they emerge between you and your client is fundamental to a relational assessment of what's wrong for him.

It's not easy, even as a relational therapist, to hold in mind this definition of what's wrong, or of "pathology"—that it is a function of the ongoing interaction of inside and outside. But clients are even more likely to slip into the assumption that what's wrong has to be something defective inside themselves, unless it is the direct result of abuse or persecution—in other words, that they must be either sick or victims. Chapter 3 opens up the possibility of a third way to think about what's wrong, one that slowly but surely can begin to make sense to your client.

In Chapter 4 I take up an important issue that can't be avoided once organizing principles are on the table, the issue of the relationship between past and present, especially a traumatic past and the work of healing in the present. Those principles that organize a client's sense of self-in-relation came into being over time and in certain relational contexts. Most often, clients who work the longest and most intensely in therapy are those who are struggling to recover from the imprint of relational trauma that they suffered early in their lives. For many of them, painful early relationships included significant neglect and physical or sexual abuse. They may not know that this is what's hurting them. More likely they do make some connection between past and present because ideas about traumatic childhood abuse, repressed memories, and recovered memories have become commonplace in popular culture.

What remains very unclear, though, in media stories of abuse and recovery and in clients' understanding of their own histories, is how the past remains alive in the present. Nor is it clear how certain kinds of experiences in the present can reduce the power of the past to undermine the client's current well-being. Confused clients wonder, "Do I have to recover repressed memories in order to feel better?" "Are certain kinds of memories especially important to remember?" "Do I have to feel all that pain all over again?" "How does remembering the past help me feel better now?"

I address these questions by presenting a relational definition of trauma, one closely connected to the idea of psychological organizing principles. I maintain that specific traumatic events, however damaging, are far less powerful than the ongoing traumatic relationships in which those events are usually embedded. Reliving with a therapist the impossible binds of traumatic relationship can be the most powerful way of remembering, and this kind of remembering often makes "video" memory of specific events unnecessary. While emotional release or catharsis may be part of the work, it isn't what heals; what matters most is the consistent, caring presence of someone who hears and understands the client's pain. Finally, Chapter 4 shows how reliving the past as a here-and-now relational struggle can lead to important changes in the principles that organize a client's everyday self-with-other experience.

Reliving the past as a here-and-now relational struggle is what traditional psychodynamic therapy calls transference, and more specifically, negative transference. Chapter 5 is about so-called negative transference. I call it "the terribly hard part of relational therapy"—because that's what it is, both for you and your clients. As clients share themselves with you more deeply, they hope that you will understand them ever more deeply and completely. But at the same time, their painful relational history leads them to expect that you will fail them, judge them, and abandon them. And inevitably, in small ways at least, you do fail them. Then, suddenly and often subtly, a client's common, self-defining experience of being discounted and demeaned is happening with you. Your lapses of attention may communicate that you don't care at all. Your inevitable small mistakes are deeply wounding. These moments of misunderstanding rupture the relationship, and repairing the ruptures takes careful empathic work to understand how things went wrong between you and the client.

Some clients can go through repeated ruptures and repairs without needing to see a larger picture of what's happening. But many are frightened and ashamed of being so easily and profoundly hurt by their therapist's lapses. If you can explain what's happening in a way that validates their acute need to be understood and that makes their painful interpersonal feelings an issue of the therapy relationship, you can support and steady them through these difficult times. At the same time, in your role as therapist, you need some support and steadying too. Feeling deeply mistrusted makes even the most committed relational therapist want to pull back from a relationship. Withdrawing, however, even withdrawing to explain, is a critical mistake, for it leaves your client feeling abandoned and punished for having painful feelings. Explaining helps, but staying present and empathic helps most.

How can you manage to stay involved, and with such a mess? How can I manage to write a chapter that stays with this messiness—these complex, painful realities of this aspect of relational therapy? As fate or luck would have it, when I came to write Chapter 5, I had just fallen into trouble with my own relational analyst, so I wrote from a client's perspective about the terribly hard part of relational therapy. I kept this account in the chapter because I could think of no better way to connect the chapter firmly to a client's experience of negative transference. This, I thought, will keep our discussion of transference from withdrawing into the safety of theory.

As a relational therapist, you simply must understand how frightening, wounding, enraging, and disheartening therapy can be for clients when the therapy relationship feels a familiar kind of bad to them. You must understand this, for if you don't, the therapy will fall apart. You have to be able to feel how difficult it is for clients just to keep coming and talking about all this disturbance and pain with the very person who's making them feel so bad. To be able to do that, they have to be absolutely sure that this is what you want—to understand *their* feelings in this mess—and that you are determined to listen to them without getting defensive and blaming them.

But what if, in the face of mistrust and bitterness, your own hurt and disappointment show? What if you do get defensive and lose your empathic perspective? It's inevitable that this will happen to you sometimes. What's important is what you do after this happens, because if you don't catch yourself (with help in supervision), there is a real danger that the relationship will spiral downward into an angry, despairing standoff. In Chapter 5 I discuss how to regain your balance in this difficult work, about how to catch those downward spirals before they get out of hand. As other relational theorists do, I maintain that even tough impasses do not have to remain impossible in relational therapy. On the contrary, working through a relational impasse is often the most powerful, effective work you can do.

In the closing example of Chapter 5, my client and I are struggling to repair a rupture between us. Here, too, it's clear that we've stumbled into this trouble together because of what we each bring to the situation, because of the ways in which we are each doing the best we can. Neither of us is at fault for our feelings. Once again I emphasize the humanness and vulnerability of both partners in the therapy relationship as they try to work out troubles between them with openness, courage, and good faith.

In Chapter 6, I move from what's very hard about relational therapy to what's very good about it. The chapter is about the everyday health and well-being that relational therapy envisions for its clients, and about how the therapy process begins to make this well-being possible—through subtle but profound changes in how clients can experience themselves with others. I briefly introduce models of development that give us language for these changes: changes in what Kohut calls selfobject experiences, Stern calls RIGs, Bowlby calls working models of attachment, Lichtenberg calls motivational systems, and the Stone Center writers call capacities for connection. I don't make a special case for any one of these explanatory systems. Over against nonrelational models of human development, they seem quite similar and mutually complementary. They all envision psychological health and well-being as products of healthy relationships from infancy onward. Within any one of these systems, dependency can be redefined as your clients' ways of connecting with you, particular kinds of connection that help them grow stronger and more connected to others and to themselves.

Chapter 7 describes how relational therapy ends. But first I address how the changes that begin in the relationship between you and your client become a solid, reliable part of the client's ongoing experience of self with others. Relational therapy doesn't make clients invulnerable to further pain, but it does give them a firm grasp of where their vulnerabilities are, and of how to protect themselves as necessary, express themselves with trustworthy others, and work through injuries and misunderstandings to resolutions of mutual benefit. As therapy winds down, clients won't be happy all the time, but on the other hand, they won't always be expecting the worst and believing that they bring it on themselves. Their deepened capacity for being understood and for understanding others will support more interpersonal ease and security, and that, in turn, will bolster their confidence and support their ideals and ambitions. When all of this is true, clients are ready to let the therapy relationship become memory—an experience that lives within them as possibilities for new kinds of being and being-with.

In terminating therapy, as you and your client review the journey together, you will notice how profoundly the relationship between you has changed. Mutual respect and trust will have grown and deepened between you. So it happens that ending relational therapy becomes something more than ending a treatment process. The end of relational therapy means that there must be a good-bye spoken between persons who have come to mean something to one another. Your client will need time and space to feel this good-bye deeply, to grieve the loss of the relationship, and to sense how it will continue as memory. The two of you can end, however, with the confidence that the changes begun in therapy will continue to ripple outward in liberating and transforming ways. Thus a good ending can become a good beginning for a new phase in your client's life.

And there in brief, from beginnings to endings, is the story this book tells about how relational psychotherapy works. Before I expand on that story, however, I have two more introductory things to say. The first is about identifying the clients who need and get the most out of relational therapy. The second is about identifying the therapists who are best suited to this kind of work.

WHO NEEDS RELATIONAL THERAPY?

I've said that relational psychotherapy is a general theory of therapy that works well across a wide range of client problems. According to relational theory, this is true because very many so-called psychological difficulties are rooted in relationship, both problematic current relationships and old relationships that still have powerful effects on a client's everyday well-being. Psychotherapists of many persuasions have discovered, however, that psychological problems can be treated as if they are an individual's internal problems or, to put it another way, an individual's problems with dysfunctional patterns of feeling, thought, and behavior. From a relational perspective, this kind of treatment addresses only the symptoms of problems that are rooted in relationship—and yet it is often quite effective. How can this be?

For many clients the experience of sharing their troubles and finding a wise and helpful guide is itself a powerful relational reorientation: they're not sick or crazy in comparison to everyone else in the world, their trouble makes sense to another person, and this person wants and offers to help. In other words, the treatment, though not relational by definition, is itself a positive relational experience and changes something about what clients can expect from their relational world. Furthermore, when clients change some patterns of thought and behavior that leave them disempowered and depressed, they change—even if inadvertently—some patterns of interacting with others. From a relational perspective, these more positive and efficacious interactions have as much (or more) to do with the client's improvement than the so-called internal or individual changes the client has made. A relational perspective also explains why clients such as these don't need a specifically relational approach. It sees them as relatively healthy: even as they come for help, these clients are living within a sense of self-with-other that is relatively flexible and open to change. That is why they can receive new kinds of interpersonal help and try new kinds of interpersonal interactions. They don't need a specifically relational therapy in order to make relational change possible.

Other clients aren't so fortunate. They live within a much more dangerous self-with-other world, though very often they don't know that this is the case. They know about their symptoms, their specific fears, anxious behaviors, and addictions. They usually know about constant, insidious bad feelings about themselves, feelings of incompetence, social anxiety, depression, and shame. They may have tried self-help books, self-improvement programs, and often a course or two of therapy, but nothing much has changed for them over the long term. They suspect that maybe nothing can change for them. And yet their unhappiness draws them back to therapy, for it seems clear to them that there's some kind of psychological problem going on. Maybe, then, there could be some kind of help after all.

When you hear a story like this, with or without a history of unsuccessful previous therapy, you are probably listening to a client who could make good use of intensive, specifically relational therapy. What's gone wrong before, you might guess, is that her self-help and self-improvement efforts have done nothing to change what she can expect from the world. The self-with-other world she lives within keeps on telling her that she's defective, she's not trying hard enough, or she's bound to fail, and this self-with-other given, though mostly unconscious, is far from flexible and open. In fact, this client's relational expectations and relational self-protections are quite rigid and closed to outside influence. This means, for example, that whether she knows it or not, she can't help but see you as one more person who will judge her, feel disgust about her feelings and needs, and ask things of her she can't produce. Your kindness and good intentions may barely register in the face of her convictions. Unless you and she can find ways to address these relational problems between you, therapy will become for her just one more round of self-protection, compliance, and secret shame. On the other hand, if you can address these problems and so make way for new kinds of interactions between you, therapy can become a matrix for powerful and long-lasting change.

Sometimes these clients who have already worked hard to change themselves will ask, "How do you think you can help me?" That's a difficult question to deal with because although you want to give an honest answer, you don't want to say something that will make the situation seem even more threatening. Clients who are relationally vulnerable protect themselves as best they can from knowing the extent of their vulnerabilities. As a relational therapist, you know that they will come to trust you only insofar as you respect and understand these vulnerabilities. You know that this long, slow interaction of understanding and trust will take time, lots of time. You also know that these clients would rather locate their trouble inside themselves than in their relationships with others, for they know "for sure" that what they can get from the world can't be changed. The best they can ever do, therefore, is change themselves. Furthermore, the last thing they can bear to imagine is trouble between themselves and their therapist, because experience tells them that in any conflict, the more powerful person will blame, shame, and emotionally annihilate the less powerful person.

All that being said, there are some simple ways to talk with a client about the essence and advantages of a specifically relational course of psychotherapy. Often I say something like this:

I'm a relational therapist. So while I know that you feel bad inside, I also see that a lot of those bad feelings—worry, low self-esteem, fear of failing—exist at the boundary or interface where you meet the world. They're relational feelings as well as self-feelings. They sound like: "Am I good enough? Have I made a mistake in their eyes? Do they like me? Am I in trouble?" When you feel that the answers to those questions are negative, then you feel badly about yourself, in yourself. It seems to me that even when you're not thinking about it, you live with a lot of negative answers to those relational questions. And I think that's been true for quite a while, and it has worn you down.

In relational psychotherapy, we spend a lot of time on those relational feelings. They turn up in three main ways. First, there are your daily relationships with your family, friends, and co-workers. We'll look at what happens in those interactions that leaves you feeling badly about yourself. You might begin to notice patterns there that make you think of earlier relationships in your life. That would be the second way relational feelings would turn up in therapy. When those early relationships come to your mind, we will talk about how they told you who you are, what you're worth, and what you can get from life. Those early relationships can leave you with a powerful script about what you can expect even now. The third kind of relationship we'll keep in mind is the one between you and me, how you and I are working together. It will be especially important to notice if I'm misunderstanding you or if it feels to you that this therapy is becoming my agenda, not yours.

What I don't say in this answer, because my client probably won't understand what I mean, is that this is how relational psychotherapy proposes to "make the unconscious conscious." It's worth saying here, though, because it bears on the question at hand: Who needs relational psychotherapy? The succinct, technical answer is: Relational psychotherapy is especially good for those people who, in order to lead lives of relative well-being, need to be released from the bonds of punitive, constricting unconscious organizing principles. In this view, a view developed within relational and intersubjectivist theories of psychoanalysis, the unconscious isn't a place or a thing; it's a self-perpetuating patterning or organizing of self-in-relationship that remains out of a person's awareness but shapes all of his self-experience.

This is not the traditional psychoanalytic theory of the unconscious; and yet, in the case I'm making here, relational therapy takes a position that has traditionally been reserved for psychoanalysis. Just as traditional psychoanalysis has been proposed as a treatment that probes for the un-conscious conflicts that cause tenacious psychological symptoms, symp-toms that can't be undone in any simpler, quicker way, so relational psychotherapy proposes relational treatment as a way to bring to light the unconscious relational patterns that underlie tenacious psychological symptoms, symptoms that don't give way in shorter-term, more goal-ori-ented psychotherapies.

In simple terms, then, the question of whether a particular client might need a specifically relational approach comes down to questions such as the following: How longstanding is this trouble? How tenacious? How thoroughly does it permeate the client's experience? How deeply does it threaten the client's sense of being a cohesive, worthy self? In short, How bad is it? If it's pretty bad, a relational therapist will begin contemplating a longer term, intensive relational approach to therapy.

But let's not forget that a relational therapist envisions most psycho-logical difficulties as symptoms of conflictual and disconnected relation-ships with others and with oneself. As such a therapist, you take a relational approach in all of your work. So when you begin to think that intensive relational therapy might be especially useful for a particular client, you're thinking not of a different approach to this client, but of attending even more carefully and specifically to the client's relational history and rela-tional struggles and of focusing the therapy as explicitly as possible on the patterns that develop within the client–therapist relationship. Very often, with a client in this group, a more intensive relational treatment emerges organically from your general relational approach to the prob-lems the client brings. That kind of development serves you both well, for the client has time to test your integrity, and you have time to dis-cover something about how the relationship sets itself up between you.

Not everyone who comes to therapy and who could profit from an intensive relational approach has the patience or interest to do the work. On the other hand, sometimes the most unlikely candidates settle in for the long haul, if only out of desperation. I think that any client who can allow himself to want or need something from you in the therapy rela-tionship can be a candidate for relational therapy. No matter how con-flicted the want or how muted the need, if the client has invested some personal passion to be understood and you can meet that need with personal, responsive presence, the therapy relationship can begin to form and move. Eventually the client will need to be able to reflect somewhat on what goes on between you, but that's a capacity that can be developed as the therapy progresses.

WHO MAKES A GOOD RELATIONAL THERAPIST?

Relational psychotherapy isn't for every client, and it certainly isn't for every therapist, either. Often, therapists who are drawn to relational work have come from families of origin in which relationships were tense, conflictual, and unrewarding, and they're likely to have carried away from that formative familial experience a certain combination of characteristics: (1) a profound longing for relationship that is meaningful and supportive; (2) a sense of responsibility for supporting fragile, unhappy family members, especially unhappy parents; and (3) personal psychological organizing principles that leave them with a somewhat fragmented, precarious, or depleted sense of self. In other words, therapists drawn to relational work are often first of all very good candidates for relational therapy themselves. In fact, if they do not do their own therapy first, to bring to awareness the principles that organize their own experience, therapists who come from such families are likely to repeat their histories in their work—feeling at first both stimulated and overwhelmed by responsibility and then fragmented or depleted as they lose themselves in their efforts to help.

On the other hand, therapists who have come to terms with their own relational history, however traumatic it might have been, don't have to keep repeating that history in their personal or professional lives. They've discovered that it's possible to develop new ways of being with others in the world, ways that leave them feeling much more whole, alive, and secure in themselves. If they're drawn to learning and practicing relational therapy, no doubt they have experienced the relationship with their own therapist as the transformative element of therapy. They know what a difference it makes to be understood deeply and consistently in their own terms. They didn't enjoy living through repetitions of their worst fears with their therapist, but on the other hand, they found that coming out the other side into a relationship of open trust was profoundly liberating. They know about slow, quiet movement from anxiety to contentment, from insecurity to confidence, from low-grade, isolating depression to vital engagement with other people. Like all those who have known life-changing experiences, therapists whose self-experience has been changed by relational therapy want to share what they've learned with others in need.

I imagine that you recognize something of yourself in this picture. (After all, you are reading this book.) But you might still ask, "What does it take to practice relational psychotherapy for 20 or 30 years?" It takes the passion for the healing power of relationship that I've just described. But like any other profession, it also requires specific traits of mind and personality. If you enjoy being a relational therapist, you enjoy entering into the stories of people's lives. Those stories aren't always pleasant, but you find them meaningful, like powerful dramas or novels. You ponder meanings and consider connections between things carefully. You are able to feel your own feelings deeply, and you're not afraid of your clients' strong feelings. You're good at pattern recognition, and also at putting complicated ideas into simple, evocative language. You can think on your feet and take quick, considered risks, but you're not impulsive or reactive. You understand and manage your own emotions well. You can sit quietly for long periods of time, and you have an abundance of patience with long, slow processes. You are able to balance your life: for all the time you spend listening and caring, you spend plenty of other time being active, self-expressive, and connected to others in ways that excite and nurture you.

Those personal characteristics don't come together into a professional self, a relational therapist self, without specific training in relational psychotherapy, training that includes both book learning and practical learning from closely supervised work with clients. And though you may be exquisitely well-suited for the work and quite well-trained, you won't thrive for 20 or 30 years in a relational therapy practice without a strong community of peers with whom you can continue to grow and learn.

You may have noticed that I haven't mentioned whether you're a social worker, an educator, a psychiatric nurse, a family doctor who practices psychotherapy, a pastoral counselor, a psychiatrist, or someone trained exclusively in psychotherapy. I haven't distinguished between agency or hospital work and work in private practice. This is because I believe it's possible for relational therapy to be done by persons in many professions and settings. It's a portable model with significant efficacy even in those settings that restrict the number of sessions available to a client. The most amenable, comfortable setting for relational psychotherapy may be the office of a relational psychoanalyst, but that doesn't mean that relational psychoanalysis is the benchmark for relational therapy. In fact, many relational analysts no longer make a sharp distinction between analysis (on the couch, several times a week) and therapy (face to face, once or twice a week), as long as that therapy moves toward nondirective exploration of the patient's unconscious patterns of experience, especially as those patterns emerge in the client–therapist transference.

As you'll see, the relational theory I'm about to explore with you is informed and influenced by relational psychoanalytic theory. But I'm not writing to psychoanalysts. As I've mentioned, a wealth of relational psychoanalytic theory has appeared in the last decade or so; relational psychoanalysts have plenty to read. I'm writing to the rest of us, who want to learn how to put this wealth of insight to work in a nonanalytic psychotherapy practice.

One final note: since I identify with lay psychotherapists in a non-medical tradition of therapy, I have always spoken of the people I work with as clients, not patients. But I trust that if "patient" is the word that works for you, you'll make the translation for yourself.

1

— ⁃ —

RELATIONAL THERAPY
AND ITS CONTEXTS

In this chapter, I'll outline the most fundamental characteristics of relational psychotherapy: it's about self-with-other, and it's about how self-with-other experience is a constant, active force in anyone's life. Then I'll expand on what this means by explaining what relational therapy is not. It's not a medical model of psychotherapy, not an individualistic model, and not a rationalistic model. When I've outlined the essence of relational psychotherapy in these ways, I will compare and contrast it with other current models of psychotherapy. Finally I will introduce several relational theories of psychoanalysis and psychotherapy that converge within what I'm presenting as relational psychotherapy.

This first chapter operates on the premise that if you want to understand what relational therapy is, you not only need a basic definition of it, you also have to refer to the contexts that give the definition its meaning. In the same way, if you want to know where you stand as a relational therapist, it's important to know not only the essence of your ideas, but also where those ideas situate you in relation to other therapists. This chapter aims to help you recognize where you will find yourself if you choose to practice relational psychotherapy.

IT'S ABOUT SELF-WITH-OTHER

First of all, relational therapy is all about self-with-other. This self-with-other focus means that whatever the stories a client tells in therapy, from the distant past or from yesterday, the therapist tries to understand them in terms of what was going on between the client and others. As a rela-

1

tional therapist, you think of your client's history as a relational history. You know that without a context of others within which to be born, none of us has a personal history. You work with the relational principle that we are all creatures of social, political, and familial contexts—that we are always being formed by our interactions with others and by how we learn to perform "self" in the various contexts of our lives.

So when a client tells you a story as if there were no other people in it—last night he was desperately trying to finish a project without falling into his private pitfalls of perfectionism and procrastination—you know how thickly populated that scene really is. You know that just out of his awareness, there's how hard it is to please his father, and how his mother is on another planet, no help at all, and how his older sister can do whatever she sets her mind to. You keep the relational story in mind. It's as true for him today as it was 20 years ago, though different actors (a boss, a wife, a colleague) may be playing the main characters.

You know that public school taught all the kids of his generation that grades mattered more than the pleasure of exploration, and that as a middle-class North American he believes that individual accomplishment is the mark of a successful life. But as far as he knows, working hard to finish his project, this is just his internal, individual struggle to dodge inevitable failure. As a relational therapist, you swim against this stream of "isolated self." You nudge your client to explore how difficult expectations and painful interactions, past and present, engender his bad feelings and his paralysis. Likewise, when he feels good, you notice with him the signs of a supportive, enlivening relational environment.

As a relational therapist, you take a self-with-other view of the stories your clients tell, but that's not all. You also believe that whatever happens in a therapy session can be understood as a self-with-other story. Almost every interaction between your client and yourself puts into play some kind of interactional pattern.

Another of your clients might feel, for example, that she has to say and do certain kinds of things to make this "good" therapy. So she tries hard to bring up important events to talk about, she concentrates on feeling her feelings authentically, and she recounts insights she's had over the week. You sense how hard she's working to please you, and you don't deny her your positive feedback, but at the same time you focus on understanding exactly what she's thinking and feeling as she talks with you. Bit by bit, she begins to grasp that you are less interested in her doing therapy "right" than in understanding her reality in depth. As she experiences your understanding, being understood begins to matter more to her than your approval. A particular self-with-other meaning she carries around—that only her performance matters to others—begins to be undermined gently. All of this is important relational work, though not a word has been spoken directly about it.

After a while, your client does say something about this shift, this different way of being with you, and you meet her with words that recognize and fit what she's trying to say. This is a relational interpretation, particularly helpful because it emerges as a shared discovery. It's also one of those insights that have the most power to change things for your client because it involves and changes the relationship between the two of you. It's likely that when you and your client talk about this pattern and how it's changing, she will make connections to present relationships in her life, where this pattern remains powerful, and to past relationships in her life, where this self-with-other pattern first took shape for her. In this way, the two of you will be able to link a relational story of her life, past and present, with the relational story that develops between you.

Learning happens as things change between you and your client, and although it need not always be put into words, words can make the learning more real. Talking about history, making connections, talking about both old and new experiences in therapy, tracking the shifts between them, exploring how the new way works—all of this—helps your client. In all of this you remain careful not to be a therapist who *knows*, or who sees what's *really* going on. You signal to your client that you don't possess the truth about her; instead, the two of you are figuring things out between you as you go along. This stance may have felt strange to her at first, when she came in seeking an authority to guide her. But you continue to invite and encourage her into collaboration. For her, it's the very activity of collaboration that creates a new self-with-other experience. Now you are doing something different with her than was possible when she first came in; something different is happening.

IT'S ABOUT SELF-WITH-OTHER IN ACTION

This emphasis on doing something different is the second essential characteristic of relational therapy. This relational therapy, which is all about self-with-other, is also by nature a performative therapy. I don't mean by this that the therapy is a performance. I mean that the material with which therapy works and the changes that therapy sets in motion can all be found in the various kinds of *doing*—actions, thoughts, words, silences, feelings—that exist and play out between self and others.

Thus, from a relational perspective on therapy, particular insights ("my family history formed me in this way," "these are my self-defeating patterns," and so forth) have no power to change anything for a client unless they are performative insights, or insights that are intimately connected to interactive, emotional experience. The essence of therapy isn't in insight or interpretation—those ideas that you and your client figure out together. It's in everything that you and your client do together—how you interact to construct ideas, how those meanings move both of you, and how your interactions change over time, especially when you reflect on what goes on between you.

In this model, you can't be an expert observing your client from an objective place outside of the relational story the two of you will play out together. You have to enter right into the story, knowing full well that relational problems and impossibilities are going to turn up, and intending to work through those difficulties to make a better relationship possible. You're there to help your client understand herself; this is not your therapy. But still, there's no way you can keep yourself safely outside of the relationship and also be a full participant in it.

It's also clear that in this model the client is not the problem. Above all, the problem is not just *inside* the client. You and your client will discover how the interactive performance of his self-with-other knowledge sends him off the rails over and over again, wrecking his well-being and self-esteem. Sometimes you will have your part in sending him off the rails, but if you both pay close attention to how it unfolds and repeats itself, together you can find a way to perform your interactions differently. Whatever keeps going wrong will turn into a story you can tell together, and then there will be a way to bring a new story into being. In other words, although working it out may well involve important new understandings, things will change when the two of you can *do* your relationship in a significantly different way. That's a performative therapy.

These, then, are the two most important characteristics of relational psychotherapy: its focus on self-with-other experience and its emphasis that the doing of such experience is what both hurts and heals. In these two ways, it's different from many other kinds of therapies. It's possible to explain that difference in negative terms, too, which is what I'll do now, very briefly: (1) relational therapy isn't a medical model of therapy; (2) relational therapy doesn't hold an individualistic view of the client; and (3) relational therapy doesn't give rational, linear, cause-and-effect explanations of how change happens.

NOT A MEDICAL MODEL

Most people go to therapy because they are suffering some kind of emotional pain, and they hope that an expert, a "doctor," will make the pain go away. When clients come to you seeking such relief, you take them seriously, but you also gently disappoint their expectation of a cure administered by an expert. As a relational therapist, you offer them a different kind of experience. You say, "I don't believe I have the answers for you, but I do want to understand what the trouble is for you, how it feels to you." You move away from the position of expert in order to put yourself on the client's side. It's a calculated risk (will he leave therapy?), but it's a risk you believe in taking.

Any client who is suffering enough to search out a therapist feels isolated in his pain and at a loss to understand it. Beneath his desperation for immediate relief, there lies a profound, often inarticulate longing to be understood, not to feel so all alone. As you work to understand exactly what he is saying, his troubled thoughts and feelings, he may be able to let go of his hope of being quickly "fixed." Why? Perhaps because he senses that "fixing" isn't what he needs after all. Being understood in depth and in detail soothes his feelings of hopelessness and powerlessness. As he "makes sense" to you, he starts to feel stronger. He feels some hope just because you have listened with respect and care. Your risk is beginning to pay off.

What you hope for over the long term is that he will come to understand that what causes his distress isn't a kind of defect or illness inside of him. Instead it has a lot to do with feeling all alone and making sense to no one, experiences he has suffered over and over in his life. What therapy offers isn't a doctor to cure him but a fellow human being who will understand his longings, losses, hopes, and fears, someone who will engage with him as he struggles to work out a happier, healthier way of being with others in the world.

NOT INDIVIDUALISM

As a relational therapist, you don't take on the job of "fixer." You also refuse to see your clients as self-contained, individual objects that need fixing. You make that refusal every time you try to find out what happened between a client and somebody else that left the client feeling so bad. You make that refusal when you immerse yourself in your client's world of experience and when you acknowledge that your own behavior can have a profound effect on a client's well-being. Those kinds of refusals are a part of refusing to practice an individualistic model of psychotherapy.

I've said that relational therapy is all about self-with-other experience. That's in sharp contrast to more individualistic views of therapy. Relational therapy debunks the myth that each of us is responsible for our own happiness, that somehow we can each find a way to hold our self in well-being. It undercuts the belief that mental health is something we individually have and enjoy—or we don't. It cuts across the assumption that our individual histories are bottled up inside each of us, and that it's just those old feelings that make us feel badly here and now. It doesn't buy that if we'd just work on ourselves, we could manage to claim our power, increase our self-esteem, and improve our confidence. It doesn't promise the North American dream of self-fulfillment, self-authentication, or the autonomous, self-responsible, fully realized individual who is evolved and conscious. It doesn't believe in self-help.

As a relational therapist, you suggest to your clients that, on the contrary, they can't feel good by themselves or better on their own. You encourage and support your clients' connections with others, and you struggle with your clients for more authentic, complex, and rewarding relationship in the therapy itself. You do this because you believe that an individual can feel genuine power, agency, and well-being only in the context of healthy interpersonal connection.

NOT RATIONALISM

It's not surprising, then, that relational psychotherapy also takes a turn away from rationalism. Most Western ways of thought begin not just with the individual, but with the individual mind, with Descartes' "I think, therefore I am." The mind establishes and validates reality, and it does so through logical processes. Psychoanalysis and psychotherapy have lived firmly within this tradition since the time of Freud. Freud saw himself as a modern scientist; his medical model of treatment, which seeks to understand and change what is wrong within the individual patient, is a model well-grounded in a rationalistic, scientistic view of human nature.

This basic scheme is not changed by the fact that, in its terms, access to what's wrong is through the irrational—through dreams, fantasies, instincts, and emotions. Here reason is pitted against emotion, feeling against thought, id against ego. Therapy facilitates the translation of "primary process," the stuff of dreams and emotions, into "secondary process," the stuff of thought and mastery. In everyday language: Therapy is about getting into your feelings and then making sense of them.

Now it might seem that a nonrationalist stance would require being on the side of emotion, feeling, dreams, and primary process, and against reason and making sense of feelings. But relational psychotherapy takes a different tack, believing that this split between reason and emotion is just another tricky form of rationalism. Relational therapy doesn't work to get clients to be more rational about their feelings, but neither does it say they should get out of their heads and into their feelings.

Relational therapy doesn't buy into that split between mind and emotion. Instead, as a relational therapist, you believe that in all of the activities of their daily lives your clients are putting into play and experiencing different interconnected and complex systems of self-with-other, which include—all at once—actions, beliefs, thoughts, body-feelings, images, self-states, emotions, and energies. If things are wrong for your clients, things are wrong in those complicated systems of thinking/feeling/experiencing/responding, and before your clients can start feeling better, whole systems need to start working in different ways.

Not only does rationalism specialize in either/or thinking—either thought or feeling, mind or emotion, for example—it also specializes in straight or linear cause-and-effect thinking. Now if what I just said is true, if what's wrong for clients is wrong in complicated systems of self-with-other experience, it would be pretty difficult to say, "Change this, and it will all be better!" In other words, in its departure from rationalism, relational therapy also departs from linear sequences of working on symptoms, producing a catharsis or an insight, and then having symptom relief. As a relational therapist you know that change happens in much more complex, systemic, and non-linear ways. For example, when change begins from the inside of a client's relationship with you, the client will gradually experience many small, interconnected differences in how she relates and feels in other contexts.

These departures—from the medical model, individualism, and rationalism—help make relational therapy what it is. Next, I will use these
departures to distinguish relational therapy from some other therapies.
Once again, to identify more clearly what relational therapy is, we will
compare it with what it is not.

NOT FREUDIAN THERAPY

Sigmund Freud was the original doctor who invented talk therapy as a
cure for mental illness, and his influence on what clinicians and the
general public understand about the therapeutic process remains profound and powerful, even among those who disagree thoroughly with his
position.[1] In the opinion of classical Freudians, there is, of course, a treatment relationship between therapist and patient, but there is no real
relationship outside of the formal one of doctor–patient (sometimes called
the therapeutic alliance). Feelings that arise in the patient toward the
therapist are the patient's *transference* upon the therapist of the patient's
past feelings toward someone else. This may evoke some *countertransference* feelings within the therapist, which the therapist keeps out of the
treatment relationship in order to understand and interpret the patient's
material correctly. As we have noted, this material of dreams, feelings,
and fantasies is seen as a product of the irrational unconscious. It includes the material of transference, which becomes a very important projection—as visible as if put up on an empty screen—of the patient's illness.
     The goal of classic psychoanalytic treatment can be stated in medi-
cal terms: to cure the patient of the symptoms of neurotic illness. This
can be done by bringing the contents of the patient's unconscious into
conscious awareness. How is this accomplished? The doctor interprets to
the patient the real meanings of his or her instinctual, irrational mental
processes as they are revealed in dreams and in transference feelings and
fantasies. Symptoms are cured as previously unconscious conflicts are
resolved, or at least as such conflicts become issues guided by the patient's
rational thinking and decision-making processes.
     Individualism is a given in this medical scenario; an individual pa-
tient is cured through a process of change that takes place entirely within
the patient's inner world. And that process is fundamentally a rational
one, both in the sense that it brings rationality to the irrational, and in
that it takes place in fairly linear cause-and-effect sequences.
     This Freudian perspective is far from obsolete. Our clients can ab-

sorb this same sense of how therapy works from afternoon TV talk shows, where the story goes as follows: Memories and what they do to you unconsciously bring on all kinds of symptoms—depression, agoraphobia, anorexia, insomnia, anxiety, substance abuse, and workaholism, to name a few. To get help for these symptoms, you need to find a therapist who will help bring back your memories, especially the feelings of the memories. When you get the feelings out and make sense of the memories—when you truly know the story hidden in your unconscious—then you can be well.

Let me illustrate this way of doing therapy with an example. "Jane" is the oldest child of a father whose alcoholism exploded into violent rages and a mother whose alcoholism drifted into despair and neglect of her children. Jane learned early to be wary of her father, to cover for her mother, and to look after herself and her younger siblings. The competence she learned young has served her well: she put herself through university and social work school, married, and is now a working mom of sons aged 8 and 6. She has come to therapy because she often feels depressed for no reason she can identify, she's afraid of a growing distance from her husband, she worries a lot about being inadequate as a professional and as a mother, and on the whole, she feels "lousy" about herself.

Classic psychodynamic treatment focuses on Jane's history and hopes to unearth the feelings of abandonment, sadness, anger, loneliness, and despair that she buried in order to take competent care of herself and others. The therapist asks her to talk about her everyday feelings and experiences, slowly helps her talk about her past, and suggests links between past and present. The therapist expects that Jane will sometimes see her as the attentive mother she never had (positive transference), and sometimes as the unavailable, neglectful mother she once did have (negative transference). The therapist slowly brings this transference material into the conversation too—one more powerful way for Jane to retrieve the conflicts and emotions hidden beneath her system of defenses.

As this unconscious material becomes conscious, the therapist helps Jane work through it, make sense of the story of her life, feel her own feelings in it, and mourn her losses. In the end, Jane's ego, or conscious sense of self, will emerge far stronger and far less burdened by old feelings of anger, helplessness, and shame. The therapist will have helped Jane find and feel the conflicts within herself, enabling her to leave a lot of those old feelings behind, "resolved."

That's the classic story of how therapy works, and it's a good story—a far better story than the one in which Jane is simply prescribed antidepressants because there's no visible reason for her depression. How would relational therapy tell a different story?

First, in the relational story, the question is not, "What's wrong with Jane?" but rather, "What's wrong for Jane?" That is to say, the "wrong" she brings to therapy isn't an illness to be rooted out or cured. The trouble can't be located only in repressed memories and their symptomatic effects, because what's wrong is entangled with everything Jane knows and feels about being in the world—especially about being with others in the world. So it's not a sickness, and it's not an inner, individual problem, either. Her system knows from experience what's safe to do, feel, and say; it tells her who will listen, and with what kind of attitude and feeling toward her. It also tells her, very clearly, what's dangerous. For good reason, Jane is convinced that she needs to protect herself in very particular ways from certain threats that come with interacting with others in the world.

As a relational therapist, you will not try to uncover and treat Jane's internal illness; instead, you will try hard to understand with her how her relational world works. And so, in your work together, you will focus first of all on the present, not on the past, and not on particular repressed feelings, but on how Jane makes sense and safety for herself in the world. As a relational therapist, you'll be saying to Jane, in one way and another: "You're making the best sense you can of the cards you've been dealt; you're protecting yourself as best you can in a dangerous interpersonal world. That's not illness, but a mark of survivor health."

You'll also notice, however, how costly Jane's ways of surviving can be. Jane's extreme competence covers for a lot of self-doubt, and her driven pace is a product of anxiety. In therapy, you let her know, "Here you don't have to produce or perform." But performing hard and well is Jane's way of connecting with others and feeling like she matters to them. She may be burning herself out and missing real connection with her husband and sons, but without her performance, she's lost, anxious, depressed, and she feels lousy about herself. This relational dilemma is the core of what is wrong for Jane, and eventually it's right there in the therapy room with you.

But slowly she lets herself relax and share more of her vulnerability with you. You keep offering her a way of being together that's less worried about outcomes, less driven, less anxious, and less lonely than she's been before. As Jane gets well in this therapy, you understand her progress not as the result of the catharsis of repressed emotions, nor as an increase in her "ego" to master those emotions. What you understand is that Jane is no longer so trapped in old patterns of self-with-other interactions and feelings. Jane knows more about those patterns than she used to, but most importantly, she can have different self-with-other experiences. Certainly some of those patterns and expectations have changed inside of her, but what matters to Jane is that she feels more real, more competent, and more worthwhile in her daily life. She feels these changes because of the more relaxed and open interactions she's now having with her therapist, her husband, her sons, her friends, and her co-workers. That's what's making her feel better! And that's not how classical psychoanalytic theory would explain the process or the outcome of a successful therapy.

NOT JUNGIAN THERAPY

But of course there's a plethora of other therapies, and many of them define themselves by differing from the Freudian tradition. Carl Jung was one of the first psychoanalysts to learn from Freud and then to move in his own unique direction. Like Freud, Jung was a physician, but one who brought the spiritual and transpersonal to the problem of mental illness. In Jungian therapy and its derivatives, there's hope for a cure, but through a self-transformational journey of the soul, not through the release of repressed memory. For Jung, as for Freud, dreaming is a royal road to the unconscious. Jung's unconscious, however, is archetypal as well as personal. Jungian therapy is about resolving complexes that cause symptoms, and although those complexes are rooted in a client's relational history, they are also related to archetypal problems we all have to solve, and have been solving since the first myths were told. This journey, then, leads to a kind of medical–spiritual cure; it involves the realization of Self understood as Soul. Jungians offer a kind of spiritual–medical model of therapy.[2]

Jane's Jungian therapist encourages her to write down her dreams. In many of them, large male figures threaten violence while Jane trembles and hides. In others, Jane notices women lying wounded in the shadows, but she can't stop—she's behind schedule, and the faster she hurries, the more things keep falling apart. The therapist and Jane talk about how these male and female figures aren't just images of her parents; they are also shadow images of Jane herself. Since masculine energy has been a threat to her, she can't count on the masculine side of herself (which Jung calls her animus) to help her think clearly and act with grounded confidence in the world. Her internal image of "woman," learned first from her mother, has become her own woman-self, lying badly wounded and helpless as she hurries by.

As Jane continues to dream and talk, new dream figures and landscapes appear. Male figures become less threatening; in her journals, Jane can imagine negotiating peace with them and even getting them on her side. The women in her dreams take on many new shapes—dangerous, angry, alluring, lively, and wise. Jane begins to enjoy meeting these women as both emissaries of a power beyond her and also as parts of herself. In Jungian terms, Jane is beginning to individuate, disentangling herself from the complexes of her personal history in order to discover the self she was meant to be.

This sketch shows that although Jungians offer a different kind of cure than Freudians do, it's still a cure for something within the client. That "within" is related to a whole world of archetypes, myths, and symbols, and the client's relationship to the world is mediated through this sense of symbolic meaning. There's a world of complexity within, mirroring a symbolically complex world without, but change happens within, and only secondarily in the relationships between within and without. In short, Jungian therapy is individualistic; conflicts and resolutions take place within the individual's psyche.

Jungian therapy also makes rather rationalistic and linear connections between symbols, dreams, and images and how clients can use them to understand and live their lives better. The world of archetypes and symbols, something other than the world of everyday thoughts and actions, affects the everyday world in hidden but direct ways. From a relational perspective, what's missing in this picture is the sense that underlying both worlds is a world of countless interactive, feelingful experiences of self-with-other that have taught one and continue to teach one everything one knows about what it is to be human in the world. These experiences are what give rise to shifting symbols, dreams, and images. These symbols, whether personal or archetypal, are important expressions of experience, but from a relational perspective, they can't be seen as the ground or primary data of experience.

Jungian work can help clients change how they envision themselves and then how they feel about themselves. From a relational perspective it's clear that changes in one's symbolic view of self can affect how one experiences self with other. I would argue, though, that this is a circuitous route to self-with-other change, and it carries the risk of getting stalled within an inner, symbolic world. Relational therapy encourages clients to come out where other people are. Here, it argues, is where you can work directly on what troubles you. Your inner world is certainly involved, but it's just part of the whole picture. The whole picture can certainly be grasped through symbols, and your experience of it can be painted, danced, and dreamed. Expressing yourself in these ways may help you feel more whole and real. But on the other hand, your experience matters just as much when you use everyday language for it and we see it in the ordinary light of day.

NOT SHORT-TERM SOLUTION-FOCUSED THERAPY

These days, due to insurance company payment plans that demand quick results for money spent on therapy, and also due to cutbacks in public health spending, short-term therapies are strongly proposed as the best alternative to the longer term "analytic" or "psychodynamic" or "insight-oriented" therapies. Short-term therapy is delivered in many forms; it may, for example, be called cognitive-behavioral, solution-focused, strategic, or goal-oriented.

Like the analytic therapies, these therapies depend on a medical model of mental illness and cure. However, they find mental illness in a different place in the human being. What's wrong is not in the unconscious, in repressed feelings, drives, or archetypes. What's wrong are destructive or counterproductive thoughts, patterns of behavior, and interpersonal habits, a point of view not so different from relational perspectives on what's wrong.

Short-term therapies, however, believe they can diagnose, isolate, and treat the problem abstracted from the client's whole context of life-experience. Furthermore, and in even sharper contrast to a relational mode of work, short-term therapies are expert-oriented. The expert, not necessarily a medical doctor, but nevertheless an expert who knows and who cures, is the one who recognizes and isolates those habitual and counterproductive patterns of thought and action and who devises strategies that change them into healthier, more productive patterns.

In this kind of therapy, Jane will be helped to identify the negative beliefs she has about herself and the negative words she speaks to herself that reinforce those beliefs. She will learn to turn down the volume on those thoughts, substituting positive messages to herself about her own good qualities and many fine achievements. She will also be helped to see that her depression takes hold when she withdraws from her family in exhaustion. She will learn to notice her exhaustion earlier, ask for some help around the house, allow herself some rest, and find ways just to "hang out" with her spouse and sons. For Jane, this is all hard work and against her nature, but when she makes herself think and act in these different ways, she does notice changes in how she feels.

Here the doctor–patient interaction is one of rational common sense, and treatment is based on expectations that certain thought and behavior changes will lead to certain predictable changes in feeling. In this sense, reason can conquer emotion. At the same time, and in their favor from a relational perspective, these therapies don't believe that insight cures; they don't think that just knowing what the problem is and where it might be coming from will instigate change. For these short-term therapies, the point is not to tell your life story, outer or inner, in ways which make expanded and transformational kinds of sense—making the unconscious conscious as Freudians and Jungians do—but to set goals, change patterns, and do things differently. When you start to do things differently, different experience will follow. Relational therapy agrees with that premise, but it knows that doing and feeling interpersonal relationships differently involves a complicated process of undoing old patterns and learning new ones, a process you can't do on your own or hurry up with willpower.

How individualistic are these therapies? On the one hand, they move the focus of treatment from a client's inner world of unconscious conflict to her conscious thoughts, behaviors, and habits of daily life, most of which take place in social contexts. On the other hand, these therapies include strong emphases on autonomy, self-assertion, and taking charge of one's own life. "You have the power to make the changes that will make your life more rewarding": so goes their keynote address. By contrast, relational therapies insist that the emotional quality of your life depends on the quality of relationships that sustain you in all of the aspects of your life.

Relational therapies point out, too, that a treatment picture that includes one expert problem-solver and one person with problems is a very narrow slice of what's possible—or, in fact, of what actually happens—between any two persons engaged with one another as client and therapist. All kinds of interpersonal hopes, fears, judgments, and feelings are inevitably woven into any therapeutic treatment, for better or for worse. From a relational perspective, it just makes sense to acknowledge this reality and then to try to work with it productively.

NOT HUMANIST THERAPY

The therapist's empathy and unconditional positive regard for the client and her authentic presence with the client are the hallmarks of humanist and client-centered therapies. Since the 1940s, the humanist therapy movement has confronted the psychiatric establishment with a nonmedical model of helping people who suffer psychological and emotional distress. Its practitioners speak of personal growth instead of cure. Carl Rogers and his colleagues insisted on the term "client," not "patient," in order to emphasize that therapy isn't about illness. What clients need, they said, is not a cure, but a selfless kind of love within which they can grow into their full potential as human beings. This *agape* love comes to clients in the form of the therapist's unconditional positive regard, empathy, and genuineness.[3]

In these ways, a humanist therapist is fully "in" the interactions with a client. She does not aspire to the position of objective expert or fixer of what's wrong. She believes that the potential for healing lies within the client, as does untapped potential for self-development and self-actualization. The therapist's accepting presence is the medium within which the client sheds his fears and begins to realize his hidden potential.

This way of being with clients is, I believe, a prototype of relational practice. But it falls short of full relational awareness when the therapist sees herself as only a benign, neutral medium for growth, something like a good mix of sun and rain for the nurturance of healthy plants. The humanist therapist provides an interpersonal context for the client's growth; she does not, however, become personally entangled in that growth process. It's for this reason that Rogers can give short shrift to what psychoanalytic theory calls transference and countertransference. For Rogers, transference is just one more constriction a client leaves behind as he blossoms in response to unconditional positive regard, and this warm regard, by its very nature, is given without any countertransferential strings attached. In summary, then, this friendly, antimedical model of therapy has two strong individualistic aspects: its goal of inner self-actualization and its disavowal of relational entanglements between client and therapist.

There are humanist therapies that borrow more from psychodynamic theory than Rogers did, giving credence to interpersonal themes that they acknowledge as transference and countertransference. But they frame these relational issues in individualistic ways. Gestalt therapy, for example, encourages clients to refuse to accept projections laid on them by others, and to recognize and withdraw their own projections as the products of their own historical baggage. "Your stuff" and "my stuff" must become completely disentangled (an impossibility within relational thought). For transactional analysis, too, the goal of analyzing interpersonal transactions is to recognize the roles you're caught in—the games you play unwittingly—so that you can escape them! Nowhere does there seem to be any awareness of the inescapable embeddedness of any self with many other selves, an interdependency that is as life-giving as it is difficult to manage.

How do humanist therapies situate themselves vis-à-vis the rational? They are less tied to insight than any of the therapies I've considered so far. Cure is experiential, especially through new experiences and expressions of self. This is especially visible in gestalt, psychodrama, and transactional analysis (TA/encounter group) versions of humanist therapies. They pay a lot of attention to how we make our lives and senses of self from what we have learned with others, which we forever after reenact with others. It's important to understand how that works, they say, but changes in those scripts take place only when we feel and express the pain they cause us, and feel and express a self breaking through and moving beyond those scripted constrictions. Changes happen within us as our blocks are released, our feelings are spoken, and our alienated parts of self are reintegrated.

Let's imagine Jane with a humanist therapist who is not wedded to any particular way of helping Jane find and express her feelings. Early in therapy, Jane talks about fear—fear of making mistakes, fear of displeasing her husband, fear of terrible accidents happening to her children. After a while she can acknowledge that she feels fear in sessions, too, fear of being judged and rejected. The therapist encourages her to fully experience her fear, to stay with it. She wonders with Jane if this is an old feeling. And of course it is; suddenly Jane feels a wave of the terrible tight anxiety that would fill her body when her father had been drinking and a fight between her parents loomed.

Later, when Jane feels safer, she will talk about some of the things in her life that make her annoyed and frustrated. The therapist will help her identify these feelings as anger, affirming the energy and power of lucid, constructive anger. As Jane becomes more comfortable with feeling angry, she begins to remember the rage she felt as a child, helpless to change what kept happening. Her therapist says it might help to release some of that rage, and Jane finds herself pounding a pillow and yelling, "I hate you!" And then her rage crumbles into sobs. Beneath Jane's rage, her therapist explains, there lies a deep well of sadness that Jane has never let herself feel—until now.

Now, for a while, Jane will need to cry her sadness—for the hurt and lonely child she was, for how much she needed to be loved, for the way her drivenness has robbed her of happiness. She can even cry about wanting her therapist to be the mother she never had, as she desires this desperately and knows it can never be. So much of what might have been can never be. But through her tears of grief, Jane also feels herself more alive and more real than she has ever felt before. Nothing within her scares her terribly anymore. She knows her blinding fear, her rage, and her wrenching sadness. She may be wounded, but she has herself at last. As she looks around, she begins to see that there may be some goodness in her life after all, and hopes and promises for the future.

We see here that while the therapist is a skilled facilitator of Jane's process, the process is understood to happen inside of Jane. It happens in her feelings, not in her mind. Most humanist therapies make a mantra out of "I've gotta get out of my head." But as I've noted, this mind/body, thinking/feeling, head/gut split is one of the trickier forms of rationalism as it appears in therapy. Rationalism appears in another form when humanist therapies lead clients to believe that if they get in touch with their feelings, have a cathartic, authentic experience, release a block, and integrate a part of themselves long alienated, then they can expect that their emotional lives will change dramatically. In other words, humanist therapies tend to suggest linear cause-and-effect sequences in the doing of emotional "work." This, along with their emphasis on individual process, sets up conditions in which clients can work on themselves endlessly and blame themselves for not doing it right when they don't experience the rewards they hoped for.

By contrast, in a relational model, change always happens within relationship with another person, even while it is experienced as change in inner meanings and feelings. This slight shift of emphasis means that in relational therapy the client doesn't carry the burden of change. Furthermore, although having many emotions and expressing them in both strong and subtle ways may be part of a relational therapy, the success of the therapy doesn't depend on any particular form of emotional release. There's nothing a client has to experience or express in order to be doing therapy "right." The work is in whatever happens between a client and therapist as they talk, and in whatever thoughts and feelings arise from that conversation.

This contrast between different concepts of therapy "work" shows up well in group therapy. In a humanist model of group therapy, members of the group take turns doing "pieces of emotional work," facilitated by a therapist who is skilled in helping them access and release feelings and then identify aspects of themselves that can be integrated into a fuller, more authentic self. As each member works, the others are supportive spectators, or perhaps even participants in a psychodrama that the therapist designs to help the working member access feelings, memories, and parts of self. Each person's real opportunity for change and growth will come when it is his or her turn to work.

In a relational group, the action happens between group members, while the therapist nudges conversations toward more honest and empathic exchanges. Group members explore their mutual assumptions and misunderstandings, their interpersonal needs, hopes, and fears, and the patterns of interpersonal feelings that emerge in the group interactions. Growth happens for the participants as relationships between them deepen into networks of mutual understandings within which persons can freely assert themselves and also offer to each other genuine, thoughtful, and caring support.

How does this picture transfer to individual relational therapy? Think of a group of two, yourself and your client. You are both the facilitator of this small group and a full participant in it. You will facilitate a relationship that will give your client many chances to assert herself freely and to experience genuine, thoughtful, and caring support. You will also participate in the collaborative process of finding out how to keep this relationship between the two of you alive and well, deepening and growing. You believe that joining with you in this collaboration will turn out to be more useful and rewarding for your client than if you just helped her to "work on herself."

NOT NARRATIVE THERAPY

With its links to theories of the social construction of the self, narrative therapy makes an important acknowledgment of the limits of individual self-creation and self-realization. It suggests that in order to understand yourself, you must locate yourself within the power dynamics of your own social context, for example, as a woman or a man, as a person-of-color or a white person, as a gay/queer or straight person, as a person with working-class, middle-class, or upper-class roots. Whatever your location, it says, there are powerful political and cultural stories that speak to you in your particular context to tell you who you can be in the world, what you can do, how you can feel about yourself, and what you're worth. Within these stories, which construct your family, too, there is also your family narrative of you. All of this is imposed on you as if it were your own story, squelching who you really are, what you really need, and who you really could become. Narrative therapy helps you notice the story you are enacting, and it backs you up to try to break out of the old narrative and into new ones that suit you better.[4]

With a narrative therapist, Jane discovers that the rules she lives by and the standards she strives to meet are set by forces outside of herself. The culture of her childhood, reinforced by her parents' behavior, taught her that it was a woman's place to suffer in silence, to clean up messes, and to keep the family going no matter what. Even as a little girl, she stepped up to the task. Now she realizes that she's living out that very same story both at home and at work, and everything around her conspires to keep her in it. But she learns to resist the pressures from her husband, her children, her in-laws, and her boss, who all profit from her hyper-competence. As she resists, she also begins to develop and test out a new story for herself, one in which she matters as much as anyone else, one in which she gets to speak her mind while joining with others in working toward mutual goals.

From a relational perspective, such narrative therapy gets very high marks for the thoroughgoing relationality of its worldview. Narrative therapy also knows that it is the client's *performance* of the narratives assigned to him that determines the path of his life, his self-image, and his emotional well-being. Therefore, rather than trying for specific changes in his self-image or emotions, it tries to set in motion performative changes of narrative that will subtly alter how whole systems of his relational interactions work. This idea about change resembles relational ideas about the performative power of the therapeutic relationship to change how a client performs and experiences many other relationships.

On the other hand, and in contrast to a relational perspective, narrative therapy can be quite expert-oriented and even rationalistic in its determination of which narratives are bad for clients and why. Historically, it has been linked with emancipatory political theories such as Marxism and radical feminism, which propose strong arguments against certain narratives and in favor of others. Relationally speaking, the danger here is that the experts' ideas about what narratives hurt a client can take over the clients' own words for what hurts them, creating a false, compliant connection between themselves and their therapists.

Another danger, from a relational perspective, lies in the assumption of an authentic self who may be oppressed by false narratives right now, but who can emerge into his or her own genuine truth. This "Who you really are" or "Who you're really meant to become" can be a fairly individualistic self-actualization construct, after all. It seems to depend on the assumption that within each person there is an essentially context-free being who exists underneath layers of oppressive social construction. Relationalists protest that there's no state or moment of being human apart from context, social construction, and relationship. Who we can be is always a negotiation of what's possible within what we have been given, contextually. Alternative, liberating personal narratives become possibilities for us only when they are sustained within a context of alternative, liberating relationships.

In other words, as a relational therapist, you don't imagine that for any client there's a true, hidden story of who she is. There's the self-with-other story she lives inside of now, and there are other stories possible, which could be better for her. Better has to do with whether new self-with-other experiences give her more freedom and support than she had before, whether they allow her more self-expression, more joy and pride, and a firmer sense of herself, her goals, and her principles. As a relational therapist, you will work with your clients' self-with-other narratives, but you won't be trying to help them find alternative or "true" selves—as if the lives they have been living have been false. Instead you will help them find more comfortable, constructive, rewarding, and responsive ways to live as the selves they have always been, and within contexts that sustain them.

NOT RADICAL FEMINIST THERAPY

A fine articulation of radical feminist therapy can be found in Laura Brown's book *Subversive Dialogues*.[5] Her version of radical feminist therapy has quite a lot in common with narrative therapy. Brown, too, understands that a client's well-being is far more dependent on what comes from her social surroundings than she's likely to think; that any client's sense of self is thoroughly contextual and constructed within networks of social power. The depression, anxiety, low self-esteem, phobias, addictions, and other symptoms that clients bring to therapy are all rooted, Brown says, in many kinds of disempowerment and subjection—to which some members of society are more subject than others. However, all members suffer from living in hierarchical or patriarchal social structures that invest in and maintain subjection. Dominance is not just a problem for the "losers" but for the "winners," too, who become alienated from themselves, from their true selves, by the dominating scripts they are performing without a second thought.

With a radical feminist therapist, Jane learns that there is a very powerful reason for her pervasive sense of powerlessness: a patriarchal society is engineered to disempower women and children. This was in force when she was a child, crushing and silencing both her mother and herself, and it's still true now. Jane's early experience, supported by ubiquitous cultural stories about a woman's place, has permeated Jane's sense of herself. Any story she can tell herself about her life assumes that she has far more responsibility than power in life. Her therapist helps her notice those assumptions and then question them. She enters empathically into Jane's experience to help her know how different kinds of disempowerment have made her feel. She helps Jane notice when the expectations of her boss or her husband leave her no options but acquiescence. She encourages Jane to claim her rightful power, both right now and retrospectively.

The therapist backs Jane in her fight against the oppression she meets every day and the oppression she has internalized, which over the years has become a self-definition. As Jane finds words for what has happened to her, she also finds words for who she is now—her own words, words that resist forces that would define her in their terms. This is the critical move for Jane's well-being: for her to be no longer a pawn of patriarchal power, but to become someone who knowingly and passionately resists. To this end, in the service of resisting domination, her radical feminist therapy has been a subversive dialogue.

In this brief description you may hear that there's a certain story about a client's experience, a story about oppression and the client's need for liberation and empowerment, that the radical feminist therapist will tell the client to explain to her why she feels the way she does. Brown holds her political convictions respectfully in her work with clients, but she does allow her beliefs to come through, and for that she doesn't apologize. On the other hand, Brown allows more than some narrative therapists do for the complications of the therapeutic relationship, which she says contains many powerful symbolic elements, especially elements of power, that need to be talked about in therapy. Her work is also saturated with implicit acknowledgments of the therapeutic power of accurate empathy, enacted as hearing and speaking in the client's "mother tongue."

Nevertheless, in Brown's presentation of feminist therapy, change comes about mostly through new understandings rather than through new relational experiences. Those understandings are facilitated by an expert, this time an expert on what patriarchy does to us all. At the same time, though, that expert is intent on empowering the client, telling her that she is the expert on her own experience, and that her voice is what matters. The therapist is both an expert diagnostician of a fundamentally social disease and also an anti-expert who resists the medicalization of symptoms and the hierarchies of medical models of cure. That's a paradoxical position to hold. And so is the position that therapy work must be undertaken with individuals, but that it strives, essentially, to build feminist community. Brown acknowledges these conundrums. But working with them is just part of the challenging job of doing feminist therapy, she says.

"NOTS" ARE US

Now it's time to gather up all the "nots" I've put forward, all the disclaimers. I've proposed that relational therapy departs from a medical model, from individualism and rationalism. I've said that relational therapy is neither Freudian nor Jungian therapy. I've said that it's not solution-focused, not narrative therapy, and that although both humanists and radical feminists may practice it, it's neither humanist nor radical feminist therapy. Now it's time for me to gather up all those "nots" and disclaim them—because relational therapy is also a product of its context, and that context includes all those themes and schools against which it defines itself.

For example, relational therapy may not be a medical model, but we can hardly deny that it seeks to help, to ease suffering, and to improve a client's quality of life. Relational therapy claims not to be individualistic, yet most of the work is done with one person at a time, with concern for that individual's well-being; moreover, the positive changes that clients experience in relationship they also experience as positive changes in their personal internal patterns of expectations and responses. Though we may call relational therapy nonrational, relational therapists and their clients are always trying to make some sense of what's happening in therapy. Furthermore, droves of relational theorists keep writing carefully reasoned articles and books about how this nonrational therapeutic process works.

Relational theory makes transformative changes to Freudian theory, but it remains heavily indebted to the central Freudian ideas that much more motivates a person's behavior than that person is aware of; that prior experience influences those motivations; and that in the process of repeated intense conversations between two persons, those motivations and influences may become visible, almost palpable, in the transference that begins to shape the conversation. When a relational therapist has a Jungian kind of openness to the power of dreams and metaphors to express the nuances of a client's experience, the dimensions of her empathic understanding expand.

As we noted above, relational therapy joins with shorter-term action-oriented therapies in their suspicions that intellectual analyses of a client's unconscious might not help him move toward much change in his life. Relational therapy agrees that change in a client's sense of self requires changes in a client's actions and experiences. Of course, the humanist therapies have created the very possibility of nonmedical therapy—therapy in which clients can expect respect, empathy, and support for their own developmental process, and therapy in which the therapist will be genuinely present in the therapeutic relationship. Narrative therapy highlights the power of social context to construct personal narratives, and it shows how the power of those narratives lies in their reiterated performances, two themes crucial to relational therapy. And radical feminist therapy reminds relational therapists that social relations of unequal power and enactments of dominance and submission come right into the therapy room with any two persons who enter it. In all these ways, relational therapy joins with other therapies in common tasks and understandings.

But if it's important for me to acknowledge that relational therapy shares history and important concerns with schools of therapy that do not define themselves as relational, it's even more important for me to acknowledge that a relational perspective has been nurtured in several different schools of psychotherapy and psychoanalysis. What I am simply calling "relational therapy" is indebted in different ways to each of them. Now I will introduce those different schools of thought that provide us with a rich diversity of relational perspectives on psychotherapy.

STONE CENTER SELF-IN-RELATION THERAPY

The women of the Stone Center for Developmental Services and Studies at Wellesley College have developed a kind of feminist therapy that sets itself within the context of feminist political theory, including analyses of racism, classism, and heterosexism. At the same time, Stone Center theorists believe that the work of therapy is not the same as the work of political resistance and subversion. Their therapy does not depend, then, on a feminist expert who can explain to her clients how social and political conditions constrain their lives and how they can resist those constraints. The Stone Center's strongest emphasis is on healing that happens through the experience of connection. This emphasis makes it less rationalistic, less insight-driven, and less linear than Brown's way of working.

While Laura Brown seeks to subvert patriarchy through resistance mobilized in therapy, the Stone Center theorists seek to subvert patriarchy through women's ways of being in connection. They begin with the premise that women have particularly relational, connected ways of being with others, and that those ways of being are healthier than masculine disconnected and autonomous ways of being in the world. Disconnection is what causes trouble between and within human beings, including the wide range of troubles that come to be labeled "mental illness." In general, patriarchal society fosters autonomy and disconnection, and a more particular source of trouble is the kind of disconnection handed down from generation to generation in troubled families.

So when Jane comes in for therapy, her self-in-relation therapist is especially attuned to Jane's disconnections—from significant others in her life, from her own feelings and self-experience, and also from the therapist as the two of them talk. The therapist keeps offering her own capacity for empathy until Jane begins to bring more of her self, her real thoughts and feelings, into the conversation. In the ambiance of empathy, Jane finds herself more able to accept the fearful, hurt, and angry parts of herself. Her confidence and self-esteem grow. Her depression fades as she is able to take from the relationship with her therapist stronger capacities to engage with others in ways that bring herself and others mutual satisfaction.

The therapy process, however, is not as easy as it looks in this brief sketch. According to Stone Center theory, if a client is in ongoing emotional pain, anxiety, or other symptoms of psychological trouble, the root of her trouble is very likely a profound sense of disconnection and isolation from others. But that disconnection is usually hidden and very resistant to change. Why is this the case? It's the case because in her culture and in her family, a client like Jane has learned that in order to get along in life and not get hurt by the people closest to her, she must squelch her desires for genuine connection to them, connection in which she gets to be fully herself.

Jane wants connection and she also needs to protect herself from the dangers of connection. So Jane learns to pretend at connection, and her pretense gives her just enough connection to get by. She becomes good at being the person others want her to be, and she carries this accommodating mode of social operation out from her family of origin into the rest of her life. Eventually, of course, she finds herself profoundly disconnected and isolated from others, and not only that, disconnected from herself and feeling bad in many ways. These symptoms are what motivate her to get help. Without them, she'd hardly know she's in trouble, for this is life as she knows it.

When she comes for therapy with a Stone Center or self-in-relation therapist, Jane is invited, over and over again, into a process of genuine reconnection with others (in particular her therapist) and with herself. Her therapist tries to be fully present to Jane even when Jane stays hidden, and she doesn't give up trying to engage her. This reconnecting is a long slow process because Jane hangs on tightly to the accommodating, pleasing strategies that keep her safe from dangerous relationship. But the therapist remains steady, showing understanding and empathy whenever Jane is able to speak or to signal thoughts and feelings that belong just to her. Eventually Jane begins to feel the therapist's empathy, and then moments of empathy for herself. Finally she begins to reconnect with feelings, thoughts, and experiences she once denied were ever a part of her. Having received empathy and understanding from another and given it to herself, she can begin to find her way to mutually empathic and rewarding connections with others in her life.[6]

If this expanded story of self-in-relation therapy sounds very much like the relational psychotherapy I'm putting forward, that's because my definition of relational therapy owes a great deal to the Stone Center. So why not stop here? Certainly we can leave Jane here and trust that her therapy process will be richly relational. But I want to understand more about the process that the Stone Center calls "connection." I want to investigate more closely, for example, what happens when both client and therapist engage in behaviors that are simultaneously "connecting" and "disconnecting." I want to understand a variety of interactions and states of being that can't be defined as simply connected or disconnected. So I look beyond Stone Center self-in-relation theory for further components of a comprehensive relational psychotherapy. I look to relational

psychoanalytic theory for more information and ideas about this complicated process.

RELATIONAL PSYCHOANALYSIS–THE BIG PICTURE

Relational psychoanalysis is a complex phenomenon constantly on the
move. To try to capture the motion and fluidity of its development, I will
describe it in terms of streams: tributaries flowing into major watercourses
that then carry forward diverse currents and sub-streams. Two major tributaries flow into the contemporary river of relational psychoanalytic theory–
object relations theory, especially as developed within the British independent school (e.g. Winnicott, Guntrip, Fairbairn, and Balint), and interpersonal psychoanalysis, an American movement originating in the
work of Harry Stack Sullivan. Both interpersonal and object relations
forms of psychoanalysis are still currently practiced; they have fed the
main stream of relational theory, but they also continue along courses of
their own. For the sake of simplicity, however, I won't deal with them as
relational schools themselves but as precursors of contemporary psychoanalytic theory that self-identifies as "relational."

In my simplified sketch of the big picture, this contemporary psychoanalytic relational theory is split into two distinct streams. One calls
itself "self psychology" and the other calls itself "relational psychoanalysis."[7] The stream that calls itself "relational psychoanalysis" carries along
within it many diverse currents: the interpersonalist one, of course, but
also constructivist, feminist, and object relations forms of explicitly relational theory. In his overview of the relational field, the relational psychoanalyst Lewis Aron includes even contemporary intersubjectivist
versions of self psychology in the stream of "relational psychoanalysis."[8]
In my view, however, the self psychology stream runs quite independently,
and it will be some time before the two streams agree on a common
language and a merger of perspectives and energies.[9]

Let me outline briefly my sense of the major differences between
these two streams of contemporary relational psychoanalytic theory. First,
they have different histories. Interpersonalist theory is the strongest force
within the wide, eclectic stream that calls itself "relational psychoanalysis." Within this stream, interpersonalist theory meets object relations
theory (as well as feminist and constructivist theories) and amalgamates/
transforms it. These changes are wrought differently by different
relationalists, but in general, in this stream, object relations theory (theory

about the intrapsychic interactions of various images of self and other) becomes a complement to active, here-and-now, interpersonalist ways of engaging in the therapeutic dialogue. The theory proves useful as it provides metaphors for whatever it is that's going on inside the patient that also makes the therapy interaction go on in certain ways.

By contrast, the history of self psychology shows little interpersonalist influence. It also has a different relationship with object relations theory, having taken the theory more literally and sought to transform it directly and coherently. For example, Heinz Kohut, the founder of the self psychological movement, invented the term "selfobject" in order to focus attention on a particular kind of inner interaction between images of self and others ("objects"). This "selfobject" kind of inner interaction is an experience of self-with-other that invisibly sustains a self from infancy onward. He believed his idea filled an important gap in object relations theory, a gap in understanding the treatment needs of patients who were missing the experience of that self-sustaining relationship with another person.

Kohut's ideas took on a life of their own, however, as early self psychologists kept on exploring the selfobject relation and how it is created by the analyst's subjective empathic immersion in the patient's subjective experience. As self psychologists saw more clearly how this space of "empathy" is actually constructed by two interacting subjectivities, the intersubjective school of self psychology emerged. It's at this point that self psychology began to mature into the fully and explicitly relational theory that I refer to in this text.

In short, self psychology slowly found its way toward the question, "What's happening in the therapeutic relationship?" while forms of that question had been on the interpersonalist agenda from its beginnings. That question marked Sullivan's break from the classical Freudian tradition. He and his colleagues went on to expand the terrain of psychoanalysis outside of medicine and psychiatry, especially with the founding of the William Alanson White Institute in New York in the 1940s. The inclusion of Ph.D.s as faculty and students of that Institute, along with the Institute's historical commitment to freedom of thought and its opposition to the constraints of the American psychoanalytic establishment, created much space for philosophical and social understandings of the psychoanalytic enterprise. Over the years, various interpersonalist analysts have integrated existentialism, hermeneutics and phenomenology, social and linguistic constructivism, and feminist and post-structuralist thought into their constructions of psychoanalytic theory.

In many ways the movement that calls itself relational psychoanalysis is a direct continuation of the energies embodied in the White Institute. For example, graduates of the Institute fill positions on the editorial board of *Psychoanalytic Dialogues* and the faculty of the relational stream of the postdoctoral program in psychoanalysis at New York University. And so what I am recognizing as "relational psychoanalysis" carries forward the interpersonalist commitment to philosophical exploration and social critique. Consistent with this commitment is the emphasis relational psychoanalysis places on the mutual construction of meaning in the analytic relationship—the deconstruction of a patient's destructive, constraining life-meanings, and the reconstruction of a narrative that provides more personal satisfaction and agency in the world.

By contrast, relational self psychology focuses less on the transformation of lived meaning in analysis and more on the transformation of self-experience, especially the experience of self in relation to others. It can be argued that there's fundamentally not much difference between trying to change a patient's unconscious organizing principles of self-experience and trying to change a patient's unconscious personal meanings. Perhaps the two streams might find a point of merged purpose and language here. However, in current practice there remain significant differences between a self psychological focus on (re)developing organizing principles of self-with-other experience and a relationalist focus on (re)constructing more useful relational meanings by which to live.

I think that these differences come down to differences between the worldviews of medicine and of the humanities and social sciences, or between a relatively "objective" scientific view and a more self-consciously constructed philosophical (lately postmodern) view of psychoanalysis. With its historical links to the American medical psychoanalytic establishment and its source in object relations, self psychology tends to couch its understanding of a patient's self-experience in somewhat scientific/ medical terms rather than in philosophical terms. Object relations theory, a medical model of psychoanalysis, taught self psychology to locate a patient's pathology in damaged or stunted internal psychological structures or functions, and to understand this pathology as a direct result of faulty interactions with early caregivers. Although self psychology has made radical changes to this picture of pathology, it continues to see its new and developing picture of personality development, pathology, and treatment as "true" in a relatively objective, scientific sense.

Interpersonalist theory taught "relational psychoanalysis" that pathology is located in faulty patterns of making meaning out of interpersonal interactions, and that these patterns are best addressed directly and in the present, so that the patient can come to understand what's going on and take responsibility to deconstruct the old meanings and construct new ones. "Relational psychoanalysis" now works in subtle, indepth ways with regression and transference—with powerful, unconscious manifestations of early trauma as they become lived in the therapy relationship. Often analysts of this school use object relations language about a patient's parts of self, defenses, and projections in order to understand and explain their clinical work. But the explanation remains a tool, a meaning-making metaphor. There's not the attention self psychology pays to infant studies about mutual attunement and forms of dyadic interaction; there's not the self psychological search for ever more reliable templates of optimal development, the better to understand pathological development in infancy and childhood and the possibilities for new optimal development in adulthood; and, of course, there's not the concomitant danger self psychology always faces (danger from a relational perspective) of being pulled back into a medical model of an expert doctor who treats a patient's objectively understood pathology.

So much for the contrasts between these two major streams of relational psychoanalytic theory. I'll go on soon to expand on each of them in its own terms. But first let me say that if you are a new student of relational psychoanalysis or psychotherapy you would do well to realize two things. First, you should know that your relationalist mentors were most likely first trained in interpersonalist and/or object relations theories, and that those theories remain an important background to their thinking about their work. In their own development as clinicians and theorists, your relational mentors would have first sought ways to more fully "relationalize" those theories in their practice. This is the way relational theory came into being. The second thing for you to know, then, is that if you choose to step into a current stream of relational theory, you won't really know what this stream carries with it, especially under the surface, unless you know where it came from. I'm suggesting that a serious, sustained look into object relations theory and interpersonalist theory can only enhance your understanding of whatever relational psychoanalytic position you find yourself drawn to.

MORE ABOUT "RELATIONAL PSYCHOANALYSIS"

Since the days of Harry Stack Sullivan, the interpersonalist school has maintained that a person's learned interpersonal patterns of interaction are at the root of his psychological problems. Inevitably, these patterns will be put into play between a client and his therapist, and so paying attention to what happens in that relationship is the best way to find out what the psychological problem is and how it works. Paying attention also starts the process of changing the patterns of interaction between these two participants in the therapy, and change that happens in the therapeutic relationship will have a powerful impact on the rest of the client's relationships and self-experience.

Contemporary relational psychoanalysts move beyond the early interpersonalists when they say that a therapist cannot stand outside of the therapy process as a neutral "participant–observer" in order to observe a client's patterns with complete objectivity. They recognize, instead, that client and therapist are both involved in the mutual construction of their relationship. Very intentionally, they replace a one-body psychoanalysis with a two-body or (as I've been saying) a self-with-other model. Lewis Aron, for example, writes extensively about the inescapable mutuality of the psychoanalytic process.[10] Owen Renik's metaphor for the therapist's engagement in the therapy process is "playing with your cards face-up."[11] Darlene Ehrenberg challenges relational therapists to push the therapeutic conversation to that "intimate edge" where client and therapist are having strong, if hidden, reactions to one another moment by moment.[12]

While proposing a radically relational model of mutual interaction between client and therapist, analysts of this relational stream must also put some words to what's wrong for their clients and to what happens when their clients start to change for the better. As I noted above, many of them use object relations language to describe what they might call the intrapsychic aspects of the client's experience. In a series of influential books, Stephen Mitchell explores how theories of intrapsychic reality—both classical and object relations theory—can be understood in terms of a fundamentally relational theory of psychoanalysis.[13]

Jessica Benjamin's work is another good example of creative inclusion of object relations language within a relational imperative. Her theory refuses to collapse into each other the terms of intrapsychic (inside-self) and intersubjective (self-with-other) reality. From Benjamin's explicitly feminist perspective, intersubjectivity is an achievement of mutual recognition between two subjects—a fragile, paradoxical relational achievement that is always at risk of breaking down into the unhealthy "match" of relations of domination, where one person (often female) serves as object to the other's (often male) subjectivity. These breakdowns, with their fantasies of objectified others who are not known as subjects, and with all their unnegotiated injuries, conflicts, and frustrations, produce much of the material of intrapsychic reality, Benjamin says.

Benjamin does not suggest that psychoanalysis or feminist social action can produce a utopia of intersubjective relations. Human beings must assert themselves with each other; aggression is a psychological reality; conflicts of needs and of wills are unavoidable. Breakdowns will keep happening, and intrapsychic constructions of reality will remain powerful and formative. Benjamin's point, rather, is that we do well to sustain the tension of recognizing one another as subjects, working through our conflicts, knowing that breakdowns of mutual recognition are inevitable, and also always holding the possibility of negotiating repair between and among us.[14]

Benjamin's work illustrates the room there is for creative theorizing within the relational psychoanalytic stream. I take note of her position for another reason, too: it stands as an important critique of feminist therapy theory that would simply reverse the terms of domination and exclude "masculine" aggression from a feminine world of harmony. The work of Laura Brown and of the Stone Center theorists is somewhat vulnerable to such a critique. Benjamin's position also reminds relational therapists that those interpersonal strategies or negative expectations of the other that constrict and trouble their clients' lives can take on intrapsychic substance; what starts out as simple deficits or efforts to repair can become complex feelings, fantasies, and symptoms that permeate their clients' psychological experience.

Benjamin protects space for intrapsychic reality, but her vision of intersubjectivity demands the personal, relational presence required by all relational psychoanalysis. When analysis goes well, analyst and patient will sustain as best they can the tension of their struggle to create a relationship of mutual self-assertion and recognition of the other. In this vision of relational work, it is in the client's best interests that the therapist be a subject who communicates and negotiates directly with the client, making space for the client's reciprocal subjectivity, not an object who provides for the client's needs.

From this feminist point of view, as from more interpersonalist, social constructionist, existentialist, dialectical, and post-structuralist points of view, relational psychoanalysis agrees that the problems clients bring to therapy have their roots in clients' problematic or traumatic relationships with others, past and present. Insight about those relationships does not in itself make change happen. Change happens through experience, all of these versions of relational psychoanalysis maintain, and it happens most forcefully through experiences of relationships that embody and enact different meanings than relationships once did for the client.

Stephen Mitchell, the best known contemporary spokesperson for relational psychoanalysis, argues that the relational analyst's expertise lies solely in her ability to engage the client in the active creation of new life-meanings, meanings that offer him a wider range for personal engagement, authenticity, and freedom.[15] And so the relational analyst tries to find the best mix of safety and challenge in how she relates to each client, in order to keep each client actively involved in the therapy. A relational analyst doesn't expect that any particular notion about developmental process will be true for a particular client. But she offers different ideas as tools with which a client may construct his own meaningful narratives about his experiences. She won't serve up any particular meanings as truth for the client, because for her what matters is the authentic process of making meaning, and making it in relationship. This is what gets a client sprung free from old, constricting meanings. This is what gets change happening. Doing this process together produces the transformative power of therapy. Clearly the process of relational psychoanalysis is not a process undertaken by an isolated mind, nor are its meanings simply the products of linear, rational thought.

So would this kind of work feel any different than working with someone committed to a Stone Center self-in-relation model? It's likely that certain differences would emerge. First of all, for relational psychoanalysis, the mutuality of a therapy relationship isn't a moral issue, as it tends to be in Stone Center thought. In relational psychoanalysis, mutuality isn't a desired state of being-together that signals successful therapeutic work. In its basic form, mutual influence between persons is just an inescapable fact: in any relationship, it's impossible for two persons not to affect one another in countless overt and subliminal ways all the time. For both participants, this mutual influence might feel quite good—or it might feel quite horrible. Even in Jessica Benjamin's more normative sense of mutuality, mutual recognition is a tenuous, paradoxical achievement, by its nature always vulnerable to forces of breakdown, aggression, and destruction, forces that never disappear from human relations or from the psychotherapy relationship.

So the relational analyst won't concentrate on helping a client move from the "bad" of disconnection to the "good" of connection, from isolation to a steady state of mutuality. She'll assume that some kind of connection and mutuality will happen, some mix of useful and destructive forms of relating. She'll wait to see what troublesome kinds of mutual influence will emerge in the therapy relationship, so that she can better understand them and, through the pushes and pulls of her own subjective engagement, help to transform them into a therapeutic relationship that makes more space for the client's knowing of self and of others.

A relational psychoanalyst won't assume that less constricted ways of being together will always feel good. Less constriction means a wider range of possibilities, which might mean new space for disappointment, aggression, and anger. The therapist working from a relational psychoanalytic perspective won't isolate the experience of connection as the reason for a client's growing emotional health. She will understand that feeling more connected is but one of many new experiences open to a client as he starts to experience self-with-other differently. He might just find new ways to stand on his own two feet, to speak his own truth, and to pursue his own agendas. In summary, a relational psychoanalyst counts on the therapy relationship to unsettle clients' accustomed ways of being, to stir things up and to get clients moving toward new meanings and options in life. This has a significantly different "feel" than counting on the therapy relationship to provide clients with a core experience of more genuine connection.

MORE ABOUT SELF PSYCHOLOGY

We turn now to self psychology, the other major relational school of psychoanalysis. With a self psychologist, a client can always count on empathy—a certain specific kind of relational connection with the therapist. Therapists of the more interpersonalist relational stream believe that such empathy is a limited, one-way connection. Too much empathy can be infantilizing, the practitioner of "relational psychoanalysis" suspects, and she believes that therapy for adults should include learning to deal with interpersonal problems and differences, even—or especially—when they occur between client and therapist. And so, always keeping within the limits of what she believes is in the client's best interests, she shares her thoughts and reactions as they occur during the process of therapy. By contrast, all the streams of thought within self psychology are wary of putting much of the therapist's self into the interaction, at least in its early stages. Why? To answer that question, we need to return briefly to the historical roots of self psychology.

We've noted that Kohut invented the idea of "selfobject" to fill a gap in object relations theory, a gap about how to understand and treat patients whose sense of self is quite fragile and easily depleted or fragmented. He proposed that they suffer from deficits of selfobject experience—or experiences of being able to count on another person to take the actions necessary to sustain one's own cohesion, vitality, and self-esteem. Obviously, these are first of all parental actions, and such deficits are most likely to stem from a patient's childhood experiences of being parented. However, in Kohut's theory, therapists can step into that gap and perform some of those essential actions for a while, strengthening the adult patient's cohesion, vitality, and self-esteem.

On the one hand, Kohut's move is deeply relational. It breaks with classical Freudian psychoanalysis and much of object relations theory to say that individual autonomy is a bogus therapeutic goal. It says that in fact we all depend on others our whole lives long for our psychological and emotional well-being. And so therapists are not infantilizing clients when they support their clients' legitimate and important needs to be understood, supported, and affirmed. In this context it's easy to see that many clients come to therapy precisely because they have not been well enough understood and supported to develop selves that are sturdy, cohesive, and energetic. A *relationship* with the therapist is what creates the medium in which derailed self-development can begin again.[16]

On the other hand, however, this classical formulation of self psychology is not yet a fully relational theory. As analysts from "relational psychoanalysis" and Stone Center theorists point out, this approach is still rather "one-body" (the therapist is involved only as empathy-provider), individualistic (attention is focused on the client's self-development), rationalistic (interpretation in service of insight is the main way of working), and linear (self-development follows certain predictable routes when the therapist responds in certain prescribed ways).

However, a strong current within self psychology, most visible in the work of Robert Stolorow, George Atwood, and Donna Orange, has put its energies into exploring the intersubjective context of the therapeutic relationship. Intersubjective theory and practice seeks to root out the myth that it's an isolated mind that suffers psychological trouble, a myth that persists even when self psychology says that this trouble can be cured through empathic understanding.[17]

Intersubjectivists describe the therapeutic situation as an "intersubjective field." The rules and emotions of the games played in "the field" are set up by the interacting subjective worlds of both the therapist and the client. The therapist keeps bringing empathy and a search for understanding to the field, but the changes that happen there aren't simply responses to his empathy, nor do they happen just because of the client's new insights or understanding. Most importantly, as therapist and client interact, something changes in how the intersubjective dynamic gets set up and plays out between them. This experienced change in interaction, this "something different" in action, is what leads to change in the client's self-experience.

Howard Bacal's phrase "optimal responsiveness" brings together the classic self psychological concern for accurate empathy and the intersubjectivists' awareness that therapists keep finding themselves in very different kinds of intersubjective fields. A therapist seeking to give optimal responses to different clients can't work according to standard rules for empathy. On the contrary, as Bacal describes his own work, he tries to respond to each client in specific ways that will create the best conditions for positive change in this unique intersubjective field, this two-person relationship.[18]

Self psychology has always had a strong developmental component. Kohut wrote about certain trajectories of childhood self-development that therapists could support when the trajectories appeared, belatedly, in therapy. Intersubjective field theory backs itself up with studies that show how infants and their caretakers are involved in intricate dances of mutual influence.[19] Self psychologists are likely to hold in mind particular developmental themes in individual experience, noticing in adult clients analogues of specific patterns of infant and child behavior. In their view, healthy development depends above all on caretakers' supportive, nonintrusive, emotionally attuned responses to a child's needs. The Stone Center has a similar model of healthy development, but it explains attuned response in terms of women's ways of being in empathic connection. In contrast to both, "relational psychoanalysis" speaks of mutual influence in relationships from infancy onward, but it doesn't commit to any developmental scheme, keeping itself free to work with whatever might help clients make meaning of their contemporary experience.

How does it feel to work with a self psychologist? I doubt it feels much different from work with a therapist influenced by the Stone Center, but the differences might be noticeable. As a self-in-relation therapist does, a self psychological therapist attunes carefully to the details and

nuances of the client's experience, whether it be past or present experience outside of therapy, or what's happening in the therapy room. He
strives for an accurate empathic connection with the client's thoughts
and feelings. His empathic immersion in the client's experience will help
the client develop a sense of connection with him and also help her
connect better with her own self-experience.

Unlike a self-in-relation therapist, however, a self psychologist understands these connections not as ends in themselves but rather as ways
to help the client redevelop how she can be her own self in the world,
especially in the world of her relationships with others. This self, he believes, can have many kinds of positive self-with-other experiences in addition to the experience of connection. And so, in no hurry to achieve a
"connected" feeling, a self psychologist investigates carefully the dynamics and meanings of interactions when a client feels afraid of him or hurt
by him. He helps the client notice when particular relational experiences
in and out of therapy leave her feeling fragmented, shaky, or disheart-
ened, and he trusts that this understanding will help her regain whatever
connection—or strength, equilibrium, or energy—she needs.

The differences between self psychological therapy and the therapy
of "relational psychoanalysis" lie along other lines. Relational psychoanalysis doubts that empathy unbroken by experiences of difference and
challenge is the best facilitator of growth and development. The relational analyst doesn't think of herself as a temporary stand-in for faulty
parents, and she doesn't just understand her client's self-protections until he no longer needs to use them. As a more proactive participant in her
client's therapy, she will share what she thinks and feels in the therapy,
and since she does not work in terms of a developmental model that
always sees the hurt child in the anxious adult, she worries less than a self
psychologist might about whether a client is ready to hear what she has to
say.

By contrast, a self psychologist will stick to his empathy for all the
different ways clients protect themselves from further injury. He might
explain his understanding that they learned their self-protections in dangerous circumstances. He might sketch for them a contrasting picture of
circumstances in which children get what they need from caregivers so
that they can trust people more and expect more from life. He will want
to explore with clients their thoughts, memories, and feelings about what
they missed in their formative years, and he will have no qualms about
providing for them some of the secure attachment they crave.

Classical self psychologists believe that helping clients achieve insight about their unfulfilled needs will help repair self-deficits that clients still experience. A more relational self psychologist believes that a relationally "optimal" way of being with a client can, all by itself, help fill in some of those gaps. For example, for clients neglected by distracted, depressed parents, a spontaneous, interested, talkative way of being might be very important. On the other hand, a client with intrusive, demanding parents and older siblings might find a silent, nonintrusive presence just what she needs for long stretches of time. These tailor-made ways of being-with are extensions of the self psychologist's empathy, variations on what the relational self psychologist Howard Bacal would call optimal responsiveness. Many self psychologists, while they know that the concept is slippery (what's "optimal"?), find that the concept of optimal responsiveness catches the spirit or feel of self psychological work.

TOWARD A SYNTHESIS OF RELATIONAL THEORY

Despite the different emphases of the relational schools we've looked at, I still believe that self-in-relation theory, "relational psychoanalysis," and self psychology are fundamentally more alike than different in what they have to say about how relational psychotherapy works. In later chapters, I will be drawing on all of these resources as I introduce the principles of relational practice. I will take a moment here to show how, in spite of their differences, they each add something to enhance a relational picture of therapy. We will look in on Jane one last time. She's with an eclectic relational therapist who is using several relational models to understand their work together.

Stone Center theory helps the therapist understand how Jane uses strategies of care-taking and competence to stay in a semblance of relationship while keeping herself out of more vulnerable kinds of connection in which she might get hurt. Her strategies, however, are wreaking long-term havoc with her emotional well-being. When her relational therapist thinks along Stone Center lines, she knows that Jane will be helped through reconnection—with the therapist, with herself, and with others in her life.

Relational psychoanalysis helps the therapist notice how these self-protective and self-destructive strategies are played out again and again between Jane and herself. And so the therapist keeps trying to establish real connection with Jane, even if that sometimes means putting her own feelings on the table or challenging Jane's strategies. But, retaining a self psychological sensitivity, the therapist is careful never to stray far from an empathic grasp of Jane's experience, and especially of her experience of the therapy. She knows that if she is to provide the support that will help Jane grow stronger, she cannot undercut or second-guess Jane's experience of reality.

Developmental self psychological theories tell the therapist how Jane's strategies for self-protection come from unconscious principles that organize how she makes sense of her life experiences, be they large or small, traumatic or benign. Thinking developmentally, Jane's therapist sees how her disconnecting strategies are but one part of Jane's complex and deep-seated way of being a self in the world. This is what Jane's relational psychotherapy is taking on: her deeply ingrained patterns of being a self-with-others.

Intersubjectivity theory increases the complexity of the scene exponentially when it notices that not only Jane's organizing principles but also her therapist's organizing principles are creating the field within which the therapy will be played out. Each participant's strategies for safe connection and safe disconnection will match, miss, excite, and upset the other's strategies, as each participant works toward being understood and understanding the other.

As Jane starts to feel better, Stone Center theory will point out to the therapist the developing good connection between herself and Jane and between Jane and many others in her life. "Relational psychoanalysis" will prompt her to celebrate Jane's developing ability to create new life-meanings for herself, full of new possibilities for interpersonal engagement, authenticity, and freedom. And from a self psychological perspective, the therapist will understand Jane's progress as different kinds of re-development and new development of self.

Classical self psychology puts that self-development in terms of positive selfobject transferences holding firm for Jane, giving her security while her self grows stronger. Bacal roots it in the many good experiences of self-with-other, elicited by a therapist's optimal responsiveness that Jane needs in order to thrive. As we shall see in more detail in Chapter 6, self psychologists believe that if Jane's therapist can anticipate the different and sometimes surprising forms good connection can take between the two of them, she will be able to work more comfortably and productively with these positive powers as they are unleashed. And that will give Jane even more room to get stronger, to shine, and to enjoy participating in life.

I'm using this last look at Jane to sketch the possibility of a relational psychotherapy that draws quite freely on different schools of relational theory. The relational therapy I'm writing about isn't to be found in only one of the relational schools. Each school has its limits, I believe. For example, striving for immersion in the client's experience can fool self psychologists into thinking they're not in the picture of what's happening right there in the room. On the other hand, the question, "What's going on around here?" can be too threatening for a client to face, or else enormously complex as it's untangled in relational psychoanalysis. Sometimes clients don't want or need to know much about this complexity as long as the relationship is working well enough for them. At the same time, however, user-friendly Stone Center theory, with its emphasis on connection, wears a bit thin without the technical support of psychoanalytic theory, especially when the therapeutic connection is full of ruptures and conundrums. And so I treasure my freedom to be bound by no school but to try to work out a useful synthesis of these different relational theories.

An eclectic or synthetic theory has its limits, too, perhaps inherent in not putting any one theory into practice with single-minded passion. Another of the inherent limits of any relational approach lies in the fact that so much that is wrong for our clients is wrong because of the relations of domination that permeate their social worlds, and ours. Our society does not teach us to recognize each other as subjects across our differences or to negotiate our separate intentions and desires with mutual respect. Many of us who are drawn to relational psychotherapy work are also deeply concerned about this larger picture of relational breakdown. Sometimes working with one client at a time can seem like trying to empty an ocean with a bucket. But we persist. As we have seen, relational therapists of various persuasions speak out about the social and political contexts and meanings of their work.[20] It's clear to me that any relational therapy worth the name must at least deal honestly with the effects of differing social powers upon the life experience of our clients and upon the construction of the social relation of psychotherapy as it develops between each client and ourselves.

Other factors that construct and therefore limit any practitioner's relational theory are the givens of his or her personal and professional history. As we've seen in the last part of this chapter, relational theory about psychoanalysis and psychotherapy is a domain of many diverse waters and much eclecticism even within defined streams of practice. All of us relationalists have our own ways of locating ourselves within this complex domain. Now that I have described the complexity of relational theory, the time has come for me to acknowledge, as clearly as I can, my bias within it.

MY THEORETICAL BIAS

I have been influenced by each of the relational schools, but I have been most profoundly and thoroughly influenced by self psychology, especially the intersubjectivity and infant development branches of self psychological theory. How did this happen—when I am a woman committed to the challenges and joys of connection (a natural for Stone Center theory) and a Ph.D. by way of a thesis on the intersection of post-structuralist educational theory and relational psychoanalysis?

It happened, I think, because my first training in psychotherapy, in both a faculty of social work and a private therapy training institute, was in object relations theory. I learned to think about therapy through those developmental and quasi-medical categories, and as I pursued my special interest in working with trauma survivors who were classified as "borderline," the self psychology that was just then emerging out of object relations theory gave me more and more of what I needed to understand my work with my clients. How might I have structured my understanding of relational therapy if I had started in a different place? Or with a different client population? I'll never know—and we all have to start somewhere.

There's more to the story, for self psychology has influenced me not only professionally, but also personally. Over the years I have been a client (or patient) in several different kinds of therapies, short-term and long-term, expressive and analytic, and the therapists with whom I connected most usefully were themselves influenced by self psychology. Most recently I have been in a long-term psychoanalysis with a self psychologist. In that relationship I have grown stronger, more authentic, and more alive in myself and in my connections with others, and I have understood my growth in theoretical terms that I have come to share with him—terms that belong to an intersubjectivist, developmental self psychology. As generations of therapists and analysts can testify, there's nothing more deeply formative of a certain understanding of therapy than a powerful and positive experience "inside" it.

Of course I can find support for my bias. In my experience as both client and therapist, I've become convinced that empathy creates a better context for growth and change than explanation or confrontation does. I've found that I can hope for "connection" with very frightened clients, but what I need most to carry us through hard times is some intersubjectivist understanding about how we inhabit disconnected relational spaces together. I believe that the profound changes facilitated by relational therapy can best be understood as changes in the *experience* of self-with-other. These mutative experiences don't need to be constructed or remembered as new meanings; perhaps they don't even need to be thought about consciously. That's because profound new relational experience itself engenders change in what's relationally possible for a person. And finally, I believe that infant studies, though observer-constructed and culture-specific, reveal something reliable about how formative interpersonal dyads work and about how interpersonal development goes off track and can be brought back on track in a therapeutic dyad. All of these convictions will determine how I go on to tell the story of how relational psychotherapy works. My bias will shine through clearly.

I might say that for all of these reasons I am most drawn to intersubjectivist, developmentally-minded, self psychological relational theory. But the truth, I think, is that my bias constructs even the "reasons" I use to support it. My bias has certainly helped construct my sketch of the Big Picture of contemporary relational psychoanalytic theory. So it goes with bias and theorizing. If you are new to relational theory, you need to know that bias is inevitable in this complex field. As you try to find your way in it, it will be important for you to understand how various biases shape various modes of relational theory. It will be important that you pay attention, over time, to your own biases and to how they determine what you understand and what you want to pursue.

On the whole, it behooves relational therapists to remember that even their theory is a relational activity, a self-with-other phenomenon that emerges from interaction and is held in being—for a while—in communities of shared thoughts and experiences. After a while, their theory will be on its way to new interactions and new constructions. Knowing all of this, relationalists can both throw themselves into the creative tussle of theorizing and also remember to hold their theories lightly.

THE RELATIONAL VISION: REPRISE

In spite of all its biased diversity and eclectic complexity, relational theory does rest on some shared givens, on what we might call a common relational bias, and in ordinary language it goes something like this: All human beings are indeed creatures formed by their social contexts. There's no escaping this reality. But sometimes some of us have opportunities to reflect on what forms us, and through that reflection, to make room for changes we hope for. Therapy offers such opportunities.

As a relational therapist, you will offer a client a particular kind of opportunity to grapple with the relational forces that have formed him. You will offer him the chance to engage in a relationship that will put those forces into play. It's a real relationship, and your own formative forces will be in it, too. In this relationship, for his benefit, you will reflect together on his past and present experience in the world and on what the two of you experience together. You will hope for new meanings to emerge, a new narrative that makes better sense of his experiences, and a new way of being in relationship together. You will hope, ultimately, that this will all lead to significant changes in how he can experience himself in his social contexts—as less depressed and anxious, as more connected and alive, more secure, more able to tolerate risk and loss, more empathic with others, more confident in his own agendas, and more firmly committed to important values and ideals.

None of these hopes for change is unique to relational therapy. What's unique about relational therapy, in all of its incarnations, is how it proposes to get to those changes—through a relationship lived out for real, together, between you and your client. This relationship is a mutual risk, a joint commitment, an interactive process, a shared journey. The rest of this book tells the story of the journey.

ENDNOTES

1. Freud's writings are collected in a multi-volume work: Sigmund Freud, *The Standard Edition of the Complete Psychological Works of Sigmund Freud*, translated by James Strachey and published between 1953 and 1966 by Hogarth Press, London.
2. See Carl Jung and Marie-Louise von Franz, Eds., *Man and His Symbols* (New York: Doubleday, 1964).
3. Carl Rogers, *Counseling and Psychotherapy* (Boston: Houghton Mifflin, 1942), and *On Becoming a Person* (Boston: Houghton Mifflin, 1961).
4. Michael White and David Epston, *Narrative Means to Therapeutic Ends* (New York: W.W. Norton & Co., 1990). Also of interest: Sheila McNamee and Kenneth J. Gergen, Eds., *Therapy as Social Construction* (Newbury Park, CA: Sage Publications, 1992).
5. Laura Brown, *Subversive Dialogues: Theory in Feminist Therapy* (New York: Basic Books, 1994).
6. Judith V. Jordan, Alexandra G. Kaplan, Jean Baker Miller, Irene P. Stiver, and Janet L. Surrey, *Women's Growth in Connection: Writings from the Stone Center* (New York: Guilford Press, 1991).
7. In this text I will put "relational psychoanalysis" in quotation marks when I'm not

sure that the reader will otherwise understand that I'm talking about the school of thought that's a counterpart to self psychology. In this text, the self-designated school of "relational psychoanalysis" is a subset of relational psychoanalysis—that whole relational movement within psychoanalysis that includes self psychology.

8. Lewis Aron, *A Meeting of Minds: Mutuality in Psychoanalysis* (Hillsdale, NJ: Analytic Press, 1996), 56.

9. This state of affairs is reflected in the conference history of the relational psychoanalytic movement. Self psychological relationalists generate and attend a conference of their own every year; 2002 marks the twenty-fifth year of the annual International Conference on the Psychology of the Self. Simultaneously, for many years analysts from more diverse and eclectic relational positions, including many interpersonalists, have gathered and presented papers at meetings of the Psychoanalytic Division (Division 39) of the American Psychological Association. In 2002 a new conference was initiated by a new association, the International Association for Relational Psychoanalysis and Psychotherapy. Named in honor of the late relational psychoanalyst Stephen Mitchell, the conference was designed to engender conversations between the diverse streams of relational psychoanalysis, including self psychology, and to include psychotherapists—not just psychoanalysts— in those conversations. Perhaps this marks the beginning of a new era of common cause and inclusivity among relational psychoanalysts and psychotherapists, but only time will tell.

10. Aron, *A Meeting of Minds*, 25–26.

11. "Playing with Your Cards Face-up" was the title of a seminar Owen Renik presented in Toronto in 1999. In "The Perils of Neutrality," *Psychoanalytic Quarterly* 65, 495– 517 (1996), Renik argues persuasively for a dialectical kind of learning in psychoanalysis that requires that the analyst own up to his or her intentions to influence the patient in ways that the analyst believes will be in the patient's best interests. When these feelings and intentions are on the table, the patient can engage with them as the analyst's personal and fallible opinions, not as moral or scientific authority, and use them to learn more about his or her own reality.

12. Darlene Bregman Ehrenberg, *The Intimate Edge: Extending the Reach of Psychoanalytic Interaction* (New York: W.W. Norton, 1992).

13. Stephen Mitchell, *Relational Concepts in Psychoanalysis: An Integration* (Cambridge, MA: Harvard University Press, 1988); *Hope and Dread in Psychoanalysis* (New York: Basic Books, 1993); *Influence and Autonomy in Psychoanalysis* (Hillsdale, NJ: Analytic Press, 1997); *Relationality: From Attachment to Intersubjectivity* (Hillsdale, NJ: Analytic Press, 2000).

14. Jessica Benjamin, *The Bonds of Love: Psychoanalysis, Feminism, and the Problem of Domination* (New York: Pantheon, 1988), and *Like Subjects, Love Objects: Essays on Recognition and Sexual Difference* (New Haven and London: Yale University Press, 1995).

15. Mitchell, *Influence and Autonomy in Psychoanalysis*.

16. Heinz Kohut, *How Does Analysis Cure?* (Chicago: University of Chicago Press, 1984). Ernest Wolf, *Treating the Self: Elements of Clinical Self Psychology* (New York: Guilford Press, 1988).

17. Robert D. Stolorow and George E. Atwood, *Contexts of Being: The Intersubjective Foundations of Psychological Life* (Hillsdale, NJ: Analytic Press, 1992). Donna M. Orange, *Emotional Understanding: Studies in Psychoanalytic Epistemology* (New York: Guilford Press, 1995).

18. Howard Bacal, Ed., *Optimal Responsiveness: How Therapists Heal Their Patients* (Northvale, NJ: Jason Aronson, 1998).

19. Daniel Stern, *The Interpersonal World of the Infant: A View from Psychoanalysis and Developmental Psychology* (New York: Basic Books, 1985). Joseph Lichtenberg, *Psychoanalysis and Motivation* (Hillsdale, NJ: Analytic Press, 1989).
20. For example, Stone Center theory attends not only to gender but also to culture, race, class, and sexual orientation. Jessica Benjamin consistently positions herself at the intersection of feminist and relational psychoanalytic theory. Neil Altman, writing as a relational psychoanalyst who also uses projective-introjective object relations theory to understand the intrapsychic and relational power of social constructs, envisions the realities of economics, race, and class entering the therapeutic relationship as concretely as a third person, with profound effects on both client and therapist and on their relationship: Neil Altman, *The Analyst in the Inner City: Race, Class, and Culture through a Psychoanalytic Lens* (Hillsdale, NJ: Analytic Press, 1995). Relational analysts and therapists are among the contributors to a collection of essays that explore similar questions about connections between multiculturalism and social diversity on the one hand and psychoanalytic or psychodynamic theory on the other: RoseMarie Pérez Foster, Michael Moskowitz, and Rafael Art Javier, Eds., *Reaching across Boundaries of Culture and Class: Widening the Scope of Psychotherapy* (Northvale, NJ: Jason Aronson, 1996).

2

BEGINNING WITH THE BASICS
Structure, Ethics, and Empathy

FIRST SESSIONS, FIRST QUESTIONS

In order to look at the basics of relational psychotherapy, we'll start from the vantage point of your first meeting with a particular client. Let's say that a week ago this client left you a phone message. A friend had recommended you, she said. You returned her call, and in your brief conversation, she volunteered that she's having trouble with different things in her life right now, work and relationships. Things aren't going well, and she thinks she needs someone to talk to. She told you that she hasn't tried therapy before, and she asked if you could say something about how you work.

You said, "I think it will be important for us pay careful attention to what's troubling you, and then we'll go from there. We'll stay with your sense of what you need from therapy. That's my approach to therapy—it's client-centered." You established a time and fee with her and made sure she knows where your office is. She asked about parking, and how long a session would last, and you answered her questions.

Now, as you meet her in the waiting room and introduce yourself, she greets you anxiously. You're aware of some performance anxiety yourself, something that's always around when you meet a new client, but you manage it by concentrating on putting her at ease. You invite her into your office, and as she settles into the chair opposite yours, you suggest that she tell you what the trouble is, what's on her mind. She outlines the trouble in her life while you listen quietly, making brief comments that show you're getting it, and asking a few questions for clarification. After a long, complex story has emerged and you're nearing the end of the session, she asks, "So, do you think you can help me?"

You reiterate what you said on the phone, something like, "I think what you need from me, right now, is that I really understand what you're going through." Her face says she doesn't quite get it, so you go on. "Just understanding it together can make a big difference. Sometimes the next part—what to do differently—comes clear as soon as you've had a chance to explore what's actually happening. We've made a good start on that today, I think." The idea of a good start satisfies her.

Since it's time to end, you ask her whether she would like to make another appointment, and she says she would like to do that. "See you next week," you say warmly as you see her to the door. You close the door and sit down for a moment, wondering, "How did that go for her? What's she feeling now?" You feel it went pretty well; it seemed that she was able to take in your understanding. How did that happen? What did you do to help make that happen?

It's second nature by now—how you let your feelings show on your face, how you tell a client you're there with "Mmhmm" and "Yes" from time to time. You check in with her, saying things like, "It sounds like that was the hardest part," or "If I'm getting it, you had really mixed feelings about that event." With this client, as with every client, you paid attention to what seemed to put her at ease. Some clients need questions and prompting, especially in a first session. Open space and time make them too nervous to know what to say. This client seemed to need you to be quiet while she organized her thoughts. You didn't think that out while you were with her. You just fit your energy level and rhythms of speech to hers, easing her way. So although you never said a word about the therapy relationship, already you've begun to work on it from your side as you interact with the cues she has given you.

Near the end of the session, your client remarked, "That was easier than I thought it would be! The time just flew!" It seems this is one of those clients who from the beginning can experience you as someone who wants to understand who they are, who tries to put them at ease and draw them out. You're happy to do your part to make that experience possible. This is a comfortable and promising way to begin therapy.

Now your client is on the street, maybe in a coffee shop, thinking about what happened. Maybe she's mulling over how comfortable it felt. But questions and worries begin to swirl around, too. Was it too comfortable? She wonders, "Exactly what kind of a relationship is this? If it's not clinical, if the therapist isn't going to diagnose the problem and prescribe a treatment, how is it different from a friendship?" She remembers what you said about how understanding helps. She didn't know what it would feel like to be understood, but now she wants more of that; she wants to count on that. She wonders how much she can count on your understanding. If she were feeling really rotten tomorrow, could she call you on the phone? Would you come to her rescue? What are the boundaries of this relationship?

Because you know these questions will come up soon for your client, early in the next session you talk about some of the practical boundaries of the therapy, things you didn't get around to in the first session—policies about how you respond to phone messages, about payments and receipts, cancellations, extra sessions, and vacations (hers and yours). If you think the two of you might frequent some of the same organizations or areas of town, you ask how she'd like to handle accidental meetings. Would she like you to acknowledge her or not? Paying attention to the many small ways in which therapy is a strange, specialized relationship with its own boundaries and protocols helps to settle her anxiety about how to continue in this relationship. She can relax when she knows that you know how to handle this strangeness.

You can handle the strange situation of a therapy relationship because you've given it a lot of thought. You won't spell it all out unless your client asks you to, but behind all the ways in which you set up the parameters of how the two of you will be together, there stands your coherent sense of the structure and boundaries of any therapy relationship. Since you are a relational therapist, it fits together something like this:

At the heart of relational therapy there is the therapist's commitment to be present, with caring and focus, in the relationship. That commitment is particularly about being present while in session in the therapy room. You will be available for emergencies at other times, but you know very well that the most useful therapy work you can do with your client happens within the boundaries of regular sessions at regular times. You will express that conviction in various ways. If your client makes a phone call when in distress, you will be considerate and understanding. You will acknowledge and affirm your client's need to make a connection for reassurance, but you will probably also keep the call short and suggest that the two of you discuss this issue in much more detail when you next meet. And when you do meet, you will want to spend time trying to understand what happened to so distress your client. What your client begins to realize is that the kind of being-with that she counts on and longs for is best available to her in session. But as she settles into that rhythm, she also realizes how much more available you are to her in session than she ever imagined could be possible.

Those feelings that scared her after the first session—feelings that she needed your care and understanding far more than she ever wanted to—may not go away. And your client's feeling of not wanting to need you may become an angry emotion tangled up with resentment that you can't be available to her all the time. Whatever you start to stand for in her daily thoughts, however powerful her feelings toward you may become, as a relational therapist you hold firm in the belief that those feelings are a rich resource for the work of therapy. You want to hear about those feelings. That's how available you are to her in session. There is nothing between the two of you that she's not allowed to talk about, and the more she is able to talk about, the better. This kind of talking may be frightening for her, but it makes for powerful learning and change.

All of this is to say that the important boundaries in therapy—no social contact between yourself and your client, no other kinds of dual relationships, meeting only at set times and in a set place, and doing the important work of therapy in sessions—have a critically important function. The point of them all is to make a safe space for honest talk in the therapy relationship. Because this is therapy, and only therapy, you and your client can explore what's happening between the two of you. Together you can note her responses to how you treat her—her fears, fantasies, wishes, assumptions, hopes, and resentments. It's the very firmness of your mutual contract to do therapy, something the two of you do together at regular times, that creates the freedom to be deeply real within that time. No ordinary relationship could bear this kind of intense working on what happens between two persons, in the interest of one of those parties being profoundly understood.

It's also very important to note that for a relational therapist, boundaries are not about avoiding or subverting your client's dependency on you. In the first place, dependency, with its negative connotations, isn't a useful word for what happens in therapy. Secondly, what is often called dependency will be an important platform for the changes therapy fosters. As I'll explain later (in Chapter 6), the relational therapist believes that the therapy relationship can meet some important needs that might help a client jump-start some blocked personal growth. And it will be just as important for the client to talk about her good relational feelings in therapy as it is for her to be open about the things that worry and upset her.

If your client expresses misgivings about the boundaries of relational therapy, you can tell her straightforwardly that although the relationship involves both of you, it is there entirely for her benefit and well-being. You might say something like, "What I get out of this is just to do good work with you, to be the best therapist I can be with you; the relationship is for you." You might add, "And I find this especially important to say to people who have been manipulated and used in relationships." You know that if your client has already been abused, tricked, and taken advantage of in relationships with powerful people, she will need to hear that said out loud. Her fears of it happening again won't dissolve with your reassurance, but at least she'll know that the question, "Who is this for?" can be spoken, and that you know what the question means to her.

In beginning sessions, various aspects of your professional ethics will emerge as you tell your client about your understanding of your contractual obligations to her—for example, that you will return her telephone calls as soon as possible, that you will give her as much notice as you can of any changes in your schedule, that whatever she tells you (unless it reveals child abuse or the endangerment of life) will be entirely confidential, and that although you consult with a supervisor about your work, you will never refer to her by name or reveal any other identifying information. With time and experience with you, your client's understanding of the ethic of this relationship will deepen. She'll begin to see how the "contract" of relational therapy, including the ethical obligations implicit in it, is entirely consistent with how the therapy works. To put it simply, you want to engage with her in ways that are clear, honest, and always with her benefit and well-being in mind, and you invite her to engage with you as honestly as she can, too. The better you can do that together, the better the therapy works. You tell your client that if anything you say or do feels not right or good for her and her well-being, it's important to say so as soon as possible—because those are exactly the realities in the relationship that need to be attended to very carefully, if a relational way of working is to live up to its potential.

As your client tries to understand what she's getting herself into with this relational therapy, she may well ask you, "How long will this take?"

What's an honest and ethical answer to that question? Many relational therapists say simply, "I really don't know. I think we'll find out as we go along." Others might elaborate, "Sometimes there's a very particular trouble that needs an understanding ear so that you can get your balance back, find your way, and get to feeling okay again. That can happen in a few weeks or months. Other times there's a whole lot out of whack in your life, and what you need is a lot more time to talk about it, more time to get to feeling stronger and more okay. It will be your choice—how long we do this. I imagine you'll choose on the basis of what you're getting out of it, how you feel it's helping you as we go along." With practice, you'll find answers that feel both useful and honest in various client situations.

WHAT'S ALL THIS ABOUT EMPATHY?

We've been noting that as your client begins relational therapy, she enters a particular kind of relationship with well-defined boundaries and ethics. The structure of this therapy relationship comes from establishing a special, protected, repetitive time and place for talking together. The ambiance or "soul" of this relationship, however, comes from something else—from your intentional and thoroughgoing empathy. A relational therapist without empathy is like a tennis player without a racquet or a lifeguard who can't swim. Empathy is your relational mode of operation, your way to keep things moving. Empathy is the primary tool of your work and the skill that makes it possible for you to be a therapist. Let's take a closer look at this empathy.

Able to Feel

What is empathy? The essence and movement of any human feeling—fear, anger, respect, shame, love—are difficult to describe. Empathy is no exception. But since it is so crucial in the unfolding of relational therapy, there's a lot of talk in the field about what empathy is and how it works. Perhaps it is better described as a capacity or ability than as a feeling—in fact, a capacity to feel many different kinds of feelings.

Heinz Kohut, the father of self psychology, defined empathy as "vicarious introspection," or "the capacity to think and feel oneself into the inner life of another person."[1] Years earlier, Carl Rogers built a therapeutic system on the therapist's ability to let himself go in order to deeply understand each particular client, with "no inner barriers [to] keep him from sensing what it feels like to be the client at each moment of the relationship."[2]

The empathic therapist, then, is not afraid to feel. But aren't we all afraid to feel? Isn't that what a lot of therapy is about—helping people tolerate feelings that would be too much to bear alone? How can an empathic therapist be not afraid to feel? There's a simple answer to that question, if not so simply attained: a therapist who is not afraid to enter the experience of the darkest and most painful moments of clients' lives is a therapist who has done her own therapy. She has been helped by someone else to face her own fears and feel what she could not bear to feel alone. This puts a different spin on the Freudian insistence that analysts undergo their own analysis. The point is not that you come to know all there is to know about your own inner workings, but that you develop the inner courage and resilience to be able to feel whatever needs to be felt—that you have, as Rogers put it, no inner barriers.

In the humanist tradition of psychotherapy, therapists are often trained in groups that encourage authentic encounters and expression of feelings among members. Behind this practice is the belief that intense group experience does even more than individual therapy can do to help a therapist become comfortable with a wide range of feelings within herself and others. But however you come to it, this capacity is crucial for a therapist—to be able to be with and to endure many kinds of suffering. Of course, you need not have experienced all the varieties of loss, humiliation, betrayal, abandonment, unfulfilled longing, loneliness, despair, and helplessness that others bring to you, but you do need to have truly felt your own experience of any of those kinds of suffering. If you haven't faced what hurts you, you will flinch away from clients' stories in order to protect yourself from your own history.

When you have felt your own history, you can also make links between your experience and your clients' experiences, the better to understand them. Sometimes you will still feel afraid of a story that's especially horrific or hopeless or strikes very close to home. But when you have done your own work in therapy, you will know when you feel afraid, and you will know to talk about your feelings in supportive relationships with supervisors and experienced peers. Your experience in therapy will have taught you how to get the help you need in order to acknowledge, understand, and bear whatever feelings come up for you as you immerse yourself in your clients' experiences.

Able to Communicate Feeling

Rogers also believed that it was essential for the therapist to be able to communicate the flow of her "feeling-with" the client in an immediate, moment-to-moment kind of way. This communication was to be an expression of the therapist's genuineness; the goal was a kind of emotional transparency. This authentic communication of the therapist's empathic connection with the client's experience would make it possible for the client to be more fully within the stream of her own feelings, integrating them experientially into what humanists envisioned as a fuller, deeper, and more authentic sense of self.

As the self-authenticating, here-and-now 1960s gave way to the 1970s, a certain group of psychoanalysts began to emphasize empathy too. Their leading theorist, Heinz Kohut, called this new stream of psychoanalytic thinking "self psychology," and, as I've said, he described empathy as vicarious introspection, or immersion in the patient's subjective world.

Early self psychologists assumed that this empathy was a tool readily available to therapists, and they saw the communication of empathy not so much as a gateway to the patient's authentic experience as a gateway to the patient's insight. For them, vicarious introspection would lead eventually to the patient's ability to be introspective herself and thus to develop that marriage of emotional and cognitive insight that would free her from her internal conflicts. A self psychological communication of empathy tended, then, to be in the form of ideas about the patient's experience that would lead the patient gently toward new understandings of herself. The therapist's empathy had to include the ability to translate feelings into ideas that didn't get too far away from the original feelings.

In the psychoanalytic world, it was revolutionary for self psychology to suggest that the therapist's empathy was as important as the patient's insight for the resolution of psychological problems. Self psychologists noted that their empathic understanding from a patient's point of view eased the patient's shame and thus broadened space for self-reflection. Such empathy also encouraged the patient to count on the therapist for those particular kinds of understanding that had been missing for the patient in childhood. In the presence of these particular kinds of empathic connection, certain kinds of aborted or stunted self-development could begin again for the patient, filling in deficits in her previously shaky self-structure. For example, in the presence of someone strong and supportive, the patient could begin to feel safe and strong herself, and in the presence of affirmation, she could begin to enjoy her own competence.

In this self psychological use of empathy, the therapist's communications to the patient are constantly adjusted according to the therapist's developing sense of which particular kinds of connection the patient needs for optimal growth. Perhaps she needs a kind of empathy, for example, that only reflects her experience, for anything added feels intrusive or controlling. Or maybe, on the other hand, she needs to hear something more from the therapist, something that will allow her to feel secure in the presence of someone wiser and stronger, or something that will let her know she's not the only one who has ever felt this way.

Now when empathy is fine-tuned according to the patient's needs, whether they be needs to gain particular insights or particular kinds of growth, it's clear that the therapist is no longer being simply authentic and transparent, sharing whatever comes up in himself in response to the patient's flow of feeling. Unlike the humanist therapist, who shares his own experience, the self psychologist shapes his responses around what he understands the patient's experience to be. In other words, these early sources on empathy, self psychological and humanist, are proposing two very different kinds of communication of empathy. But neither of them has the last word, because several decades after Rogers began writing and a decade after self psychology came onto the psychoanalytic scene, infant studies began to complicate and enrich the picture of how empathy is communicated between infants and their caretakers, and, by extension, between any two human beings.

As we noted in Chapter 1, although Rogers and other humanists had a profound and prophetic understanding of the power of empathy, they still worked from an individualistic worldview. For them, empathy was a neutral medium, created by the therapist's authenticity, within which a client's authenticity could emerge. They didn't pay much attention to how the therapist and client co-created the limits and freedoms of their mutual relationship, or the shape and feel of the empathy possible between them, and how they thus co-created the very modes through which "self" and "other" could be known in this relationship. Likewise, although early self psychologists believed that human selves need others like human bodies need oxygen, their understanding of the exchange between these selves was fairly linear and usually one way—from the provider of empathy (therapist/parent) to the receiver of empathy (client/child).

A more systemic and mutual sense of the empathic exchange didn't emerge until the 1980s, when therapists began to look at what Daniel Stern called "the interpersonal world of the infant." Baby studies began to show two things about empathy: (1) instead of being a neutral medium offered by one who has the capacity for it to another who needs it, empathy is a system active between participants who are each constantly contributing to how that system works; and (2) the communications that establish and regulate a system of empathy are subtle and ongoing, and they include a wide variety of nonverbal and verbal cues. Often, instead of "empathy," baby-watchers speak of the parent's attunement to the infant and the infant's reciprocal attunement to the parent. These attunements, with all of their shadings and near-misses, become patterns of infant–caregiver mutual regulation—a shape and feel of relationship that is formed by and that forms a certain kind of baby and a certain kind of parent. In other words, in this view empathy is not just an understanding to be communicated between two entirely separate selves; it is itself a complex system of communication that, while the communication is happening, is shaping the sense of "self" of the persons who are communicating, be they infant, child, or adult.

This much more complex view of how empathy is elicited, communicated, and received leaves contemporary relational therapists with a different set of considerations about how to do their work. Authenticity between two persons becomes a contradictory concept if what either person is feeling at any given moment cannot escape the influence of the other. But rather than trying to purify empathy of this mutual influence, today's relationalists pay close attention to the unique ways in which connection takes shape between themselves and each of their clients. This view also makes obsolete the idea of empathy as a one-way movement from the therapist's vicarious introspection to well-crafted expressions of his understanding, which will help fill in the client's deficits.

As a contemporary relational therapist, you work in a much more complicated, bi-directional field. You don't have to worry, however, that you won't be objective enough to know what to provide for a client in need. Objectivity is no longer the point. Instead, with a systemic view of empathy, you trust that in the push and pull of what goes on between you and your client, you will together find ways of connecting that work for both of you. Exploring, understanding, and improving that mutual connection is the point. In this systemic and mutual view of empathy, the communicated, shared experience of empathic connection between persons becomes far more of a mystery to enter than a tool to master. "Able to communicate empathy" means able to persist in that mysterious dance, making connections happen around, through, and beyond inevitable misses and disconnections.

Able to Know Who Is Who (and What Is What)

Empathy is a system of mutual cues and responses that regulate each participant's experience of self and the other in the system. But at the same time, each participant is a separate person, with his or her unique subjective reality. Empathy is a mutual activity, and yet the empathy that therapists and the parents of young children put into play does not expect an equivalent empathy in return. Therapists, like parents, practice intentional, purposeful, and self-reflexive empathy. The therapists and parents concentrate on understanding what the client or child is experiencing. Often they do much of the work of suggesting words and meanings for what's happening. They carry the responsibility of keeping clear whose feelings are whose. They hold in mind the separate uniqueness of their own and the other's experience. We might call this constructive empathy, an empathy that knows what it's doing. This knowing may not be conscious or articulated, but it is present even between adult friends who know that when one is in trouble, the other provides a special kind of listening, listening full of caring and feeling-with, but listening that doesn't take over the other's hurt or get lost in it.

The Stone Center theorists argue that such mature, intentional empathy is the work that has fallen to women in our culture—and therefore it has not been honored as a gift or a special capacity. In fact, it has been devalued, just as "we-ness" has been set up as the flawed opposite of autonomy. And so, while fully appreciating the interactive mutual nature of empathy, Judith Jordan, one of the Stone Center writers, also highlights the strengths and powers embedded in the intentional practice of empathy: (1) a secure, well-differentiated sense of self, including the flexible self-boundaries that make it possible to step into—and out of—the other person's shoes, feeling both sameness and difference; (2) the ability not only to feel-with but also to give meaning to that feeling with thought; and (3) the ability to use these feeling–thoughts to help the other understand his or her inner world better.

Those who have the good fortune to be held within this kind of intentional empathic connection are given a wonderful chance to learn that people can be at the same time both uniquely separate and self-directed and also joined in their feelings and understandings. In time, the recipients of such empathy will be able to extend this kind of empathic understanding to others. In therapy, a client can also turn this fledgling capacity for empathy toward herself, allowing for the integration of feelings, memories, and self-representations that had been shut away by shame.[3]

WHAT DOES THIS EMPATHY DO FOR YOUR CLIENT?

This is all very interesting, you might say, but how does it play out when a client sits down to talk with me? Let's explore that question for a while. First of all, what does it mean for your client that you have been in therapy yourself, facing your own fears and bearing your own most painful feelings? It means that you know what it's like to be in the client's chair right now. Remembering how it was for you, you understand how ashamed she may be to tell her story, or how frightened she may be of her emotions. It means that even though you never speak of your own experience, your responses to her feel grounded and sure, and she can begin to count on you for understanding that runs deeper than words.

Your commitment to doing your own emotional work means that no matter how harrowing your client's memories, how intense her fear or rage, or how bone-wearying her depression, you're there for it all. If you start to feel overwhelmed, you take care of yourself so that you won't abandon her or disappear. While the two of you work together, she can be sure that you are paying close attention to how it feels be with her, so that if you sense some scare in yourself, some resistance or defense against what she feels, you will get the help you need to be able to return fully to the relationship. You will be especially careful to know about the feelings you have when the feelings she has are all about you. Her feelings about you matter profoundly to her therapy, and if your feelings get in the way, you won't be able to hear how the therapy is for her. Your ongoing connection with your own emotional responses and your ability to deal with them appropriately means that the two of you will be able to work together with all of the very important information that emerges in the give and take of your relationship.

What does it mean for your client, then, that in addition to being able to be with her in her feelings, you consistently try to communicate your empathy? Well, without some communicative effort on your part, she might never know that you get it! What's more, your ways of communicating through eye contact, facial expression, body language, and verbal response add up to the experience of being with a real person—a real person who is affected by who your client is and what she has to say. As she watches you trying hard to understand how it is for her, she may be able to feel the care and attention in your effort and in your further concern about how your responses affect her. All of that may help her feel more like a real person herself, with a story and feelings that actually matter.

As a contemporary relational therapist, you will try to balance your genuine presence with efforts to give your client the kind of response that seems most helpful in a given moment. You know that you will never strike the perfect balance between expressing your authentic responses and meeting your client's needs, for those two intentions exist in tension. You know, furthermore, that this tension is part of a much more complex picture in which empathy is a dance of separateness and connection all at once, as infant studies demonstrate.

What does it mean for your client that you have listened to what some of those baby-watchers have said about the mutuality of empathy? It means that you attend to how the two of you keep co-constructing your ways of connection. At first this will be just part of your careful listening. Later, as appropriate, you may share with her what you notice about your mutual style of connection and invite her to do her own noticing. As the two of you pay attention to the kinds of responses that help or hinder her, to what scares her and what makes her feel safe, the therapy becomes slowly cleared for freer expressions of who she is and what she feels.

What's the overall effect of this kind of attention to the process of connecting with each other? After a while your client begins to realize that you aren't sifting through her feelings in order to find out the real truth about her, something she might never have guessed. On the contrary, she, her being, is what is real to you. Her immediate experience is what matters. Her experience matters even more than the various narratives she constructs to explain her experience. From day to day and over time her stories may shift and change in feeling and emphasis. But the bottom-line "real" for her remains the reality of the connection between the two of you and the fact that you believe her. You know that her story is who she's come to be and how she's come to know herself through years of other relationships. Her story is as real as she is; in fact, she and her story are one and the same bundle of meanings as she tells them to you. And yet even the telling puts those meanings into further motion. The meanings move between the two of you, and your client finds herself moving and changing along with them. Eventually she might even find herself enjoying the adventure of not knowing what she'll say today, what will happen next, or what it will mean.

We noted above that although the therapy relationship is formed through mutual attunement, the empathy mobilized in therapy has one purpose: the client's emotional health and well-being. What does it mean for your client that you take responsibility for maintaining empathy for her without expecting empathy in return? She might find that situation unthinkable, for it's not how social relationships work. Or perhaps she's been well-trained in other relationships to look after the other person's emotional well-being before her own. This training is most potent when it happens to children who must look after emotionally needy parents. If this was the case for her, she may slowly realize how diligently she looks after you whether you need looking after or not (she has to assume you do). At first it will disorient her whole system to realize that maybe she doesn't have to be "good" in therapy, the parentified child ever careful of a fragile mom or dad. Eventually, though, she may be able to relax, becoming secure in the presence of a competent, emotionally sturdy adult whose chief concern is her well-being.

What does it mean for your client that you can feel her feelings with her and at the same time be clear that you aren't her? Let's put the question the other way around. What if, as she talked, you would fill up the space between you with your own emotions? What if you seemed to believe that she is just like you, or that you know better than she does what she is feeling and why? This sort of emotional takeover is as disturbing for a client—for anyone!—as emotional abandonment. Actually, it's just the other side of the same coin; to take over another's emotional space is a very powerful way to fail to be with a person, and thus to abandon her without seeming to. Straightforward desertion can be far easier to cope with, because then at least a person can be clear about what has happened.

Clients who come to therapy hoping against hope to be understood, wanting understanding but believing it just can't happen, have very likely suffered some combination of emotional neglect and emotional takeover. Whichever side of that coin was up, what happened to them was a massive failure of empathy. Here and now with you, if on the one hand you won't disappear on them, and on the other hand you won't take over their emotional space with your feelings, needs, and agendas, they may finally discover a space in which they can find out who they really are through expressing what they really think and feel.

Infant studies support the claim that anyone's felt sense of self ("I know who I am, what I want, how I feel") comes into being only as there is response to a self's developing motivations, desires, and feelings. Where there is a dearth of empathy or very inaccurate, intrusive attunement to an infant's or a child's communication of wants and feelings, the child's sense of self begins to fade and fragment. A therapy of empathy offers someone who will listen and not intrude, who will wait for and celebrate the return of a self's own feelings. A client will find her own lost self not in the misty past but in her current moment-to-moment experience, when she can finally pay attention to it. That's exactly where her self got lost once, when nobody paid attention or they paid the kind of attention that had little or nothing to do with her.

How can you show care not to take over your client's feelings? You can respond in the form of "wondering." You can use the word "maybe" a lot. You can indicate that you're *trying* to get it; this is what you understand so far, but you'd like to get it better. Clients will begin to count on this respectful, open-ended curiosity, and then they will join in the shared process of "getting it." In fact, the process of creating understanding will become more important to them than getting a perfect empathic response right off the bat from you. Why is this? Because what they need is not perfect empathy, but the experience of a relationship in which they are free to work out mutual understanding with a reliable partner. (Infants and young children don't need perfect empathy, either; in fact, over-attunement can be stifling and intrusive. On the other hand, they do badly need the experience of ongoing relationships in which misattunements and misunderstandings can be repaired and the relationship put back on track.)[4]

You can be sure that your client will know, if only vaguely, that there's a very good reason for you to be tentative with your empathy. You can't ever assume that you know exactly how it is for her, because you aren't her. Neither she nor you can ever get out of your own skins, your own histories and current social locations. You can only see her from where you are, and she will be reassured to sense that you know that this is true, and that therefore you won't try to "know it all" or in some subtle way tell her how she feels or what's true for her. She might sometimes wish that you had a "God's eye view" of her and all the answers that go along with that, but on the whole and in the end, she'll be glad that you're a fallible real person trying to understand her the best you can.

Your understanding involves more than just respectful feeling into your client's feelings. Your empathy comes with thought. In your own mind, you construct an ongoing narrative of your client's life, past and present. You think about patterns in her life, her recurring fears, assumptions, and hopes, and how they play out. You think about how she is able to express herself and what seems to block her. You ponder the experiences you share in therapy and wonder how they affect her feelings.

What does it mean to your client that you bring a great deal of thought to your emotional understanding? It might mean that for the first time in her life your client begins to sense that she does really exist over time as a three-dimensional person who can be known in depth by someone else. As your client experiences your thoughtful connection to her inner world, she learns not *what* is going on for her—that's hers to discover with your help—but *how* to wonder and think about the workings of her own inner world. As her capacity to self-reflect expands, her sense of self grows stronger and more resilient.

And at the same time, it can be a great relief to your client not to have to be thinking all the time, making sense of things, self-reflecting, connecting the dots. It's a great relief to know that someone else is minding the store, to know that she can trust you not to lose track of what's going on, not to forget the way she's come or all the things she's learned about herself. Sometimes, especially if your client always had to keep herself safe by understanding everything, it can be quite wonderful for her to just let herself be, feel, talk, float, and know that someone she trusts is doing the understanding for a while. You're on top of it, so right now she doesn't have to take care of a thing, control for chaos, or make any sense of what's happening. Part of what makes those moments of letting go possible is her repeated experience of always being able to come back with you to making meaning and finding understanding when she wants to.

We took note above of the Stone Center idea that through experiencing a therapist's empathy, a client can begin to have empathy for herself. This process often begins with a client's gentler sensitivity to what she's going through right now. As you listen with care and empathy to her story, she begins to realize that whatever is hurting her, it isn't trivial, stupid, or a product of her own weakness. Then she might begin to notice links between the current trouble and what she remembers of similar situations and feelings in her years of growing up—*when it wasn't her fault, either.* Another layer of empathy has become available to her: feelings for the child that she was, a child who made sense of what troubled her by deciding that something was wrong with her—*she* was the problem. Now the shame or disgust she has felt about that child can give way to understanding and then to grief for what she lost, and to loving respect for how she did the best she could anyway.

When there's more room in your client's imagination for the reality of her own struggles, she begins to see other people differently, too. We might say she has more empathy for them—or more knowing that life is not a simple process of doing things right or wrong, that almost everybody gets burdened by family legacies of shame or guilt, and that the secrets of being okay lie not in escaping trouble but in living through trouble with others, supported in mutual networks of care and understanding. These new thoughts and feelings will help her find a more grounded, balanced, and secure place in her own present life. Sometimes the people she will come to see differently are some of the people who once hurt her most: a frightening, rageful father tormented by the demons of his own depression, an unavailable mom silenced by her own self-doubts, a partner whose childhood pain got so entangled with hers that there was nothing to do but separate.

What's happening to your client? Because she is being understood, she can know what has happened to her, who she is, and what she feels. Now she can move from the emotional traps of old relationships into her own place in the world. As she feels your understanding empathy, she begins to feel in her bones how a body can be both separate, a "self," and connected at the same time. She is coming into a real sense of self not because she's gaining her independence, but because someone else has been there with her. And from that alive and resilient place of knowing "This is me!" she is reaching out for more connection, for relationships in which she both understands and is understood, and in which each participant can come to feel more fully alive, more confident of his or her own unique value.

So in summary, what does empathy mean for your client? What does it do for her? It's a way of being together that you will keep on offering to her. It's both of you tuning in to what she feels, thinks, fears, wants, and hopes for. It's a system of understanding within which you and she discover the meanings and passions of her life. It's the way she can recover her own self-experience and self-esteem, and the way she can find out how to live with others and be both connected with them and her own separate self, all at the same time.

THE SCOPE OF EMPATHY WORK

The power of empathy makes relational therapy a very versatile way to work. For example, although relational therapy doesn't organize itself around the belief that understanding what's wrong will make clients feel better, it often happens that as your empathy draws more of their memories, beliefs, and feelings into the light, many new understanding do emerge, and often just knowing what it's all about does help them feel better—less confused, helpless, and "crazy." Likewise, relational therapy doesn't try particularly hard to unearth clients' memories. It doesn't in any special way go after their feelings, in hopes of release or catharsis, nor does it try to pin down their faulty belief systems and negative thought patterns in order to change them. Nevertheless, as empathy creates new safe space for feeling and remembering, clients may well remember feelings and events they had forgotten, or they may find themselves remembering things in different ways, with feelings that were never safe to have before. As empathy allows them to shake off some shame, they can explore what they actually believe and think, a process that in itself makes space for new ways of thinking. And there's nothing like looking at the therapy relationship itself, through eyes of empathy, in order for clients to experience the hidden power of their core belief systems: how they believe others see them and what kinds of connections they assume are possible between themselves and anyone else.

Relational therapy doesn't make a special point of helping a client make specific changes in his life, unless that's the client's agenda. Your empathy, however, might highlight a client's restless, "stuck" unhappiness and get him moving. Your acceptance of a client's self-doubt might, paradoxically, give that client space to reclaim his confidence. If he is entangled in difficult relationships, you can help him untangle what he needs to say to his parents in order finally to "leave home," or discover his sense of entitlement with his boss, or figure out how he wants to negotiate better ways of give and take with friends and lovers. When there's somebody who really understands how tricky and difficult these issues are for him and who stands right behind him helping him know what he wants, he can find his own way through it all, bit by bit.

Relational therapy doesn't advertise as bereavement counseling, but when a client has suffered a loss, as a relational therapist you will stay with a client's pain and sadness, his anger, loneliness, and despair, and the full range of his memories, regrets, and farewells for as long as he needs you to be there. Sooner or later any client's experience of relational therapy becomes, for a while at least, an experience of grieving—allowing the pain of the past to be real, acknowledging that certain longed-for experiences will never happen, and mourning lost opportunities, failed hopes, and broken dreams.

And finally, although relational therapy wouldn't characterize itself as a spiritual therapy, there's something about creating a quiet space in which to know oneself and be known that invites clients to meditate on the meanings of life, in all of its pain, loss, and beauty.

Such is the breadth of a relational mode of therapy. But don't certain kinds of psychological trouble call for particular kinds of therapeutic expertise? Yes. For example, phobias, obsessions, and compulsions often respond well to desensitization and relaxation techniques, as do the intrusive symptoms associated with recent, sudden trauma. Some relational therapists will have developed additional expertise in these and other special modes of treatment. On the other hand, all relational therapists will suspect that there is more to any story than the symptoms a client describes. For example, sudden unexpected trauma will bring on intrusive symptoms associated with acute fear and anxiety, but it will also, in more hidden ways, shake the victim's entire sense of being safe in a predictable world, and this deeper fear may extend to the world of his relationships with others. Phobias and obsessive-compulsive patterns are also often symptoms of more longstanding and deeply felt assumptions that the world is not safe, and although a person's efforts to control the danger may focus on physical events and objects, usually the danger has a strong interpersonal core. It is not safe to be in the world of people, and by some psychological sleight of mind, avoiding or controlling certain events or thoughts will make it safer. This is where relational therapy can help, gently uncovering the roots of interpersonal fear and slowly establishing a relationship that can be tested and expanded toward more and more interpersonal safety.

Another way to make a scary world feel safer is to become addicted to a mind-numbing, feeling-erasing activity or substance. If a client's presenting problem is an addictive and disordered relationship to food, drink, drugs, sex, gambling, or other repetitive activities, you may, as a relational therapist, refer him to a treatment center that specializes in getting the problem behavior under control, or if you have the training, you may do that work with him yourself. But after the behavior is under control, the real work starts. What is it that he hasn't wanted to know about or feel? Now that he's not numb, what's it like for him to be in his own skin? Can he talk about the emptiness inside, the restlessness and the craving?

As a relational therapist, you will know that the anxious emptiness that drives his craving is itself only a symptom—what he's left with because there's nobody around who sees him or takes time to know who he is, or at least that's how it was in his formative years. By now, his disconnection from others is just a given, and it's a long road back, not just from his addiction but from his conviction that this aloneness is his life. It may take you a long time to get in, to convince him that you're really there and that he matters. But you're in it for the long haul. If he's ever going to get over it, not just the addiction but what drives him to it, this is the kind of long-term help he will need.

People who have suffered childhood physical and sexual abuse (which always includes emotional intrusion and abandonment) also need long-term help. Therapists who work with abuse survivors have a special body of knowledge about the symptoms survivors suffer—various kinds of dissociation, hypervigilance, crippling anxiety, flashbacks, intense shame and self-hatred, and using self-harm to manage overwhelming feelings. Therapists of many schools have learned how to help survivors understand and manage these symptoms in order to create safer everyday environments for themselves.

At the root of all these symptoms, of course, is a devastating betrayal of trust. The very person(s) the child looked to for love and protection also abused him. And yet, to stay alive emotionally and physically, the child had to stay connected to the caregiver(s). If this is your client's story, at the dark, silent center of all of his symptoms, that betrayal lives on, making him sick at heart. No one can be trusted. Love is a lie, a trick. If he doesn't look out for himself, nobody else will. And chances are, no matter how well he watches out and is careful, he's going to get hurt again. Why on earth would he trust a therapist, someone who offers care?

As a relational therapist, you not only help manage and quiet the symptoms that follow traumatic stress, you also step with your client into the impossibility of the new relationship. You know you cannot hope for his trust; you also know that he needs your help desperately. None of this bleak reality is glossed over in relational therapy; to accept it and to understand how it pushes and pulls the client and yourself is where an empathic process must begin. If there is ever to be any undoing of the knot of betrayal inside your client, it will be through a long, hard process of learning to trust you anyway—in spite of all he knows about what's dangerous, and in spite of all the little ways you will fail him, scare him, and in those ways hurt him all over again. This book includes an entire chapter (Chapter 4) about the trials and tribulations of this sort of interpersonal journey; for now the point is, quite simply, that the deep, persistent empathy of relational therapy may be the most fitting therapeutic response to the relational devastation suffered by survivors of childhood abuse.

Indeed, in almost every kind of therapeutic intervention in special situations, the therapist's empathy is a crucial part of the treatment. Furthermore, empathy work links up well with other modes of experience and expression in therapy. For example, when clients express themselves in sculpture, painting, dance, and music, or in dreams, stories, and psychodramas, they need someone present to receive their expression, to feel into it and wonder aloud about its energies, feelings, and meanings. Some relational therapists bring these other modalities into their practice. They seek to broaden and deepen the empathy system between themselves and certain clients by inviting those clients to explore some of these other ways of expressing themselves—nonverbal ways, and ways of talking in story and metaphor.

And then there are all the possibilities alive in relational work with more than one person at a time. What better place for the active, self-reflexive use of empathy than in work with a couple or with several family members? As a relational therapist you can extend empathy freely and equally to every person in the consulting room, knowing that they all have their own subjective truths about what happens in the family and suspecting that every one of them is feeling misunderstood. As their joint therapist, you hope, first of all, that your understanding will slowly quiet the anxiety and defensive anger that prevent them from hearing each other. Even if they can't talk to each other, they can see how feelings change as you put yourself in the shoes of each of them in turn. Without words you will be telling them, over and over, "This is what listening looks like. This is what being heard feels like. When there's empathy in this room, everything gets safer, doesn't it? Wouldn't you like to try it?"

In your relational work with couples, long before the hurt, angry partners are able to try to extend empathy to one another in conversation, each begins to hear secondhand, while the other talks to you, the other's hurts and fears, vulnerabilities that had been hidden behind walls of defense and blame. Each also has the experience of sharing those vulnerabilities with you, someone who listens without jumping in to disagree or to fix or change something. Slowly—how slowly depends on how badly hurt and betrayed each of them feels—you will encourage them to talk with one another and really listen. You may be even more specific. You may give them rules for how they may respond to each other in each step of their dialogue, at least until it becomes easy for each of them not only to hear the other but also to answer in a way that shows emotional understanding of·what the other is trying to say. Couples take home from this process a lot of new information about each other. But none of what they learn matters as much to them as their newfound ability to put empathy to use in their everyday communication.

Finally, a word about relational group therapy. A group set up as relational, set up so that group members will learn from their exchanges and relationships with each other, offers wonderful chances for unleashing the power of empathy. On the one hand there's the chance for a client to be heard and understood by a peer—not a therapist who's been trained to do this "empathy thing." Sometimes empathy can feel more trustworthy when it comes that way. And on the other hand, a client has chances to reciprocate genuinely and find out that his own empathy is powerful, too. A mutual exchange of empathy is always rewarding, and for those who grew up with tight, cold silence or with disrespectful, careless chaos, the giving and receiving of meaningful empathy can be exhilarating. Here at last are opportunities to put into intentional, reflective practice that dance of being open and boundaried, separate and connected; here a client can find out exactly what it feels like to make his own choices from within a web of influence, and to be that self who is a self-in-relation.

Probably the therapeutic scope of empathy is far broader than I have been able to sketch here. On the other hand, as you've made your way through this section, maybe you've begun to wonder if there's anything a relational therapist doesn't take on. Are my claims for the power of empathy too sweeping? I hope I have made it clear that in situations of special injury and special symptoms, it's important to have specialized training. Yet all psychological difficulties require careful, caring understanding of the client's experience of the problem, and relational therapists are very well suited to provide such understanding. Often it turns out that such understanding is also very effective treatment.

Why would this be? Not because empathy is a magic bullet, but because almost any psychological problem can be traced to a self-with-other problem. And most self-with-other problems happen when empathic connection between the selves and others in question has broken down. It makes sense, then, that bringing empathy back into any self-with-other system will begin to ravel up what has become unraveled through disconnection. The relational therapist tries to carry this process as far as it will go. That's why, no matter what problem or symptoms a client brings to therapy, there can be a generic answer to the question, "What's it like to get into relational psychotherapy?" It's like stepping into empathy.

But sometimes even relational therapy doesn't work, and clients leave feeling they didn't get the help they needed. What might have happened?

When would a relational, empathic approach be likely to fail? What are the limits of therapeutic empathy? Well, first of all, since so much depends on forging a relationship, the therapy can run aground if you and the client just don't hit it off. We could call this situation a "personality clash" or, if we could find a way to investigate, we might find that something about you stirred up the client's fear of authority. Or something stirred his fear of becoming vulnerable. And then maybe the client's aggressive mode of protecting himself set off old warning bells for you. It could be that the negative cycle of interaction began with you, not the client. But in any case, what looked like personality clash was just plain fear—on both sides.

Fear is what usually undermines the work of empathy, fear of being hurt again in the same old ways. Sometimes it's fear of just certain interpersonal dangers, for example, fear of being belittled by someone with more power, fear of "being boring," fear of being suddenly unwelcome or "in trouble" for no reason the client can figure out, or fear of having assumptions made about the meanings of his gender, race, class, or sexual orientation. If a client can be helped to express such fears early in the therapy, and if you respond by recognizing them as valid, the therapeutic relationship can be saved. In fact, the relationship grows stronger when its scary aspects are brought honestly into the open. If those fears are strong but remain underground, the therapy probably won't last long. But short or long, it will have been an unsatisfying experience for both client and therapist.

Sometimes the fear that a client brings into therapy is a more universal dread of every kind of interpersonal connection. Any real connection is a powerful threat, for it makes him unbearably vulnerable to being hurt. Often this client hardly knows he's scared, because his life is built around ways to live out his roles and take care of the business of life without feeling much at all. He expects you, as his therapist, to tell him why he has his symptoms of depression and obsessive thoughts; he wants to set goals and devise strategies for solving his problems. What he'd really like is a book to read and a homework assignment. What he really doesn't want is a relationship that's alive and moving between himself and the therapist. (What a terrifying thought!) Surely, we might think, in this case relational therapy will be a failure in its own terms.

Often failure does, indeed, turn out to be the case here. As therapist, you must respect whatever the client needs to do to keep himself safe. However, you will usually hang in with such a scared and rigidly protected client for as long as the client wants to come. Why? Because you believe that underneath all that disconnection and terror, there may still be a spark of longing to connect. Perhaps that spark is exactly why the client keeps coming. Maybe somewhere the client knows that what you offer is his best chance at a better life, and maybe if you keep offering empathy instead of cure, one day that spark of longing might become a spark of relationship between the two of you. That would be only the beginning of a long journey of self-recovery for your client, but relational therapy is made for those long journeys. In other words, even when it looks like empathy isn't going to work, it might just work after all. In fact, paradoxically, this is just the kind of situation that relational psychotherapy is best suited to.

I've been saying that empathy-work can address a broad range of specific problems clients bring to therapy, but relational psychotherapy does have its own central focus. The kind of pain it addresses best is exactly that kind of pain that's locked away in a scared and rigid client who can't bear connection because he knows it will hurt. But at the same time, his self-protection is slowly smothering the life out of him. Fundamentally, this is a situation of painful relational dilemma, of relationship that feels impossible. This kind of situation, whatever its severity, however it is masked or expressed by varieties of symptoms, is the situation that relational therapy enters over and over, in hopes that empathy will begin to make relationship possible again.

Chapter 3 is all about how situations of relational dilemma get to be that way. How do painful interpersonal experiences become self-protections that end up feeling like jail cells? Or as we therapists often hear the question put, "Why do I keep feeling so bad when I try so hard to feel better?"

ENDNOTES

1. Kohut, *How Does Analysis Cure?*, 82.
2. Rogers, *On Becoming a Person*, 184–185.
3. Jordan, "Empathy and Self Boundaries," in Jordan et al., *Women's Growth in Connection*, 67–80.
4. Cf. Beatrice Beebe et al., "Systems Models in Development and Psychoanalysis: The Case of Vocal Rhythm Coordination and Attachment," *Infant Mental Health Journal*, 21(1–2), 99–122.

3

ASSESSMENT

What's Wrong When Your Client Feels Bad?

A PARTICULAR KIND OF BAD FEELING

Some clients come to us for help with situational troubles in their lives. Others come suffering from what's often called emotional disturbance, psychological dysfunction, or mental illness. But such words say nothing about the essence of their more pervasive, persistent trouble. As these clients try to tell us what's wrong, they search for more meaningful words, words they think we'll understand: "I'm depressed. I feel anxious all the time. I have low self-esteem." Or else they just tell us how they feel—all strung out, dreading another day, lousy, rotten, utterly worthless. These are the sorts of "feeling bad" this chapter explores.

For such clients, the ongoing distress they feel is not just an emotional reaction to a life crisis such as the death of a loved one, a business failure, or the diagnosis of chronic illness. Their trouble runs deeper than the effects of stress. They usually know that it's appropriate to feel sad and angry in response to loss, and they can recognize and manage the ordinary stress in their lives, the demands of family, work, and mortgages. They also know that something else is wrong, a "feeling bad" that doesn't go away even when life runs smoothly. This kind of feeling bad has been part of their lives, part of their self-experience, for a very long time, and often they think it will never be any better.

At times of loss and stress, however, the bad feeling can suddenly get worse. That's often when such clients come for help. As a relational therapist, you will take such a client's present crisis seriously. Allied with your client, you will feel the punch the crisis packs, the meanings it holds.

In your presence, she will find some strength to cope with what she faces. But as the crisis eases, you won't be surprised to hear that what you and your client have dealt with is only the tip of an iceberg. Much lies below the surface, "bad feelings" that have been lurking for a long time. Now, perhaps, your client will decide that it's time to face those deeper issues.

Whether she came in because of a crisis or not, when your depressed or anxious client looks for a generic term for how she feels most of the time, "dissatisfied" comes up. Not with anything in particular—or, perhaps, with many things in particular—but the general feeling is that life isn't what she thinks it could be. For a long time she thought that if she got that degree or made enough money or met the right person, she'd be happy. But she's got a career now and her relationship is okay . . . so what's missing? Sometimes she thinks maybe a better job, a new city, a long vacation. Maybe having a baby. But that thought scares her. It's a big responsibility, and what if having a baby doesn't help either? By now she knows that she can't blame her dissatisfaction, her low-grade depression, on the circumstances of her life. Would it even be fair to bring a child into this scenario?

Another word for her dissatisfaction might be "dissonance." Her hopes aren't matching up with what she's getting out of life, and it's not the straightforward kind of dissonance that achievements and possessions can resolve. It's not a situational dissonance; it's psychological. Relational psychotherapy says that when a person is living in states of psychological dissonance, most likely what's behind and underneath her discomfort is relational dissonance—longstanding relational dilemmas and impossibilities that she has never been able to resolve. They've become so much a part of her everyday life that she hardly notices them. But she certainly notices their effects.

This is but one more way to say that almost any psychological problem can be traced to a self-with-other problem. The problems aren't coming just from outside, from circumstances, but on the other hand, they aren't coming just from inside, either.[1] Where do your client's psychological "bad feelings" come from, then? They are almost always produced by something that's happening, in one way or another, between your client and other people. She's not a closed system, making her own emotional weather. Emotional weather is an interpersonal, systemic kind of weather, and in many ways her personal psychology comes down to how she manages to play her parts in the ecosystems in which she finds herself.

SYSTEMS MAKE A "SELF"

A person's psychology, or sense of self, is produced by at least three different kinds of systems operating at the same time. First, there's what's happening right now or what just happened between that person and another person. Second, each person brings a great deal of self-experience to any interaction—his position of relative power in the relationship, his memories of previous mutual contact, his desires, fears, and hopes, and the moods and feelings that color the moment of interaction. These complex systems of perception, thought, feeling, and belief that make up a person's experience at any given time can be called "self-states." Changes in emotional tone often signal changes in self-states—from cheerful confidence to shame-laced anxiety, for example.

Let's put these first two systems, the interactive system and the self-state system, into play. Let's say a client of yours called Ben goes out for a beer after work with a friend, Jim, and Ben decides to talk about an idea he has for a new little business. Ben has been thinking about it for a while, working out the glitches, and he thinks it could fly. He launches in happily and Jim listens, but without showing much feeling, certainly no enthusiasm. And suddenly, instead of feeling excited about his idea, Ben feels deflated and almost ashamed of having brought it up. His self-state has changed drastically. If he could do a comprehensive self-state review, he'd find that not only have his feelings changed, but he has also started to think his idea might be stupid, he has begun to doubt his ability to make it happen, and he's much less likely, in this state, to take any action to move his idea forward.

Of course, happy excitement and self-doubting shame are both self-state possibilities for Ben that predate his exchange with Jim. Jim's response didn't create what a deflated state feels like for Ben, or how quickly Ben can fall into it. On the other hand, if there were a video recording of their conversation, an observer could point out exactly where Jim failed to match Ben's energy and where Jim missed the cues that invited his positive response. The tape would show just how systemically produced Ben's deflated feeling state was.

Jim's self-state wasn't what Ben expected. Afterward he wished he had asked Jim more questions before he launched into his own ideas. Is Jim afraid of losing his job? Or has he had a bad fight with his wife? Maybe, Ben thinks, he was annoyed with me about something I'd forgotten. Or maybe he had a headache. Or maybe he was thinking of a business idea he'd had once, but it went sour. Ben doesn't know how his words affected Jim. But they did, and at the very same time, Jim's response was affecting Ben. Two selves, or "organized worlds of subjective experience," met in the pub, and another small, systemic world was created in the moments of their interaction.[2] That two-person system affected both of the self-state systems present there, if to different degrees and in different ways. So it goes in human interaction.

A SYSTEM THAT MAKES SENSE
OF INTERPERSONAL PROCESS

But the plot thickens. In addition to the self-state systems each man brought into the interaction, systems of continual flux and change, and in addition to the two-person interactive system created during their conversation, there was a third kind of system at work to produce Ben's sense of self in that pub. We might call that system his interpersonal process memory. It's made up not of specific memories of interactions between Ben and others, but of generalizations of how many similar interactions have gone before and of how, therefore, they are likely to go again. If his system didn't streamline discrete event memory into generalized process memory, Ben would have to work his way through every action and interaction as if it were his first.

Daniel Stern says that infants begin streamlining their interpersonal learning very early, developing what he calls RIGs, an acronym for "Representations of Interactions which have been Generalized."[3] For example, when Ben was a baby, like most of us he probably developed a RIG around the sequence of crying, hearing footsteps, and being picked up and comforted. Not only did that RIG contain action sequences, it was also full of affect exchanged between him and his caregiver, and so it also contained a tone or feeling of "self" for him. So almost from the very beginning, even before he had a toddler's awareness of a "me," his affectively toned self-feelings were bound up in repetitive self-with-other interactions. Making these RIGs wasn't anything he ever had to work at; it was just the way his system automatically made sense of many bits of experience— after those bits of experience had been repeated in similar sequences many times.

As an adult, he doesn't have to be aware of his RIGs, either. They are still just the way the world works and how he gets along in it. But we might hypothesize certain RIGs at work for Ben in the pub this afternoon. He was enacting a certain RIG as he entered with his excitement, expecting some enthusiasm in return. He had an expectation of a particular kind of interaction, with all the positive self-feelings that go with it. But it turned into a different kind of interaction, and a different RIG slipped in, one in which his energy is met with flatness. The deflation that followed the interchange led to Ben's self-feeling of shame. Both the expectant and the deflated RIGs were readily available to Ben as active components of his process memory. Each was a response to unfolding imagined and experienced events, and at the same time, each was a construction of events and of certain senses of Ben's self.

I hope that this example makes clear that process memory is a system, too, not a closed book. It's an active system, constantly *making* sense, and to a certain extent creating much of the reality a person experiences. Perhaps a better term for process memory is "organizing principles."[4] The work of organizing experience into recognizable patterns is never finished. Organizing principles can be as small as one little RIG and as large as the networks of RIGs that make up a worldview. The word "principles" catches the sense that something has been generalized (from memory) that helps a person manage the task of organizing. Later in this chapter we'll look at organizing principles more closely. For now it's important just to know that they're there—that third system that was interacting with Ben's self-state and also with whatever was going on between Ben and Jim.

The question of this chapter is, "What's wrong when your client is feeling bad?" So far I've said that the "feeling bad" I'm talking about isn't just an expectable, healthy reaction to crisis or stress. It feels more like chronic dissatisfaction. It's a kind of psychological dissonance that, I'm arguing, has its origins in relational dissonance. And I have sketched out the three kinds of systems that are involved in any relational interactions. Now I can explain that relational dissonance—that feeling of being jarred by people or disconnected from them—can originate in any of the three systems. When, for example, Ben's self-state is under the influence of financial worries or a nasty cold, it can be difficult for him to enjoy any interactions. When there's something off about an interaction, as there was with Jim, the interaction itself can disturb both participants, whatever the self-states and organizing principles each brought to it. But the kind of relational dissonance that has the most power to produce psychological dissonance is the kind that originates with organizing principles.

Let's go back to Ben in the pub. What happened made him feel bad. But his bad feelings don't count as the kind of psychological trouble we're trying to understand unless he can't shake them off. The relational dissonance he experienced doesn't grow into psychological dissonance until what's wrong begins to feel like it's something wrong about *him*, and it doesn't become chronic psychological dissonance until that wrongness stays with him as an uncomfortable, dissatisfied, troubled feeling about himself.

As it happened, some of that psychological trouble did start to set in for Ben. He was understandably deflated by Jim's flat response, and then he started to feel stupid about having been so excited. Rather than protest to Jim, "Hey! What's up? You're pretty flat today!" or try to get a different response from him, Ben went quiet and began to feel what therapists call "shame." It's a feeling Ben knows all too well, he tells you in therapy. Once it happens, it's difficult to shake off. Let's explore Ben's situation further.

"SOMETHING IS WRONG WITH ME!"

The shame Ben feels did not come simply from his deflated self-state or from the interaction with Jim. Although the interaction led to shame, it wasn't Jim's intention, Ben knows, to make him feel stupid or ashamed. The shame took hold of Ben as Ben's organizing principles made sense of the interaction and of the changes in his self-state as his excitement fell away. He didn't decide or think it, he just knew it: His feelings of disconnection and deflation were something wrong with him. What was wrong with him? The first word that came to his mind was "stupid," and it stuck.

Ben tells you that "stupid" is the word that usually comes to mind when he's feeling bad in this way, and now that he thinks about it, he knows that he often worries about doing or saying dumb things, or that his co-workers or friends think of him as stupid. Sometimes, when he's feeling anxious and out of sorts, he has intrusive flashbacks of stupid moments from his past. Clearly, Ben has developed a story about the psychological dissonance he suffers, and the story says it's all about feeling stupid. If only he wouldn't be stupid, or feel stupid, he would feel better. That's what Ben assumes, even though he has never been able to talk himself out of the problem.

Ben, however, won't be able to talk himself out of it, because his problem isn't really about feeling stupid; it's about feeling shame. The problem for Ben is that when something is off or jarring or disconnected between him and someone else, his system organizes that information to mean that there's something wrong with him. The name of this basic feeling is shame, and shame spawns many different kinds of stories, defeated stories like "I'm stupid and worthless," defensive stories like "Nobody understands me," and counterattack stories like "I don't get mad, I get even." Some people's organizing principles tell them they are defective most of the time—for long periods, and after quite innocuous interactions. They may be able to block out some of this dissonance with strong defenses or counterattacks, but a strong undertone of feeling bad remains a constant for them.

I hope that Ben's story has clarified the idea of psychological dissonance. On the one hand, Ben responds to invitations to connect with others in the world. The truth is that he needs to connect, in his workplace and with neighbors and family, if nowhere else. This is how human life is lived: one has to interact with others to feel productive and valued in the world. In fact, Ben does the very best he can, wanting to contribute and to experience life as meaningful and good. Understandably, despite his best efforts, many of his interactions with others are less than perfect. That's life. The real problem for Ben, however, is that each of those imperfections or "misses" leaves him feeling that there's something wrong with *him*. It seems he should experience more inner harmony, especially when he tries hard to be responsible and responsive to others. But no, there's dissonance.

How does it happen that some people experience difficulties in interpersonal interactions as problems that can be ignored or solved while other people experience them as their own defectiveness? As I've been saying, it's a matter of different organizing principles. These principles come by way of powerful, nonlinear learning; they are automatic, unthought generalizations that follow upon repetitive interpersonal interactions. So it makes no sense for Ben to blame himself for feeling defective or for failing to change his feelings by thinking better thoughts. Ben needs help to understand his shame feelings as the product of interactions, both present and past. This kind of help will, in itself, ease some of his shame. And he needs not to think that now it's his organizing principles that are "wrong with him"!

As a relational therapist you know that Ben's organizing principles may be contributing to a great deal of dissonance and discomfort for Ben. But you also know that they lie dormant until they are pulled into action to make sense of specific things that happen to Ben. So you can explain to Ben, "I don't think the problems you're struggling with are just inside you. They're problems you have living in the world and feeling okay doing that. I think that in some basic ways, the world doesn't feel safe to you. When things happen between you and other people, you worry whether they are actually on your side, or whether they like you very much. I think that's what's getting you down. Certain things keep happening, they lead to the same old kinds of bad feelings, and then you think there's something really wrong with you."

WHERE INSIDE AND OUTSIDE MEET AND MINGLE

This discussion has been leading up to a very important point, implicit in what I've just suggested you might explain to Ben. Now I want to make that point explicit: It's not the case that psychological problems come from either inside of a person or outside of a person. Instead, they come from the in-between spaces where the data of the outside world and that person's capacities to make sense of it meet and mingle. Here it's not clear what's objective and what's subjective, for one can't get outside of how one's own mind shapes the data in order to know what's "really" out there, nor does one's mind or subjective self have any substance—anything to think and feel about—apart from what comes from "out there." Think of Ben's simple, early RIG of "crying . . . footsteps . . . being picked up . . . feeling comforted." It has substance, feeling, and meaning that are deeper and fuller than a simple sequence of events. We might imagine that it exists inside Ben's mind, and yet the RIG with its associated feelings doesn't exist unless the sequence happens.

Furthermore, even for an infant, many representations of interactions develop simultaneously; organizing principles may dovetail or conflict in complex ways. In short, there's a lot to sort out and track in this inside/outside place of making sense of interactions. For example, what if something drastically different happens to young Ben sometimes, say, "crying . . . footsteps . . . being yelled at . . . feeling overwhelmed"? Then another RIG will have to develop in tandem with the first, and it will be part of Ben's work, as he grows and develops psychologically, to organize a world that holds both RIGs, that is, both of those interactive sequences that have been generalized to include particular, recognizable sets of feelings and meanings.

Later the young Ben might be able to hold both RIGs simultaneously by knowing his mother as reliably loving, but sometimes moody and stressed. Or he might make sense of feeling overwhelmed by experiencing himself as bad whenever the unpleasant interaction happens. If that's the case, he will try to keep the bad away by doing whatever it takes not to get yelled at. This solution involves efforts to undo or cover over the second RIG. But the RIG doesn't disappear. It stays available to organize other overwhelming or dissonant experience into an "I'm bad" feeling. We could guess that Ben's current feelings of shame may have links to organizing principles rooted that far back in his experience.

Earlier we were asking, "How is it that some people can work comfortably with interpersonal conflicts and disconnections, while others experience them as their own defectiveness?" These different ways of managing disturbing RIGs is where such patterns begin to diverge. We haven't yet said why a child might use one or the other of those ways of managing, the one that integrates positive and negative experience or the one that tries to separate good experience from bad and keep the bad away (storing the bad as shame). We'll return to this question in the Chapter 4, when we investigate the nature and effects of interpersonal trauma. But this is at least a snapshot of how a pattern of feeling bad gets put into motion, influenced not just by the outside or by the inside, but by both at once, by both the data and the process of organizing it.

This "place" between outside and inside (probably it's more an activity than a place) is where infant senses of self come into being and where adult senses of self are held in being. When what's being processed are the meanings of interpersonal interactions, this place of making sense also makes a personal "psychology," full of the meanings and feelings a person has about himself. Here the three systems I've been talking about—self-state systems, current interaction systems, and systems of organizing principles—are constantly busy, making and exchanging the information that gets turned into personal meaning and feeling.

Now that we have established that the "feeling bad" we're discussing comes from this complex activity or place where organizing principles are making sense of what's coming at them, we can look at how both outside and inside contribute to psychological dissonance without having to choose either location as the sole cause of the trouble. We'll begin with what comes at your clients from the outside.

PROBLEMS THAT START FROM THE OUTSIDE

Feminists have been saying for a long time, at least since the publication of Phyllis Chesler's *Women and Madness* in 1972,[5] that women's psychological problems are not in women's heads; that they come from "outside." The story goes something like this: June Cleaver, Beaver's mom, may look fine on camera, but really, when nobody's looking, she's depressed. She drinks secretly to numb her anxiety, and sometimes she feels that it's not safe to leave the house. Why? Because she can't remember who she is or what she's worth. Her value lies in what she does for others. She's bored with repetitive, undervalued housework, she's isolated from other women, she's starved for adult company (Ward is a good man, but he doesn't talk much), and she feels empty nest coming on. Actually, she's really quite angry that her life has come to this. But everything around her tells her it's a wonderful life; it's exactly as it should be; she has absolutely no reason to be angry. So she squelches her anger—all of her feelings, in fact—and she gets depressed instead. She sees a psychiatrist who prescribes valium for her nervous problems. Mixed with a little alcohol, the pills do take the edge off, and they leave her with enough energy to vacuum, mop, dust, and get meals on the table. So on she goes, a woman with her psychological problems under control for now.

Feminists took a good look at June Cleaver and said, she's not sick! The problem isn't inside her, it's all the messages and pressures coming at her from the outside, telling her who she is and what she's supposed to do. Her assigned role is a form of oppression, and she's being kept in her place for a reason. Ward and the boys get more from her life than she does, but they never notice; that's just how it should be, they assume. And in fact a whole patriarchal establishment, including psychiatry, is making that same assumption: that a white, middle-class woman should be satisfied with her place in the home, with her role as provider of physical and emotional care. To keep things this way is in the interest of those who have more social power than she does. That's what makes the pressure to conform so powerful. If June is at all aware that she wants to do some other things, or if she has some feelings besides satisfaction, the system tells her there's something wrong with her. What can she do but agree?—unless she finds the support of a group of women who understand what's being done to them, who see what's coming at them for what it is, and who respond, "We're not crazy, we're angry!"

In other words, what looks like mental illness here is actually a healthy response to a sick system. Psychological dissonance builds as an oppressive system forces its truth on people, denying them the truth of their own experience. More recently, radical multicultural feminists like Laura Brown add more complexity to this idea that oppressive systems produce mental illness. If you are a woman, they say, but also, and in special ways, if you are a woman of color, a lesbian, a disabled woman, a single mother, or a poor woman, the social system that privileges able-bodied, hetero-sexual, affluent white males will make your life even harder. The way privilege works in our society, you don't just *feel* oppressed and devalued, it's really happening to you. The pressures on you to feel not good enough, second-rate, and defective are powerful. And even though it feels like your shame, the problem is what's coming at you. It's not inside you; it's out there.

Relational psychotherapy takes this reality very seriously. Many clients come into therapy feeling bad about themselves because they have been told in thousands of overt and subliminal ways that they are second-class citizens, persons of secondary value. These clients first need help to hear those messages clearly, to see where the messages are coming from and what effects they have on them. Often the pressures to devalue themselves slip in unnoticed; what these clients notice are just their own general bad feelings about themselves. The self-with-other contexts of their negative self-states have become invisible. An important part of your work will be to trace these bad feelings back to the everyday interactions they come from.

I'm thinking of a lesbian client, "Sue," who told me she had a seasonal depression that settled on her every December. "Just a bad funk," she said. "By February it's gone. Maybe it's the lack of daylight." I asked her what December was like for her. For her, December meant holiday parties at the office, seasonal cocktail parties with friends and acquaintances from her "previous life," and various festive meals and celebrations with members of her own family and her partner's family. Luckily, she was an extrovert who liked socializing. "It's my antidote to depression," she laughed. She also explained to me that she'd been out for about eight years now and was quite comfortable with her orientation. Sue and her partner, "Lyn," had been together for five years, and each of their families seemed to have accepted their relationship. Sue wasn't out at work, she said, because that didn't feel entirely safe. But most of the old friends from her previous life knew about her life now.

As we moved into December, we tracked quite carefully the ups and downs of Sue's daily life. We noticed that at the office parties she couldn't talk about her holiday travel plans when the topic came up. In fact, to stay safely closeted, she couldn't say much about her life at all. So in spite of all the banter Sue could exchange with workmates, those necessary omissions left her feeling on the outside and a bit of a stranger. "Not a good feeling!" she said, but she hadn't really noticed it before. At the cocktail party reunions, she did mention her partner and their new home—

three different times!—and each time the conversation got steered in another direction. It felt like her old friends were happy to see her, but they really didn't want to know about her new life. "That feels bad, too," Sue said. "It's like there's something just too weird about being queer, though they'd never say so. I don't like them thinking that way about me."

Sue decided to pay more attention to what she felt when she and Lyn went visiting family. She noticed how carefully polite—distantly polite—Lyn's brothers and sisters were to her. She wondered if their unfailing niceness meant something like, "See what a good, broad-minded person I am, making this effort to be nice to you." She explained, "They're not interested in me! Their niceness doesn't have any me in it. I could be anyone, any dyke they have to be nice to! Am I turning into a cynic?" I told her I didn't think she was becoming a cynic; she was just paying more attention to the nuances of interactions.

The most difficult nuances for Sue that Christmas were tangled up in interactions with her father. "He treats Lyn like a buddy of mine," she said. "Like we're college roommates, not a grown-up couple. And then he puts his arm around me like he always does, and says I'm still his little girl." After letting herself know how bad that interaction felt, Sue tried to understand the feeling. After a while she guessed, "It's like if only he could keep me little, then maybe I'd grow up right—grow up and marry somebody just like him!"

All through that December we kept noticing the homophobia that was just an ordinary part of Sue's social life, a subtle oppression that intensified as her social life intensified. After we had noticed, she would often say, "It's not about me; they don't mean it," or "It doesn't matter. I'm used to it." But when we paid close attention, we found that it was right after those events that "didn't matter" that she felt especially worthless, flat, and depressed. Each time, as soon as we talked about what had really happened to her, her funk dissipated. What she had thought was an inner ailment turned out to be her expectable responses to interactions that told her that she wasn't completely okay, or normal, or a person whose adult life-choices should be celebrated. It was this subtle oppression that left her feeling isolated, different, and worthless.

Subtle, systemic oppression isn't just outside of therapy; it comes right into the room. To protect herself, a client like Sue has to assume that the therapist will take advantage of her position of social power in relation to Sue. In symbolic terms, the therapist certainly does have more power, if only because she is the professional in the relationship and represents some kind of authority. She is more blatantly implicated in systemic oppression if she is straight in relation to her client's queerness—or white in relation to her client's color, affluent in relation to her poverty, or able-bodied in relation to her disability.

Such relations of difference enforce oppression and generate what's wrong for a client on a daily basis in her life. If a relational therapist fails to acknowledge the differences in social location and power that are in the room, she becomes an ongoing part of a system of social power that tries to make itself invisible while it continues to oppress. Not much real relationship can develop between client and therapist when their important differences are covered over. Not much can be worked out in a relationship that has large pockets of falseness, and it's doubtful that such a relationship can do much to improve a client's sense of self-definition and intrinsic value.

So if you work with clients who come from different social worlds than you do, different daily experiences of power and privilege, it's crucial that you acknowledge this reality and encourage them to take as much time as they need to explore it. If your social location gives you a position of more power, it's important not to pretend that this isn't so. As a responsible relational therapist, you won't make light of your own privilege or downplay the social powers that your clients are up against. But at the same time, it's important that you don't feel guilty because of your privilege and try to make it up to your clients somehow. That reaction to difference will tangle up the lines of the relationships just as thoroughly. What matters is to hear your clients' truths, their experiences. As you hear them, and as you don't deny or try to fix what's wrong for them, it can become tolerable to have these differences between you. When they are acknowledged fairly, differences probably won't stand in the way of positive working relationships. In fact, honest work around real, painful difference can build your clients' confidence in the potential of the therapy. Doing this work with your clients is a very important way for you to make clear to them that you believe that what's wrong for them comes at them from the outside—even from you, and from the powers of your own social position.

THE TROUBLE COMES FROM FAMILIES, TOO

Stone Center feminists add another dimension to the idea that bad feelings are responses to what comes at clients from the outside. They say that clients' psychological dissonance is produced by interpersonal disconnection. Disconnection includes oppression, for oppression is fundamentally the oppressors' refusal to connect respectfully and mutually with those whom they oppress. Disconnection is also a prime characteristic of a patriarchal society that values autonomy, power-over, and winning more than the feminine values of empathy, connection, and cooperation.

The Stone Center theorists argue that the power of disconnection can be mitigated through experiences of connection in genuinely mutual relationships. Such connection, they maintain, is the key to psychological health for both women and men. They hope to see the values of connection and mutuality make significant differences in the structure of our society. As they focus on the emotional work women do to keep connection going in families, they also look very carefully at the disconnections inside of families. They show how family systems of disconnection have incredible power to spin a person's self-systems toward dissonance.

Jean Baker Miller and Irene Stiver identify certain patterns of disconnection in families that lead to severe psychological difficulties for children raised in those families.[6] One pattern is secrecy in the family, or a conspiracy of silence, to deny an unacceptable reality. An extreme example is the secret of sexual abuse in the family, but families keep silent about many other kinds of skeletons in the closet, too, such as abortion, suicide, mental illness, and babies born out of wedlock.

In a second pattern, parents are emotionally inaccessible; their children don't have permission or opportunities to get to know them. Alcoholic parents, for example, are absent when intoxicated, and usually they lack the emotional skills to make contact when they are sober. Parents who have been traumatized by war, death camps, or familial violence often want to put those memories behind them and spare their children knowledge of such horror. But in blanking out their own histories, they can make themselves strangers to those closest to them. This black hole in the family history then also becomes another kind of family secret.

The third pattern of disconnection that Miller and Stiver identify is the one that therapists call "parentification." In many families, because of economic stresses, separation and divorce, parental illness, or parental emotional fragility, children learn to take on responsibilities beyond their years. Many children manage these challenges well, and knowing that their help is honored, welcome, and important to the family gives them confidence and self-esteem. However, in many other families, there is no acknowledgment of the child's efforts, and even worse, the parent does not reciprocate by taking the kinds of responsibility appropriate for a parent. In important respects this child is put in the role of parent to the parent, and then there is no interpersonal place for the child to be a child, with a child's anxieties, confusions, and needs. This is where the disconnection happens that later proves to be so psychologically devastating. The child may know a great deal about the parent's feelings, but there is no place in the relationship for her own frightened, needy, vulnerable self. To keep performing the role of competent caretaker, she needs to disconnect radically from those parts of herself. This, you might remember, was the case for Jane, whom we followed through different modes of therapy in Chapter 1.

Whatever its pattern or reason, if disconnection is what came at a client from her family of origin, it has left her with a certain kind of psychological dissonance: she both desires and fears connection. At the very same time that she seeks to be in relationships where she belongs and is valued, she also "knows" that those relationships will be dangerous unless she hides a great deal of who she is and how she feels. It may not even be clear to her why bringing her whole self to relationship would be so risky, but she has to assume that if her parents and family were that scared to be real, there must be a very good reason to be careful.

It may seem that this family-systems sense of what comes at clients from the outside is completely different from the more radical feminist sense of the oppression that comes at them. But these terms of disconnection can be applied usefully outside of the family, too. When social systems oppress and injure clients by failing to see them and to respect who they are, they also perpetrate profound disconnection. To protect themselves from further disappointment and hurt, clients have to put up their own barriers. These resistances and disconnections protect them while they find ways to stay connected enough to make a life within the social systems in which they find themselves. So they carry on in a semblance of belonging, but they keep themselves basically hidden and apart. Whether it is happening between clients and their everyday social surroundings or between clients and their families, this disconnected semblance of connection can all too easily turn into feelings of isolation and worthlessness, a deeply dissonant sense of being at odds with others and with themselves. And then they begin to feel that what's wrong is inside them.

How does it happen that the wrong that comes at people from the outside starts to feel like it's inside them? That's the question we'll turn to now.

THE BEDTIME STORY CLIENTS TELL THEMSELVES

Those therapies that emphasize the social construction of self maintain that psychological dissonance is a direct effect of social forces. We have seen how feminism has taken the illness out of mental illness and located it in patriarchal systems of oppression. But according to almost all theories of psychotherapy, what's called mental illness or psychological disturbance involves more than just a self being attacked by outside forces. Somehow that self has become divided against itself; the outer conflict has become an inner tension. How do social-construction therapies explain this inner tension without capitulating to the idea of individual psychopathology—to the idea that something is wrong inside a person?

Often those therapies use the idea of narrative. They note that in systems of oppression, people in power propagate powerful stories about how the world works. In those stories, the losers in the system deserve to lose because they are lazy, inferior, weak, or prone to making bad choices. These stories are woven into the fabric of everyday life, popular culture, and mainstream media and politics. If a client lives on the "loser" side of social difference, and if she doesn't have a strong community and family speaking another story to her more insistently, she will start to believe those stories about herself. There's nothing else available to believe. And it's not like anyone can escape living out a story of her own life. That's what human beings do, narrative theorists say.[7]

Your client can't escape doing it, but she can pay attention to what her story is telling her about how she can live. She can listen in on what Laura Brown calls the bedtime story she always tells herself.[8] She might hear herself saying things about herself that "they" say, those who live on the "winner" side of certain social differences. She sees herself through their eyes. She hopes for only what they think she can achieve; she values herself by their standards. She looks back over her history with their sense of how she's failed, and she looks forward to more of the same. And every morning when she gets up, she goes out to live another day of this particular story, because it's hers, the only one she knows. This is how narrative therapy explains "internalized oppression." The oppression isn't really internal, and even the story keeps coming at your client from the outside, but there's no alternative story for her to live.

If within your client's society and the confines of her life, there is truly no alternative story to live, then there's no point in her paying attention to the story she's been given. In the history of human cultures, many of the losers—serfs, slaves, untouchables, prisoners, and women—

had no chance of a different story. Many still don't. But if a client can afford to notice her story, already she has some inkling that maybe something could be different. Besides suffering the effects of oppression, she's feeling tension between the story she's been given and something else she knows, suspects, hopes, or wonders about herself and her life. This uncomfortable psychological dissonance is the first step toward change; it's what gets her to therapy, for example.

The next step in narrative therapy is for your client to understand the power of the narrative she is living right now. The longer she listens in on the bedtime story she tells herself, the more she feels what it does to her. It's good for her to have some help while she listens, someone to put the real names to her experiences, names like "abuse," "sexual harassment," "racism," "incest," or "homophobia." Your empathic presence makes it easier for her to bear the pain of understanding what the story has done and continues to do to her. She also needs someone there to tell her that another story is possible. A new story won't burst upon her. It won't be easy for her to find her own real experience or her own voice for speaking. But when she does, she will have undone a great deal of the damage done to her by forces outside her. Those forces are beyond her control, but in her own voice and from within her own real story, she can keep on resisting their power over her.

RELATIONAL STRATEGIES AND RELATIONAL IMAGES

Stone Center theorists, too, resist the notion that psychological problems are internal to individuals. Psychological trouble, they say, is a self-in-relation problem. A social and family history of disconnection generates specific kinds of self-in-relation experience. In families where important things cannot be said, where children have to grow themselves up, and where parents remain emotionally unavailable, the children develop the habit of emotional isolation. They learn to keep large parts of their own experience out of sight, and out of their own awareness, too, eventually. Their lives become narrow, rigid, and joyless, but this is the best they know. They may create elaborate inner worlds to which they can safely retreat. They may comfort themselves with compulsions, obsessions, or substance abuse, or they might sink into depression and feelings of self-loathing and despair. All of these self-states are symptoms of isolation, an isolation that is no longer imposed from the outside, but has become a habit of being.

With this picture as background to what goes wrong for their clients, Stone Center theorists offer two more ideas about how this isolating disconnection becomes a seemingly internal phenomenon. They speak of clients' *strategies* for maintaining disconnected kinds of connection, and also of the *relational images* that construct their clients' self-images.

As Miller and Stiver describe the situation, various forms of self-isolating behaviors are actually clients' best efforts at remaining connected with others. These disconnecting/connecting strategies are a complicated negotiation of inner needs and outer reality. Experience has taught a client how to keep apparently "bad" or unacceptable parts of himself disguised or far away from others. He also knows how to bring forward some acceptable parts of himself, the parts others will like and can use. In a nonresponsive or abusive environment, this knowledge once served him well. But now he experiences psychological dissonance—constriction, anxiety, depression—as he keeps on making those same strategic relational moves. His strategies protect him, but over the long term they leave him quite isolated and unknown. Thus, the impact of the client's social surroundings comes to be, in a certain sense, "inside" him in the form of strategies he learned to use to keep himself out of connection while seeming to be in connection with others. In describing his situation in this way, self-in-relation theorists avoid attributing some kind of illness or flaw to him, while also acknowledging that what's happened to him has affected him in a way that keeps the pain of his early experience alive.

Stone Center writers also mention "relational images" as they explain the connections between external and internal reality. Relational images are generalized pictures your clients hold, pictures of how they have been and can be in relation with others. These self-in-relation pictures strongly influence how they feel about themselves. Sometimes the best access to those pictures is through childhood images that first appear as frozen vignettes of memory. One client remembers standing alone on the playground, left out of all the games. Another recalls huddling for hours at a locked door in the winter, her house key lost. A third can't forget the awful moment of getting caught cheating in grade five. For each client, the image isn't about relationship, it just represents something bad that's true about herself.

As they tell these stories in therapy, however, your clients begin to see these images in context. Your first client was ignored and left out because her family moved a lot and she was always the new kid. Your second client was only eight that time she got locked out in the cold; she was scared and her hands and feet hurt terribly. But when her mom finally hurried up the walk, she didn't see her kid's fear or pain. Her mom's eyes were just angry that she'd lost the key—*again!* For your third client, getting high marks was the only thing she was good at. So when she didn't know the answers on a test, she had to try very hard not to cheat. But sometimes she peeked anyway.

As you and your clients live with these stories, your clients begin to understand that the relationships in them are what give them their meaning. Certain interactions with people told your clients who they were and what they were worth. When the kids on the playground ignored your first client, they told her she was ugly and unlikable—or that's what she could make of their behavior. Her mom's angry eyes told your client who had lost her key that her troubles were all because of her own stupid mistakes. When your third client was caught cheating, the teacher seemed to see only the one bad thing she'd done. To the teacher, right then, there was nothing good about your client—and that's how she felt, too.

In each case, the interaction left the client feeling, "There's something wrong with me!" Those kinds of relational experiences hurt. When they happen often, children develop strategies to protect themselves. They disconnect from people, while making sure to present a safe front. As adults they will strive to be seen as competent, honest, reliable persons both at home and at work. Underneath they may be quite depressed and angry. That will keep people away, too. In any case, no one comes close enough to discover all that's wrong with them.

A self-in-relation therapist expects that when clients like this come for help, it's because their strategies for disconnected, "safe" kinds of connection have isolated them in ways that are becoming unbearable, and because their relational images keep on telling them mostly bad things about themselves. Doing self-in-relation therapy means creating relationships with your clients that will subvert and undo some of those strategies. You will talk about the old, shamed pictures of themselves and see them with new eyes—as images of a small, vulnerable self in relation with others who weren't able to give them what they needed.

The "bad" that gets changed in this process is not something pathological inside your clients. Instead, the "bad" is the pain caused by their everyday self-protections and their everyday memories. They haven't known any other ways to connect with others or with their past. Now they have some new ways of connection. They can see their early relational contexts more clearly and feel more empathy for their younger selves. Now those old ways of acting, thinking, and feeling can change, and they can begin to find themselves in relationships with others that feel completely different, relationships in which they aren't bad or wrong. Those bad feelings that have tormented them forever can now begin to fade.

A BRIEF DETOUR THROUGH OBJECT RELATIONS THEORY

We've seen the Stone Center picture of how difficulties coming at your clients from the outside turn into their own bad feelings about themselves. To see what relational psychoanalytic theory might add to this picture, we'll first take a brief look at the stream of psychoanalytic theory that has become known as object relations theory. Behind most of relational theory, there's a long history of psychoanalytic theory. Within that general history, it was object relations theory that began a movement toward more relational understandings of psychological processes. As we noted in Chapter 1, object relations theory has influenced, in different ways, both self psychology and the school that calls itself "relational psychoanalysis."

In a classically Freudian scheme, a patient's bad feelings (guilt, anxiety, depression, and other symptoms of neurosis) come from psychic energy, usually sexual drive, which has been blocked or trapped by becoming tangled up in memory or fantasy that the patient cannot tolerate knowing about consciously. Hidden conflict between instinctual drives (id) and a punishing, silencing containment of those drives (superego) expresses itself as symptoms. (In Freud's day, the symptoms first addressed were not what we would recognize as psychological dissonance, but rather the "hysterical" conversions of psychological conflicts and blocks into physical symptoms.)

After Freud's death, many psychoanalytic theorists began to suspect that not all adult psychological conflicts originate from the oedipal period (ages 4–6) and from the child's oedipal struggle to find his or her appropriate sexual self-definition in relation to both parents. They proposed that many significant conflicts originate in earlier childhood and even in infancy. They located these conflicts inside the child, not between child and parent, and mapped them out as the child's relationships to "internal objects." Their adult clients, they reasoned, were suffering from still-unresolved problems in the ongoing relations between themselves and their early internal objects.

So in object relations theory, bad feelings are still coming from conflicted, blocked, and tangled-up drives. But the field of conflict has become more complicated. More attention is given to the existence of the internal objects (images of others) to whom the drives are directed, and there are important questions asked about the relationships between the adult patient and those internal objects. The conflict going on in those relationships is more complex than a struggle and standoff between id and superego. Object relations theorists remain true to Freud in their assumption that the child's conflicts, like the rest of the child's psychological development, are powered by drives. But they begin to talk of the drives not just in terms of innate sexual and aggressive instincts but also in terms of the child's need to attach, and in terms of innate psychological energies that can be turned to adaptive, developmental tasks.

How would this theory describe our earlier example of the two RIGs, one that links crying to feeling comforted and the other that links crying to overwhelming negative feeling? For object relations theorists, more is going on in these pictures than a child's pleasure-seeking instincts being gratified, or else being frustrated so that her aggressive instincts are aroused. The child is also busy making an internal map of what's happening, and the components of the map are her drives (the passions of love and hate entangled with attachment longings), the internal images of the others who respond to her drives, and internal images of herself that correspond to those internal Others. So, for example, the child dealing with the problem of the two RIGs has an internalized comforting Good Mother and an internalized frightening Bad Mother, with corresponding images of Good Self and Bad Self. In healthy development, the intense feelings bound up in the Bad Mother–Bad Self relation are neutralized as the different fragmentary good and bad images coalesce into the image of a consistently good enough mother, in whose presence the child can enjoy a free range of self-expression and be good enough, too.

Or the child's internal objects may remain fragmentary, the bad ones bound up with intense psychic energy and also wrapped tightly within strong defense mechanisms such as denial and repression. Then these unresolved early childhood object relations sink out of sight, into the unconscious. But they reappear in a patient's adult life as projections—as seeing those Bad images in the faces and actions of the patient's significant others.

As object relations theory describes this situation, the adult patient who suffers these pervasive experiences of Bad Other and Bad Self has no idea about their origins. He knows and feels only the fear, sadness, despair and hate they stir up in him. He may also long desperately for a powerfully Good Other who will turn his Bad Self into Good. What can he do to help himself? He can act out his experiences to get some relief from feeling them, turning against others and ultimately against himself. He can flee from his acutely painful experience into the less acute pain of depression. He can block his feelings with addictions or medication. Or he can take his experience, with all of its painful feelings, to therapy.

In psychoanalysis or therapy guided by object relations theory, the therapist expects that as she becomes a significant attachment object to her client, his projections will surely come at her, too. As his intense feelings rise into his consciousness and toward her, she helps him allow into his awareness the internal dramas of Other and Self that generate the feelings. At last he is able to revisit the internal scene where his early conflicts were laid down. As he feels, once again, those early passions of longing and fear, love and hate, but this time in the presence of someone who can reliably contain them, the fragmented images of Good and Bad Other and Self slowly coalesce into a much healthier picture of a good enough other in relation to a self of many aspects, both "good" and "bad." Through this process, and because the client has owned or taken back his projections of his internal conflicts, eventually he finds himself able to live in comfortable, autonomous relationships with real others in the world, relationships now far less weighed down and troubled by the past.

In this model, then, the bad that a client experiences as psychological dissonance came at him mostly long ago. That's when he internalized it. And it's not entirely clear how bad it really was then and how much the fragmentation and repression of his internal objects were due to his infantile inability to integrate powerful feelings of desire and rage. Different object relations theorists take different positions on these issues. But in any case, the psychological entanglements and dissonance of the client's present life are understood as unconsciously driven repetitions of connections to bad internal objects, and/or as projections of those painful but unconscious Bad Self–Bad Other connections on his present relationships.

In other words, although at some time in the past, bad feelings were this client's response to what came at him from the outside, they very soon became an "inside" problem, a problem of internal object relations, which then began to wreak their own havoc on his "outside" world. This sense of how past experience becomes a powerful force in present-day life is captured in the metaphor many clients learn to use in psychodynamic therapy: "It's not my real, present-day Mother (or Father) who's the problem; it's the Mother (or Father) I carry inside. And then I project, so that the people around me turn into my Mother (or Father)!"

Object relations theory is fundamentally a theory about what happens inside clients, and about helping them to clear up the confusion between inside and outside. And yet, far more than the classic Freudian scheme does, it pays attention to interpersonal relationships, even if mostly in internalized or projected forms. In object relations theory "self" (or ego) comes into being not where drives are recognized and tamed, but in the ongoing interface between "outside" and "inside"—even though that interface is internalized. It is this strong movement toward relational reality that makes object relations theory useful to "relational psychoanalysis" and also a bridge to self psychology.

"RELATIONAL PSYCHOANALYSIS" AND OBJECT RELATIONS THEORY ABOUT "WHAT'S WRONG"

Many analysts with roots in interpersonal theory and who now call themselves "relational" use object relations theory to understand what's wrong for their clients. Sullivan himself set the stage for this when he included the concepts "good mother," "good me," "bad mother," and "bad me" within his transactional and interpersonal practice of psychiatry.[9] Contemporary practitioners of relational psychoanalysis, less opposed than Sullivan was to "the unconscious" and "transference," include ideas about trauma-induced splitting and about the unconscious projection of a client's powerful dissociated feelings onto the therapist. They try to engage with split-off parts of a client's self, and their hope is that the client will become able to reintegrate previously dissociated experiences, feelings, and parts of self.[10]

Incorporating an object relations sort of theory into an interactive interpersonalist mode of therapy allows a relational psychoanalyst to move back and forth between the intrapsychic and the intersubjective, between inside and outside, always keeping an eye on how each "side" gives form and substance to the other. To keep this movement going, the relational psychoanalyst constantly invites the client's troubled psyche to engage directly with her: "Talk to me; connect with me; push me away; tell me what you're thinking just now; tell me how you feel about me right now; want something from me; hate something about me—*with* me—and then together we will be able to sort out what the 'inside' trouble is."

Though such words may never be spoken, these are the kinds of interactions through which the client's intrapsychic Self–Other conflicts become interpersonal dynamics. First they are lived out, and then they are deconstructed in the therapy. Intrapsychic splits are healed as the analyst draws dissociated parts of the client's inner experience into human contact and interaction on the "outside." An intersubjective relationship with the analyst creates a safe, containing context where the client can experience as safe his own "bad feelings" and the most painful parts of his internalized history.

In summary, the client's unconscious object relations are slowly drawn out onto an interpersonal playing field where, over the course of many replays, they lose their unconscious power. In the process of playing on that field, the client wakes up to new possibilities for play that he couldn't have imagined before. Those new possibilities for self-with-other interactions are internalized as new object relations that produce an internal world of more freedom and comfort. And those internal changes keep on paying off as newly satisfying interpersonal interactions.

BETWEEN "INSIDE" AND "OUTSIDE"
IN SELF PSYCHOLOGY

Self psychology does something very different with object relations theory, something that in another way is just as radically relational.[11] It doesn't use it to map what's wrong in a client's inner world. Instead, self psychology has made a considered move beyond object relations theory in order to explore a new locus for therapeutic discovery and change, the space of empathy. It proposes that in this space the significant relations of therapy happen. Over the years, self psychology has come to understand this shared therapeutic space as fundamentally intersubjective. The client's and the therapist's self-systems, conscious and unconscious, are present in the space of empathic understanding, and so this is a space in which several kinds of "inside" and "outside" meet and mingle. Instead of moving between an interpersonal "outside" and an "inside" of object relations, self psychologists focus on this in-between, intersubjective space or activity in which senses of self take shape.

At this point in this chapter, I'm not giving you new information. In fact, this is the language I've been using all along in order to describe what's wrong when your client is feeling bad. Intersubjective and developmental self psychological theory was behind my story about Ben and Jim, and it guided my descriptions of self-states, RIGs, and organizing principles. It is, as I admitted in Chapter 1, my bias within relational theory. I lean toward the most radically relational and systemic forms of self psychological theory, and so that's what you've heard about so far. In the following section, I will talk about the wider scope of what self psychology has to offer on the topic of "What's wrong when your client feels bad?"

With its roots in object relations, self psychology has always been developmentally minded. Since its earliest days, self psychology has located the origins of psychopathology in a patient's relational history. Today it continues to offer relational–developmental answers to our question of how the bad experience that comes at a person from "outside" turns into her own bad feelings about herself. But in order to understand what self psychology offers, we first need to understand what it means by "selfobject experience"—which, paired with "empathy," is one of the most important concepts in self psychology. (The therapeutic space of empathy creates for a client a new chance for necessary selfobject experience.)

As we've seen, in the history of psychoanalysis, "object" has come to mean a person's internal experience of another person. Our object relationships are our relationships to internal images of important other people in our lives. What would a "selfobject" be, then? In self psychology theory, a selfobject is the internalized presence of another person when the presence of that person is necessary for a positive experience of self. The other's presence provides the self with experiences of identity, agency, and value: "This is me; I can do it; I matter!" It may seem that these feelings belong just to the self in question, whether that self be an infant, child, or adult. But although they do "belong" to that self, the good feelings wouldn't be there without the presence of others—both real and fantasized or internalized others.

Selfobject theory also explains the reciprocal negative parts of self-experience. When the presence of others fails to support a self's cohesion, power, and goodness, the self feels weak, fragmented, depleted, or flawed. With this vision of where at least some psychological dissonance originates, early self psychology added a whole new arena of bad feelings to the psychoanalytic picture. "Feeling bad" can stem not just from internal conflict but also from deficit, deficit originating in self-with-other experience.

If that's the case, then what's wrong for your clients comes not just from bad things that happened to them, but from good things that didn't happen for them. Their senses of self are not as coherent, resilient, cohesive, or sturdy as they might be. This kind of "what's wrong" often means that clients are especially susceptible to disturbing episodes of shame that fragment their somewhat fragile sense of self. That's self psychological language for what happened to Ben when he shared his excitement with Jim and found himself deflated.

Self psychology not only recognizes clients' vulnerabilities in this regard, it traces these vulnerabilities to caretakers' failures to provide the supportive, empathic selfobject experiences clients needed when they were young. Self psychology also holds therapists responsible for providing the kind of understanding that will help clients feel more cohesive, safer, and stronger, not more shamed and fragmented. The self psychological therapist becomes the selfobject, or (more accurately put) the provider of selfobject experience, that a client needs in order to repair deficits in his self-structure. This repair comes partly by way of his new, good experience of his therapist's in-depth empathy for him. It also comes partly through the strength he gains when the therapist's empathy is not quite right, and client and therapist have a chance to find out together what went wrong and to repair the "miss."

In other words, self psychology makes the therapy relationship a crucial scene for the reworking of a client's principles that organize his relational experience. Thus self psychology also takes in stride the fact that as a therapist you will fail your clients sometimes, and that then their bad feelings will be coming directly from the therapy. Their experience of being misunderstood, criticized, belittled, or abandoned by you will set off that powerful psychological dissonance called shame, that experience of themselves as weak, crumbled, or severely flawed. When this kind of shame overwhelms and silences a client in therapy, it's crucial to look for the origins of the shame in moments of misunderstanding between the two of you. When together you are able to understand where exactly the break in empathy occurred, your client's feelings of falling apart or becoming worthless will quickly diminish.

At this point we might ask: When both shame and repair happen in the here and now, where are the bad feelings really coming from—from old RIGs that turned present disappointment and hurt into "there's something wrong with me"? Or from just the current experience between client and therapist? Or do the bad feelings, the fragmentations, happen only when old and current experiences interact? It seems our answer must encompass all of these possibilities in some way. So perhaps the question is more usefully put like this: What was the relationship between "outside" and "inside" when this particular client's organizing principles around this issue were being formed, what's the relationship between "outside" and "inside" now, and how are those two times related? With these questions we approach a more radically relational version of self psychology.

But it wasn't until intersubjectivity theory and studies of infant–caretaker interactions appeared on the scene that it became possible to ask such questions about connections between past and present. A new paradigm made a new way of understanding possible. In early self psychology theory, a self was seen as a substantial, structured entity that could be firm or shaky, solid or riddled with deficit. In the new paradigm, a self is understood to be a subjective world of experience continually coming into being and held in being in intersubjective networks. In this view, selves exist as systems interacting, with some level of self-awareness, with other systems.

This is the case, first of all, for the selves of infants and their caretakers. The overall feeling quality of their interactions indicates when things are going well or poorly between them. Repeated intrusive or disconnected interactions create dissonance in the infant's system. The problem shows up in the infant's distressed responses to feeling overwhelmed or understimulated and also in the infant's attempts to regain equilibrium through avoiding, clinging, or self-distracting behaviors. When the caretaker's behaviors change, so do the infant's reactions, and what's wrong can be repaired. Of course, as Stern points out, when interactions are repeated, they begin to become generalized. Repeated interactions start turning into "principles" that organize experience in patterns that have become predictable. Yet when recurring problems are noticed early, often it takes only some careful coaching to help a caretaker develop interactions that work better in a particular infant–caretaker relationship.

A client's current adult relationships follow the same kinds of patterns: affectively loaded interactions between persons, or "self-systems," have powerful influences on each person or system. It could be that two self-systems are threatening to annihilate each other, or they may be providing each other life-giving support. Or in the territory between those two extremes, a client's systemic interactions with important others may leave him feeling disorganized, unhappy, or vaguely out of sorts. It's important for this client to understand the connection between what happened in these interactions and how he feels afterward. It may also be important for him to understand the relationship between what happened yesterday to make him feel this way, and what happened over and over in his childhood—that also left him feeling this way. Probably most important is that the two of you notice when that very same bad thing happens in an interaction with you. This gives both of you a close-up view of how your actions elicit certain reactions from him. His perceptions and reactions will be organized by convictions refined since childhood, organizing principles that make sense of how others engage with him and that also produce certain predictable meanings and feelings about who he is and what he's worth.

Your client's organizing principles might tell him, for example, that in order to keep his psychological equilibrium, he must keep others well out of his personal space, for if he doesn't, their anxiety or agendas for him might throw him off kilter quite badly. All he knows when you come too close with a "helpful" question or suggestion is that he must retreat and disappear. But the two of you are beginning to understand that your anxiety to help might be causing this particular problem for him. Neither of you know it, but his mother's anxiety was the problem when he was an infant and he learned to turn his face away from a spoon and her insistence that he eat more. These days he's quite aware of how he withdraws to protect his personal space from what he experiences as his partner's intrusion. His trouble in that relationship is part of what sent him to therapy.

ORGANIZING PRINCIPLES AND A WORST-CASE SCENARIO

Let's look more closely at this situation from an "organizing principle" way of understanding how inside and outside interact to create problems for your client. Your client's psychological organizing principles are telling him that for his own well-being he must protect his personal psychological space from his partner. He "knows" that if he doesn't, something bad will happen. But these organizing principles, like all his experiences of self, aren't a closed system. They can change as experience demands or invites a change.

Your client's partner loves him and wants to know him better. Frustrated about being shut out of important parts of his life, she proposes a deal to him: she promises not to worry out loud or meddle if he will share with her some of his plans for a project that's important to him. With some trepidation, he does so, and he finds, to his great surprise, that her interest doesn't feel like a threat after all. In fact, now that she knows more about his hopes and fears, he feels more energy and strength to carry on with the project. A loneliness he hadn't even noticed is suddenly eased. In this scenario, your client's ways of organizing interpersonal experience are, after all, quite flexible and open to new information. It's not too much work to find ways to revise and expand them.

But it might be the case that your client's earliest anxieties were so well-reinforced by childhood experiences of invasion of privacy that he can barely risk negotiating the deal his partner wants. Then, when he does try to let her in, her first comments feel like an invasion. (Her own organizing principles produce anxious reactions to being shut out.) Your client retreats and closes up. That doesn't mean that his system is locked irrevocably into the old organizing principle, but that his present operating principle locks very tightly onto suspicious information in order to give him quick protection from major danger. Loosening up this automatic reaction will take lots of exploration of how it works—when his wife's somewhat anxious approach (or yours) sets off his experience that he's not safe. It will also take many instances of finding out that in spite of his fears, sharing himself turns out to be safe after all.

This scenario illustrates that some kinds of feeling bad remain very resistant to being changed by new input from the outside, for they involve very strong organizing principles. Donna Orange, an intersubjectivist self psychologist, calls these strong organizers "convictions"—emotional convictions rooted in emotional memory.[12] Powerful emotional convictions that other people are dangerous can turn even the possibility for good experience into bad experience. When a client suffers from powerful negative emotional convictions, he must avoid real connection in order to avoid what he anticipates—inevitable humiliation, abandonment, or violation. When invitations to connect come his way, he's hamstrung by how he makes sense of them. When a person who suffers in this way comes to therapy, your central work as a therapist will be patient, persistent, gentle efforts to engage him in a relationship that slowly begins to feel safe to him.

In a worst-case scenario, even therapy never feels safe; a client's organizing principles have set like cement, blocking all exits to more interpersonal freedom. In such a case, her early history was probably what some self psychologists call a history of "pathological accommodation," that is, an accommodation of herself to a powerful other, likely a parent, in which her own thoughts, feelings, and experiences were no longer her own but were determined by what the other needed her to feel, want, and experience. The substance and dynamics of her own self-system were swallowed up by the self-system of the needy and more powerful other. Your client had no choice in the matter; she had to submit to this takeover of her core emotional self or be psychologically abandoned or destroyed. Wholesale accommodation was the only way to keep the connection she needed in order to survive.[13]

The problem for her, then, is far worse than inauthenticity. She's not "there" enough to pretend to be someone other than herself or to hide who she really is. Who she really is has been flattened, denied, twisted, and obscured. Who she thinks she is and what she thinks she feels are mirrors of someone else's needs and extensions of that person's organizing principles. Beneath this ostensible self, there is a vague, dissociated, and scrambled system made up of her own real experiences and feelings. They don't fit the prescribed picture—what to do with them, then? Her self-system will have expended immense quantities of psychological energy to get rid of her own experience, in order to make sure that the rules that ensure her survival are locked into place. Her organizing principles will be especially rigid because they are designed to hold in place a system in which there is very little margin for error.

But then she finds herself in another, later life. The Powerful Other in question is no longer physically present. She is free now—but she isn't. This is when psychological dissonance becomes acute for her. She begins to long for freedom from anxiety and for supportive connection in her life. But the rules of what she must do in order to survive annihilation remain in force. She is a prisoner of her own emotional convictions about what's possible for her.

Yet even in this worst-case scenario, there remains a chance that your client's self-system and her self-with-other system may still have some openings to influence, openings to being altered, if ever so slowly, by having different experiences in a therapy that finally does prove itself safe enough. These different experiences are made more powerful when you and your client notice them together in therapy. You'll have to do that over and over, and you'll also need to pay careful attention to how the old organizing principles keep trying to kill the positive effects of new opportunities and invitations. This will be the central work of her psychotherapy. It's very hard work, but the good news is that it's *possible*—within this self psychological understanding of what's wrong for a client who feels this bad.

WHAT'S WRONG WHEN YOUR CLIENT
IS FEELING BAD? A SUMMARY

Each of the relational theories we've visited has a useful angle on what's wrong when your client is feeling bad. I believe that there are important ways in which these views come together. Each maintains that psychological kinds of feeling bad don't arise from inside your client or begin with her. Rather, they are her involuntary reactions and habitual responses to what once came at her and continues to come at her. In other words, what's wrong exists at the interface of outside forces and inside effects and responses, whatever that interface is called. As we have seen, the interface between outside forces and inside responses may be called oppression and resistance, or disconnection and strategies for safe connection, or the creation and management of relational images, or empathic failure, fragmentation, and efforts to self-repair, or organizing principles that support accommodations to the other that are simultaneously self-protective and self-destructive.

Each of these explanations of what happens at the outside–inside interface has a distinct flavor. Some are constructed with a determination to keep the struggle located entirely outside of the client, while others allow the struggle to be staged more internally. But for all of them, the "feeling bad" that a client suffers is fundamentally a systemic phenomenon, something that happens in the reality of self-with-other.

What kind of a self-with-other system can keep a client feeling bad? We've seen it described as a narrative of oppression that a client can't stop telling and living, and as a practice of strategic disconnections that both protect and isolate a client. We've seen it manifested in a client's anxious efforts to hold a shamed and shaky self together in the absence of support, and, in more desperate circumstances, as self-immolating accommodations of a client's own desires, thoughts, and feelings to the needs of a powerful other.

What all of these descriptions have in common is that the systems they describe are active ways of being, or complicated sets of interactive doing, made up of many aspects—thoughts, feelings, choices, and actions. Changing the systems that keep in place these ways of being/doing involves, then, many different kinds of change—changes in understanding and naming what's going on, changes in repetitive patterns of thought, changes in interactions with others, and changes in clients' relations to their own feelings, so that forbidden feelings can surface, to motivate new thoughts and actions. What's wrong isn't something finished; it's something that is happening and will keep on happening unless it is interrupted. Change can begin only when the ongoing interactions of the system begin to change. In other words, both what's wrong and what can be changed are matters of what I called "the performative" in Chapter 1.

All of these theories support that idea of a performative therapy. "Relational psychoanalysis," with its links to interpersonal theory, not only believes that therapeutic change depends on changes in the therapist–client system of interpersonal interaction, it makes this belief the nexus of all its theorizing. From this perspective, it doesn't really matter whether the interface of inner and outer is called oppression and resistance, object relations, or mutually regulating organizing principles—as long as the problem is understood to be a relational matter, not an individual matter. From this perspective, what matters is to choose an explanatory system that makes the best sense of how all this unfolds in the therapy relationship and, even more crucially, to choose explanations that facilitate development and change in that relationship.

As any therapist does, you will have reasons of personal history, style of thinking, worldview, and politics to prefer one or another of these relational explanations of what's wrong when your client is feeling bad. And clients, too, come from many walks of life and thought. Some come with a well-developed political analysis and a vision for personal and social emancipation. Some have family of origin concerns and are seeking more rewarding interpersonal connections. Some come shame-ridden and looking for someone to shore up a shaky self. Others bring with them a bundle of symptoms tucked with them into a narrow, dark prison of assumptions about themselves that it seems no kindness can reach. A certain kind of relational therapy might be especially suited to each of these groups of clients.

But for all relational therapists and their clients, therapy is a process of self-with-other performative change. It's about learning how to do and to experience life differently—with others. That's the only lasting antidote for what's wrong when clients are feeling this kind of bad. Because what's wrong isn't some kind of failure or poison inside your clients. What's wrong is what they have learned to do in order to make the best of the relational experiences life has dealt them so far.

ENDNOTES

1. Some psychological problems do come from "inside." Organic and genetic factors are implicated in the development of schizophrenic illness. Hormonal imbalances can precipitate postpartum and menopausal depression. The "chemical imbalance

in the brain" of manic-depressive disorder can be effectively balanced with lithium. But these remain relatively rare conditions in the context of the millions of North Americans treated for anxiety and depression every year. Most of them are also treated with chemicals, treatment that seems to change something "inside." Does this mean, then, that something was wrong "inside"? Perhaps, but it can also be argued that the documented alterations in brain chemistry in people who are chronically anxious and depressed are an effect, not a cause, of "feeling bad," and that the primary causes (and best ameliorations) of feeling bad are still to be found in interactions between self and social environment.

2. Intersubjectivity theory proposes that we think of "self" as a world of subjective experience; see for example, Stolorow and Atwood, *Contexts of Being*, 2-4.

3. Stern, *The Interpersonal World of the Infant*, 97-99.

4. The term "organizing principles" comes from intersubjectivity theory: George Atwood and Robert Stolorow, *Structures of Subjectivity: Explorations in Psychoanalytic Phenomenology* (Hillsdale, NJ: Analytic Press, 1984). The Boston Process of Change Study Group (N. Bruschweiler-Stern, A. Harrison, K. Lyons-Ruth, A. Morgan, J. Nahum, L. Sander, D. Stern, and E. Tronick) describes how interactional processes from birth onward give rise to "procedural knowledge." They call this knowledge, which gives unconceptualized form and meaning to all of a person's further relationships, "implicit relational knowing." Karlen Lyons-Ruth, "Implicit Relational Knowing: Its Role in Development and Psychoanalytic Treatment," *Infant Mental Health Journal*, 19(3), 282-289 (1998). In the scheme I'm proposing, "organizing principles" are the (mostly unconscious) articulations of this general procedural knowledge or implicit relational knowing.

5. Phyllis Chesler, *Women and Madness* (New York: Doubleday, 1972).

6. Jean Baker Miller and Irene Stiver, *The Healing Connection: How Women Form Relationships in Therapy and in Life* (Boston: Beacon, 1997).

7. For a clear, concise explanation and example of a narrative approach, see Epston, D., White, M., and Murray, K. "A Proposal for Re-authoring Therapy: Rose's Revisioning of Her Life and a Commentary," in McNamee, S. and Gergen, K., Eds., *Therapy as Social Construction*. Newberry Park, CA: Sage Publications, 1992, pp. 96-115.

8. Laura Brown, *Subversive Dialogues*, 117.

9. Harry Stack Sullivan, *The Interpersonal Theory of Psychiatry* (New York: W.W. Norton, 1953).

10. See, for example, Darlene Bregman Ehrenberg, *The Intimate Edge: Extending the Reach of Psychoanalytic Interaction* (New York: W.W. Norton, 1992); Jody Messler Davies and Mary Gail Frawley, *Treating the Adult Survivor of Childhood Sexual Abuse: A Psychoanalytic Perspective* (New York: Basic Books, 1994); and Philip Bromberg, *Standing in the Spaces: Clinical Process, Trauma and Dissociation* (Hillsdale, NJ: Analytic Press, 1998).

11. For an in-depth account of the development and transformation of object relations theory into self psychological theory, see Howard Bacal and Kenneth Newman, *Theories of Object Relations: Bridges to Self Psychology* (New York: Columbia University Press, 1990).

12. Donna Orange, *Emotional Understanding*, 113-124.

13. Since his seminal 1993 paper, "To Free the Spirit from Its Cell," reprinted in Robert Stolorow, George Atwood, and Bernard Brandchaft, Eds., *The Intersubjective Perspective* (Northvale, NJ: Jason Aronson, 1994), Bernard Brandchaft has been developing the idea of pathological accommodation and clinical approaches to the problem.

4

BETWEEN PAST AND
PRESENT, MEMORY AND NOW

In the last chapter I explained how a client's psychological "feeling bad" comes from processes that take place among his self-with-other systems, and that the system with the most power to make him feel bad consistently is his interpersonal process memory, along with the principles it generates for organizing the meanings of his present-day interactions. In this way, a client's past self-with-other systems come to have far-reaching effects on present systems, and thus on the quality of his relational and emotional life. This is how past is present, according to a performative, relational model of therapy.

Popular conceptions of therapy link past and present, too, often with the assumption that therapy is about remembering traumatic events that clients have repressed. Sometimes it's assumed that just recovering traumatic memories will purge out the "bad" bit by bit. Or cure is thought to come through putting together the past like a puzzle, work that can include finding out how a client's past is influencing his present patterns of behavior and self-esteem. I don't disagree with the fundamental tenet here: that therapy is about dealing with the effects of the past as they live on in the present. But in this chapter I will try to show what that tenet means in a relational model of therapy, sketching out first a relational definition of trauma and its effects, and then a relational picture of the power of remembering-with.

WHAT IS TRAUMA?

"Trauma" comes from a Greek word meaning "wound." In the world of psychology, "trauma" means shocking, wounding experience that has lasting psychological effects. There are psychologists, psychiatrists, and psychotherapists who specialize in understanding the psychological processes set in motion by the sudden severe violations and prolonged brutalizations that trauma survivors have suffered. Judith Lewis Herman is one of those. She writes from a feminist, relational perspective about the psychological aftermath of having suffered war, political imprisonment, torture, camp incarceration, kidnapping, rape, domestic violence, or childhood physical and sexual abuse.[1] Along with many others in the field, she proposes the name "complex post-traumatic stress disorder" for the aftereffects of prolonged subjection to violation and domination.

Long after liberation or escape from the scene of the trauma, a survivor continues to suffer the past as if it were present. Nightmares and daytime flashbacks bring back sights, sounds, smells, and other body memories of violation. These fragments of traumatic memory remain frozen in time, frozen by the terror that still possesses the survivor with every repetition of the memory. In this daily atmosphere of persistent retraumatization, a survivor also fears real and present danger around every corner. Even when it's not a conscious thought, a survivor is vigilant, alert to threat. Insomnia, constant irritable anxiety, and repeated surges of fight or flight adrenalin can wear down a survivor's physical resilience and bring on physical symptoms of long-term stress such as hypertension, gastrointestinal disease, and chronic pain and fatigue.

When severe trauma is inflicted again and again, many survivors learn to dissociate themselves from what's happening to them, sometimes through powerful trance states. In parallel fashion, when the trauma has become history, a survivor learns to minimize its intrusive physical aftereffects by limiting the risks, encounters, and demands of daily life. In a very safe, repetitive daily routine, there will be less chance of feeling the kind of momentary scare that might set off a flashback or nightmare. If a survivor avoids new people and new situations, she doesn't have to be so hypervigilant. And if she numbs out most of her daily feelings, she can also manage to keep out of her awareness the painful feelings still entangled with her traumatic past.

But although various kinds of dissociation allow the survivor to keep those painful feelings out of her awareness, the feelings still keep breaking through in fragmented, unintegrated bits of memory, and they are what generate her pervasive anxiety and physical symptoms of stress. Constricting her feelings eases some of her pain, but rather than solving her problem, constriction keeps her problem in suspension, out of the reach of help. Constricting her interactions may also leave her isolated, depressed, and despairing of any meaningful future.

This oscillation and tension between intrusive symptoms and constricting her life in order to cope with the symptoms is only a small part of what an abuse survivor suffers. Far worse is the emotional anguish of having suffered relational violation and betrayal. Especially in the case of childhood physical, sexual, and emotional abuse at the hands of a caretaker whom the child should have been able to trust, such betrayal threatens the child's sense of self with annihilation. A secure self develops in response to secure connection with caretakers who use their power benignly, with respect for the child's person and feelings. When parental power is used to control and coerce a child with no thought for the child's perspective or emotions, the child feels helpless, powerless, and often obliterated by shame. Her desires to explore and to assert herself with confidence fade as she worries about keeping safe by being good. For in trying to make a world for herself that is tolerable, she will have decided that the bad things that happen to her are her fault (as she may have been told). She will know that she is bad and Daddy or Mommy is good. This will give her some sense of control; it's better to be a bad child in a universe that makes sense than a good child in a universe of arbitrary, random pain.

For an adult survivor of severe childhood abuse, a deep, helpless sense of "what's the use" persists, along with pervasive self-blame, shame, and guilt for whatever bad happens to her. Having had her personal dignity shattered, she carries feelings of being defiled and stigmatized, of being profoundly different from others. Having had to make sense of her childhood experience all by herself, she feels deeply and utterly alone, with no hope of ever being understood. Thoughts of her abuser bring rage and desire for revenge, but in her mind, her abuser remains bigger than life and still has supernatural power over her. Though she hates what has been done to her, often she still sees herself and the world through the abuser's eyes and belief system, the only view she was allowed to have for a long time and under duress. When she sees the world through her own eyes, she finds it difficult to see any purpose or meaning in it at all.

In her adult life, an abuse survivor's relationships are profoundly confusing and disturbing. Having known betrayal intimately, she distrusts any professions of love, care, or commitment. She knows that loving crosses over easily into using and abusing. And since as a child she found herself trusting those who hurt her, she also deeply distrusts her own ability to tell "good people" from "bad people" and thus keep herself safe. So sometimes she just takes thoughtless risks, and other times she withdraws into isolation. Somewhere she keeps on hoping against hope that someone will rescue her, even while she turns angrily away from a world of dangerous people. In intimate relationships, she fears abandonment desperately, and at the same time, she has to protect herself constantly from invasion and emotional takeover. Interpersonal conflict throws her into intolerable anxiety, for her history tells her that if she asserts herself, a dominating control or rage will come at her, and her only options will be to rage back or to submit—an absolutely no-win situation.

A CONTINUUM OF RELATIONAL TRAUMA

This is but a brief sketch of the stress, pain, and trouble a trauma survivor copes with every day. Certain clients fit this picture exactly, and it is clear that they are survivors of childhood abuse. For other clients, the pain in their lives is not quite so physically and psychologically overwhelming. They have confidence and initiative enough to make decent lives for themselves, including, perhaps, good jobs or careers and some sense of belonging to a community or neighborhood. In relationships with friends and family, they can learn to trust, feel mutual respect and caring, and even manage to work through some interpersonal conflict constructively. They also struggle, however, with pervasive anxiety and depression and with deep doubts about their worth and connection to others. Does the trauma we're talking about have anything to do with their experience?

In my clinical work both with abuse survivors and with deeply troubled clients who have not been overtly and severely abused, I have wondered for a long time whether there is more continuity or difference in their two kinds of experience. As I have become more and more aware of the relational trauma at the heart of a history of abuse, I have come to see far more continuity than difference, and I find myself placing many clients on a single continuum of relational trauma. This, I believe, does not trivialize the atrocities done to those whose experience exists at the most severe end of the continuum, and it includes their suffering in a larger human picture. A unifying relational definition of trauma also validates those whose suffering has been more psychological than physical, but no less real. Perhaps using a single continuum is most important for those many clients whose experience exists somewhere in the middle, bordering on overt abuse. They're not sure whether they can call what happened to them abusive. If it's not abuse, does their experience really matter? Is their pervasive psychological pain fraudulent, self-induced? Understood as relational trauma, their experience does matter profoundly, and their pain makes sense.

And then there are the many clients who can't remember much of what happened to them. Can they heal if they can't remember? A continuum of trauma based on traumatic relationship rather than on traumatic events takes the urgency out of such questions. Clients usually do remember the powerful relationships that hurt them, even if they haven't fully recognized the hurt and don't remember many of the details of how that hurt was inflicted. When we focus on relational trauma, we can see that it is the devastating context for violent, coercive enactments of abuse. We can also see how it wreaks quiet destruction in its more covert and subtle versions.

As you work with various kinds of relational trauma, you may have clients who remember being abused and who can now start to realize and integrate what has happened to them. But in addition to this kind of remembering, again and again they're taken aback by relational ruptures with important people in their lives and with you, their therapist. Working their way through these impasses is the most frightening and exhausting part of their work inside and outside of therapy. A relational perspective on trauma reassures them that these aren't side issues; this is exactly the work they need to be doing in order to reassemble healthier, happier ways of being in the world.

Other clients may remember being abused, but remembering seems not to have helped them much. They wonder if their previous therapy work has gotten to the heart of what happened to them. From a relational perspective, the key to healing the wounds of abuse is to work through the relational violations and betrayals that are at the heart of violently abusive acts and threats. Until these clients have a chance to attend to the relational aspects of the trauma they suffered, they won't get to the heart of what happened to them. They *do* need more help, as they suspect.

Then there are the clients who can't remember what happened to them, and the ones who are quite sure there was little overt violence or coercion in their families of origin. Yet in their daily lives with others, they feel frightened, isolated, angry, trapped, and worthless—all evidence that something relationally damaging happened to them. You—and they—are right to wonder whether the quality of their early connections to caregivers left them with deep and long-lasting, albeit hidden, relational wounds.

I'm suggesting that for clients in any of these situations, their experiences can be situated on a continuum of relational trauma. From one end of that continuum to the other, certain things hold true: (1) The injuries underlying psychological pain are at their core relational injuries: trust has been betrayed; legitimate interpersonal needs have been denied; a child's personhood has been ignored or demeaned. Particular events or times of injury have become traumatic because they were embedded in an ongoing traumatic relationship, one in which caretakers did not notice the child's distress or help the child recover. (2) Persons wounded in early relationships protect themselves from remembering and from further hurt with a wide range of dissociative strategies and behaviors—from "spacing out," to severing themselves from their emotions, to medicating themselves with substances, to losing themselves in fantasy, to giving themselves over to addictive behaviors, to forgetting themselves in non-stop, hectic cycles of responsibility. (3) The traumas of the past continue in the present not only in self-protective strategies but also in troubled relationships. All along the continuum of relational trauma, interpersonal trust is riddled with doubt and fear, though in their less severe forms those feelings can be masked. Still, the expectation of being ignored or humiliated is never far away. Holding one's own in self-assertive projects remains problematic for one who has suffered relational trauma, and situations of conflict can induce panicked flight or paralysis.

Any one of your clients may not recognize himself as a survivor of overt, severe abuse, but he may find himself quite definitely on this continuum of relational trauma. He needs to hear that with or without experiences of severe physical and sexual abuse, relational violations and betrayals count as trauma. His pain is not fraudulent. He can be sure that he isn't doing it to himself. He also needs to know more about how this trauma might have happened and how it keeps on affecting him in his present life.

FACTORS CONTRIBUTING TO RELATIONAL TRAUMA

Psychologically traumatic experience begins when something happens to a person that is more than that person's psychological system can handle.

Prisoners of war and torture victims are psychologically broken by repeated assaults intended to overwhelm them with terror and helplessness. Battered wives become prisoners in their own homes, their psychological system of self-protection destroyed, as their abuser eliminates all outside contact and support. For a small child, terror and helplessness can be inflicted much more carelessly: there's a sudden explosion of rage when she has made a mistake; she's left alone and humiliated by her badness in a dark room; she hears and sees abusive, hateful exchanges between her parents; she lives with the constant threat of violence which, even when not enacted, keeps her anxious and watchful; or she witnesses violent acts or verbal abuse inflicted on her mother or siblings.

A client may have specific memories of such overwhelming, self-disorganizing moments. She might also guess, based on what she remembers of how other children were treated in her house, that there were similar moments in her infancy, ones that survive in only her most rudimentary interpersonal process memory. Her crying might have been ignored so that she wouldn't be spoiled—until she wore herself out with helpless, overwhelmed screaming, and slept. Caretakers might have yelled at her and spanked or shaken her to make her be quiet and "good"—until her system learned the value of giving up and acquiescing. Mealtimes and toilet times may have been experiences of being invaded and controlled, of losing her bodily agency and integrity.

All of the psychologically overwhelming moments I have described are ones inflicted by caretakers. This is a very important part of what makes them traumatic. For in such situations, the child is truly helpless. When the acts and emotions of her parents scare her, there is truly nowhere else to turn. The child is literally at their mercy, as captive as a political prisoner or a battered wife, but she doesn't even know she is captive, for this is the only world she knows.

If, instead, your client had lived in a safe interpersonal world as a child, even deliberately abusive acts by strangers would have had less long-term traumatic effect on her. The abuse would have been a violent intrusion on her safe world, but it wouldn't have constructed a constantly frightening world in which she was trapped. In a safe world, if a child were hurt, her parents would notice and care about what happened to her. They would try to help her talk about her scary bad feelings so that she could get to feeling safer and stronger again.

But this is another critical point where a careless traumatizing parent fails. Not only does he or she shock, ignore, frighten, coerce, or humiliate a child without thinking what that might be like for the child, afterward the parent doesn't notice what's been done to the child. He or she is oblivious to the child's pain, a kind of obliviousness that discounts and obliterates the child's experience. It's not that the parent doesn't know what happened; in fact, he or she does know, but it just doesn't matter. It's nothing. That's what the child is left to believe. Or it's something other than he thinks it is. The child's terror doesn't matter because the truth of the scene is this: his father has a right to be so terribly angry. Someone *made* him angry. Or it's the child's own disgusting behavior that has gotten him banished to his room, and he deserves his mother's cold silence for the rest of the day. The neglectful chaos that swirls through his family is just how it is. If his father needs his help, and he's slow and makes mistakes, it's his stupidity. If he has a hard time at school, if he's an unathletic geek or overweight or very shy, his parent has a right to shame him and pressure him to change.

Children can be helped to deal with many kinds of interpersonal hurt. They can even tolerate and integrate their parents' failures, flaws, and emotions when their parents notice the effects of their actions, take responsibility for changing whatever might be out of control, explain their feelings, apologize when necessary, and help their children talk about their own feelings "when Mommy gets mad," for example. But the overwhelming events we've been talking about are burned into your clients' experience as trauma not just because they're scary events, and not just because they came at them from people they needed to trust, but also, and perhaps most importantly, because those very people didn't help them deal with what happened to them.

After a child has survived a flood of disorganizing, overwhelming feelings, he is left to make his own sense of what happened, a sense that he can use to protect and guide him the next time it happens. But he can make sense in only the simple, childlike ways we've already mentioned. If he has been shamed, he is shameful. Believing that he's the bad one in the relationship, he tries hard to be good. The more at risk he feels, the more tightly his perception of the world has to match his caregiver's perception, a loss of self we've seen described as "pathological accommodation." (Some children believe that they're bad and decide to give up and just be bad, then. But for all their apparent rebellion, they are no less tied than their "good" siblings to their parents' view of them and of the world.)

And above all, a child who survives trauma repeatedly tries not to think about the bad times. There's no future in feeling those feelings; there's no way out of them except to wait for it to be over. So although the child is ever watchful for the signs of something scary about to happen again, when a bad time has passed, he puts his feelings as far away as he can. Because no one acknowledges what has happened, he, too, has to turn that experience into something that hasn't really happened. Or even if it has happened, he turns it into something that doesn't matter. Since it's "nothing"—and also nothing he can make sense of—he turns it into his own kind of nothing. But through this act of disconnecting from it, the "nothing" is put where it can begin to take on a powerful life of its own.

THE DISCONNECTING EFFECTS
OF RELATIONAL TRAUMA

The technical term for the psychological process most responsible for putting traumatic experience where it can carry on into the present is "dissociation." And this is, of course, a paradox and an irony, since for the trauma victim the whole point of dissociation is to get rid of painful feelings and keep them away. In fact, what dissociation does is put painful feelings where they can't be integrated into a coherent narrative of a client's history. They keep causing him plenty of trouble, but he can't tell where the trouble is coming from. Strong, quick, and persistent acts of dissociation, the kind a child can learn to perform very early, keep trauma out of narrative memory. So it's not even the case that there's a whole story of what happened to your client pushed down somewhere, waiting to be recovered. The picture is more like scattered fragments of radioactive memory—body memory, event memory, emotional memory, and/or interpersonal process memory. These fragments lie strewn across your client's internal landscape, disconnected from each other and from your client's awareness, but still emitting powerful, disturbing signals.

During and after severe abuse, dissociation may be physiological as well as psychological. Many victims learn to get through traumatic events by using self-hypnosis to detach from their own consciousness. After an intense and terrifying experience, what a victim has sensed, felt, smelled, seen, and heard, along with his visceral reactions to the abuse, may be encoded in only a part of the brain that doesn't link into narrative memory. Those fragments of memory will remain there unaltered, erupting sometimes into nightmares or flashbacks, but never coming together as the victim's own story. Therapy will have to include the painstaking process of gathering up these fragments and allowing them to take more coherent patterns and meanings.

If a particular client's trauma is more psychological than physical, other kinds of dissociation will keep certain aspects of a traumatic relationship out of her awareness. She may remember disturbing events, but with no real sense of what was going on between herself and her caretakers, and without much feeling. Of course those things happened, she may say, but they don't matter anymore. She's quite sure of that. She may even have put together a story for herself of a happy childhood. Nowhere in her story are the feelings that belong to a relationship in which a self-absorbed, fragile, angry parent fails to understand the longings, needs, and fears of a vulnerable child. These are the radioactive memories that lie scattered away from this client, unintegrated and therefore still meaningless.

Furthermore, as we mentioned earlier, the traumatized client can use any of a host of ways to block the signals coming from those fragments: emotional numbness, self-medication, overwork, addictions, obsessions and compulsions, or psychosomatic illness, to name a few. Her way of being in the world with others will have a dissociative quality about it, for although she functions well enough, she's quite disconnected from her own inner feelings and processes. These particular strategies for disconnection (to use Stone Center language) keep her from being present to her self. She can't be very present to anyone else, then, and so these strategies keep her out of relationship, too.

A traumatized client has other everyday ways to protect herself from being hurt again by others—subtle strategies for emotional disengagement and safe disconnection. As we saw in Chapter 3, behind these strategies lie her interpersonal process memory and the principles it has produced to organize all the bits of her daily interpersonal experience. This is how the self-with-other system of her childhood gets replicated in her interpersonal systems today. This is what tells her, for example, that she must please her partner or she will be abandoned, that disagreement between friends is terribly dangerous, or that isolation is the most trustworthy kind of safety.

If any one kind of everyday experience runs through relational trauma and its fragmenting, disconnecting aftereffects, it's the experience of shame. For survivors of relational trauma, shame turns up in many forms. To be shamed is to become a pariah, cut off from human connection, and the reverse is also true: isolation is itself shaming. To be cut off abruptly or ignored deliberately can induce shame reactions even in very young children. When one is left alone, feeling bad, those bad feelings quickly become feelings about a bad self, for the feeling of shame carries with it the sense of being defective. As we noted in Chapter 3, when a child can't make sense of bad feelings, one explanation is always available: "There's something wrong with me."

Dissociation and disconnection riddle your client's adult life with shame. Since she can't know her feelings and motivations from the inside out, she can't feel whole and strong. She's ashamed of the disorganized anxiety she carries around, and she's ashamed of the obsessions and habits that keep her anxiety under control. Nobody knows how hard she works to present a coherent, "together" front to the world. Chronic disconnection from others robs her of the support she needs to feel good about herself; here, too, isolation breeds powerful shame. Her organizing principles quickly turn any interpersonal trouble into something she should be ashamed of. To live life in the long shadow of relational trauma is to live haunted and constricted by shame in all its guises.

HOW DOES REMEMBERING HELP?

But therapy promises relief for those whose relational past has been traumatic, relief through remembering. More specifically, relational therapy insists that to be effective, such remembering must be remembering *with*. For unless a traumatized client has someone to help her make reconnections, she won't be able to shift out of her usual self-protective, disconnected ways of remembering. She has invested a lot of psychological energy in putting difficult experience out of sight and out of mind. When she was a child she needed desperately not to feel what was going on between herself and others so that she wouldn't feel her overwhelmed, shamed confusion. She still knows in her bones that there are very good reasons not to revisit those scenes and feel those feelings again.

Yet there is also a very good reason to let herself feel how it was: Putting those experiences out of sight has not really put them out of her mind or out of her life. She struggles with physical and psychological symptoms that don't "make sense." Something keeps bothering her, sapping her energy and self-confidence. Though she can't make the connections, she suspects it's "old stuff," and so she has looked for a therapist whom she feels she can trust. She thinks that trust is probably crucial. She's absolutely right. Only when your client can feel that her therapist is on her side will she be able to let herself remember how it was. Once she pushed all the bad stuff out of sight because no one saw or cared. There was no one to help her name the feelings and understand what was happening. Just because there was no one to help, the trauma was so deeply disorganizing and shaming for her. To begin, now, to speak to you about that shamed place will be to take a major emotional risk.

Her risk starts to pay off, though, as your empathy for her experience eases her fear of being shamed again. She finds she can bring her jumble of hurt and angry feelings, and you help her sort them out, bit by bit. When you try hard to hear and respond to her experience just the way it was for her, that's the very opposite of what happened to make her experience so traumatic. This time her feelings really do matter. This time someone is saying, "Yes, what happened really hurt you!" As you listen and respond, you reassure her that it's okay if she can't be sure of all the details. What matters is that someone is here, now, to witness and validate the truth of her experience. In time she will find herself not just speaking about her shame and confusion, but speaking directly from those shamed places in herself, in the shaky but growing hope that your empathic understanding will keep on welcoming her back into connection and human community.

In the next section of this chapter, we'll look more closely at how this remembering takes place in therapy. But already it's clear that it's not an investigative search for the story of what happened to your client in exact detail. In relational trauma, the hurt comes less from particular circumstances and events than from the ongoing attitudes and feelings important people had toward your client. Things that happened showed her how other people felt toward her. What she needs to remember is how it felt to be with those people. The proof of that kind of memory is imprinted on all the ways she protects herself from being hurt again by people close to her.

It's also clear that we're not talking about revisiting scenes of trauma in hopes of cathartic expressions of emotion. This kind of remembering just activates fragments of self-with-other pain. If what happened between your client and an abusive parent left her flooded by helpless rage, it's no help for her to find herself back in that state, even if this time she can kick and scream about it. The help she needs now is the same kind of help she needed then: someone to see what was really happening, someone to care and to validate her feelings, someone to support her angry protest and her demand for fair treatment, and someone to help her integrate even unfairness and cruelty into a picture of the world as it is, and into a coherent story of who she is and what she's known and felt.

This kind of remembering helps her because it adds up slowly to new, important knowledge: "This is who I am. These are the kinds of things I had to live through. This is how I made myself strong enough to survive, and these are the vulnerable feelings I had to hide away. This is how I came to be who I am today." As these things fall slowly into place, she may feel as if she's finding a lost self or as if she's beginning to exist at the center of her own being. Now, because she is no longer a child, no longer alone and overwhelmed, she can say, "It's better to feel the pain. At least I'm here!"

Remembering *with* is what makes the pain of recovering herself bearable and meaningful for your client. The presence of someone who witnesses, understands, and cares allows her pain to be transformed into grief. While dissociation is the psychological process most responsible for keeping trauma active and destructive, grief is the opposite process. A time of grieving is a time of integrating past and present meanings and feelings. Grief is the psychological process through which trauma can be laid to rest.

Only grief can begin to heal the pain of loss, but since grief itself is acutely painful, people who have suffered loss need the close presence of others to help them grieve. Many human communities build this wisdom into burial and mourning rituals. As your client's therapist, you bring this wisdom with you as you attend her grieving process. She may mourn for the broken spirit of her young self; for the confident, optimistic young adult she wishes she could have been; for the loving intimacy she avoided for too long; for so much of her potential wasted; for how very hard she has worked just to keep herself together; for the tenor of her everyday life, far too anxious and sad; and for the understanding, affirming mother and father she always longed for but never had—and never will have.

Grieving brings past and present together into coherent meanings, dense and rich with feeling. From the crucible of mourning relational losses, a once-fragmented self emerges as a self of integrity. In the words of Judith Lewis Herman, "Integrity is the capacity to affirm the value of life in the face of death, to be reconciled with the finite limits of one's own life and the tragic limitations of the human condition, and to accept these realities without despair."[2] And though grief may always haunt certain of your traumatized client's thoughts and memories, when it has done its work, it passes. The integrating work of grief not only recovers a self for her, eventually it sets that self free to look forward and to go on.

At the time of self-recovery and beginning to move on, it's just as crucial that your client not be alone. During the long process of remembering, you have been present to her suffering and grief. Now you are the one in whose presence she is no longer fragmented and shamed. Just as the grip of shame is intensely interpersonal, so her release from shame can be fully known only in the presence of another person. If that person was once present to her shame as well, her release can be exhilarating. Energies and interests that had been blocked by shame begin to surge forward. When she has someone to respond to her newly released desires and motivations, they don't overwhelm her. She is able not just to dream new dreams but also to make new plans and to take new actions.

It was in hope of this outcome that she went to the trouble of finding out how to remember who she was. The point of remembering was to stop the mindless repetition of dissonance, anxiety, and emotional pain that plagued her subjective world. Mindful reflection brought her into the presence of what hurt her. But it also gave her the gift of grief, her integrity, and her freedom.

HOW IS THERAPEUTIC REMEMBERING DONE?

We come now to an absolutely critical question for the practice of relational psychotherapy: How, exactly, does therapy help a client do the kind of remembering that will loosen the constrictions of her past? Just the word "remembering" conjures up an image of a therapist taking a detailed history and of a client responding by telling all the stories of her childhood she can remember. But as you know from earlier chapters, that's not how relational therapy goes.

Memory Is Now and Now Is Memory

In fact, a lot of what I'm calling "remembering" doesn't look the least bit like a trip down memory lane. I need to explain that I am using the word in a very general sense: "remembering" as making mental or emotional contact with something that's past and present at the same time. This sense of remembering depends on two assumptions: first, that memory is always a here-and-now mental construction; and second, that our perception of here-and-now is constantly being formed by the sum total of all that we remember. Every day and in every way, we live our lives through our memories. And when we remember a specific event, all of our other memories and all of our feelings right now shape and color what we think is coming straight from the past.

That doesn't mean our memories aren't true. But it does mean that we have to think carefully about our definition of truth. Perhaps we would be wiser, at least in therapy, to talk about meaning instead of truth, for meaning includes not just "the facts," but also the feelings around the facts, and how those facts and feelings are woven into meanings within our subjective worlds of experience. That interpersonal system that we call a self, with all its love, hate, desire, fear, joy, and shame, is not a data bank. It's a meaning-making system. It doesn't make arbitrary meanings; whenever possible, it checks outside references for validation of the meanings it makes. But as it makes meanings about self-with-other, its first reference is always to feeling, or "affect."

That's why what we think of as the facts of memory are "filed" under feelings. What do I mean? Let me illustrate. On a certain day a client comes into therapy terribly upset about having been cheated by a colleague, and then he spontaneously remembers a childhood incident where he felt both helpless and furious about having been tricked. Another client is trying to screw up his courage to ask a special person to dinner, and he finds himself recalling his stylish mother's disapproving eye, and how he felt like a hopeless geek at his senior prom. What brought those particular scenes to mind? In both cases, we could say that a number of scenes or memories have been filed under a certain self-with-other feeling. "Tricked, helpless, and furious" opens one file. "Anticipating humiliation" opens another one.

In a client's meaning-making, the filing system matters more than the memories it contains. The filing system shows how a client has already categorized situations and emotions from reams of memory data about interpersonal processes. Certain event memories are kept at the front of each file as strong illustrations of the feeling. The arrangement of the files is much closer to the truth of who your client is than any supposed facts of his history, because his filing system is *how* he makes meaning of "facts." Obviously, this metaphor of a filing system coded according to emotions takes us back to organizing principles.

To extend the metaphor, we could say that a client's organizing principles are his automatic fact-filing and retrieval program, especially when the facts in question have to do with his relationship with others and his place in the world. These principles that organize a client's life of relationships and feelings are the most reliable form of relational memory. Their organizing actions don't depend on just a few events; on the contrary, they have been generalized from very many similar experiences of what happened between a client and other people. Just outside of his awareness, they continue their constant operations of making sense, and as they retrieve files in order to do so, they are the forces that turn memory into "now." They are also the forces that define new experience by filing it in old files that have fixed emotional meanings.

Metaphors always fall short, of course, of the reality they aim to capture. But my point is that any memory takes place within this complex activity of making meaning. It's here that the remembering of relational psychotherapy is undertaken—in this activity where then and now merge, where experiences of past and present co-determine each other.

In Chapter 3, we saw that relational therapy understands psychological bad feelings to originate from neither outside nor inside a client, but rather from that place or activity where inner and outer systems interact, producing relational meanings full of feelings. Here we have another angle on that same difficult concept, another approach to the same territory. In this chapter, I am saying that the "remembering" work of therapy is not about the past as such, but about specific ways the past is present in a client's system of living and making meaning.

A client's relational past is present in active principles that organize the feelings and meanings possible for him in his life and relationships. These are the very principles that came into being in order to make recognizable patterns out of many repetitions of interpersonal interactions. They came from that place that is neither outside nor inside, but outside and inside all at once. What your client remembers is past and present all at once. It's important to remember, however, that your client doesn't have to think about all of that while he's doing his therapy. Nor do you have to force or cajole his remembering. It will be there. The layering of now and memory will slowly reveal itself when careful attention is paid to whatever the client is experiencing, thinking, and feeling here and now.

Staying Anchored in the Present

Any client comes to therapy because of problems he has living right now. His problem isn't simply that he's forgotten what happened to him. His problem is that the meanings of what happened to him aren't good for him, he's living those meanings every day, and he doesn't know what they are. For the purposes of therapy, what happened in the past matters only in how it stays with a client now. That's why, as a relational therapist, you will keep yourself and your client anchored firmly in the present. Even if your client comes in wondering whether his problems are coming from his history, it's probably best to say, "Let's talk about what's troubling you now, and see what comes up." It's likely that what will come up are persistent patterns of feeling bad on a daily basis, which can be linked, after a while, to certain interactions your client has with other people and to the meanings and feelings of those interactions.

This was the case with "Megan," who came to see me because she was feeling lost and confused about her life and worried about the beginnings of a starve-and-binge eating pattern. She was just finishing her first year of university, and she wasn't happy in the program she had chosen. The youngest of three daughters, she was the last one living at home. Her brainy oldest sister was away at medical school and the second sister, married to a nice guy, had a beautiful new baby. In her opening sketch of the family, Megan painted herself as the quiet one who never really knew what she wanted. I couldn't get a clear picture of her parents until I began to hear clues that they weren't very happy together. Megan told me more than once that each of them loved her very much. I began to wonder whether this quiet youngest daughter had long ago become the comfort of her mother's lonely existence and the light at the end of every long, hard day for her father. I wondered whether her eating obsession helped her manage the anxiety she absorbed from her parents' relationship.

But mostly we talked about what she would do in September. First she told me, very hesitantly, that she didn't want to go to university; she wanted to go to art school. Next she dared to say, "But only part-time." Megan liked the new place where she was waitressing; management was fair and the tips were good. If she kept that job, she could make decent money and still go to school part-time, she explained. As she told me these things, she realized that she was trying to become financially independent. Then came the bigger realization, quite hard for her to face. She wanted to be independent enough to leave home! This was a large problem with many problems inside of it.

Megan knew that her parents would oppose her for many good reasons: the responsible thing would be to stay in university; the financially sensible thing would be to live at home. But what Megan feared most was hurting her parents by wanting to leave. She felt trapped and angry. She cried. She thought she would never be able to say what she wanted to say to them. Again and again we discussed all the ways she might explain herself to them, and all the ways she thought they might respond. In the end Megan invited them to come into a session with her—so that I could help look after them, she said. My presence also gave her extra strength to say what she had planned. It came down to, "I'm not my brainy sister Gwen or my bubbly sister Joan. I'm just me, and I really need to leave home in order to find out who I am. I still love you both very much, and I will visit lots, but I need a space and a life of my own."

In that session, her parents were able to hear her fairly well, and in the weeks following they were able to let her go with only sporadic guilt-inducing messages. Megan was able to tolerate her uncomfortable feelings in the face of their sadness and their subtle anger about her leaving. Soon after Megan had moved out on her own, she didn't need to come to therapy any longer. She told me that she was pretty sure that her eating wasn't going to be a problem anymore either.

You could say that in Megan's therapy, we never touched her past. Or you could say that as she experienced my listening, one of the assumptions she had made in the past, in the shadow of her competent, talk-ative, outgoing sisters, got significantly altered. She found that when somebody was listening to her, waiting to hear what she really thought, she could, indeed, figure out what she wanted. She could find her voice. And with this new possibility springing to life between us, she dared to risk an even more radical change. Perhaps she could speak her needs, even though her needs would take her away from her parents.

We never went back in time; we never had to talk about the little girl whose sense of worth depended on easing the pain of both her parents, or about the years she carried their anxieties as her own. What we did was go over and over the shape and feel of the system in which she felt trapped, and as we did so, a new, freer system was developing between us. Our new interactions had altered Megan's accommodating, care-taking organizing principles just enough to give her a crucial window of escape from them. Though we never spoke of it, something had changed in how her past was present to her, and I could hope that the change would give her freedom enough to keep on speaking her own truth to her parents and developing more self-assured ways of being in the world.

A critic might object that this was a fairly easy, straightforward six-month therapy, and that many adolescents, in order to get ready for adult-hood, are in the process of revamping their interpersonal organizing principles. To do so, they don't need to explore the past. All of this is true. A critic might then suggest that adults who have suffered more extensive relational trauma are in a different situation; they do, in fact, need to be directed to think about what happened to them in the past, at least for a little while. In answer, I will tell another story, which I will call

"A Tale of Two Hospitals." It's only a small part of a long, complicated story, for the story's heroine, "Lucy," has been in psychiatric care for half of her life, ever since her first suicide attempt at 16. She came to me from a residential treatment facility that specialized in the recovery of memory, in particular, memories of sexual abuse. I have been her therapist for 10 years now, and she also keeps contact with a psychiatrist who can prescribe medication when she needs it and who still maintains her safety-net link to a hospital, should her suicidality recur.

A Tale of Two Hospitals

When she came to me, Lucy had already remembered that between the ages of 5 and 9 she had been sexually molested and perhaps raped by her father. But her memories were in vague bits and pieces. In her previous treatment program, she'd been told that the key to her healing was to recover her memories fully, along with all the feelings that went with them.

What was wrong that needed healing? Lucy lived most of every day alone in a fog, losing large chunks of time, forgetting to eat, and sleeping irregularly. When small things went wrong, she would feel so helpless and terribly alone that she would cut herself to feel the pain—and to stop the pain. Often she was too frightened to go out, but when she had to, she could switch into a tough, bright persona who could interact with shopkeepers and bus drivers. Sometimes Lucy tried to work at menial jobs to augment her small disability pension. But inevitably her persona would get stretched too far and crack, and she would retreat, sobbing, to her apartment, sure that everyone hated her, sure that she was ugly and disgusting, sure that she should hurt herself as punishment. And at least once or twice a year, her ability to keep herself functioning would also get stretched too far, and she would start planning to die. But ever since her first suicide attempt, her plans to die had always become entangled in complicated relationships with hospitals. So once or twice a year, she would be in hospital for a week or two, getting over the urge to kill herself.

I decided that my first priority with Lucy would be to help her establish more physical safety and comfort in her life. I also wanted to help her feel safer with me. So for months stretching into years we talked about the details of her everyday life—about cleaning and painting her apartment, about starting seedlings and shopping for groceries, about fights with a boyfriend who treated her badly, about troubles at work, misun-

derstandings and fallings-out with friends, and negotiations with psychiatrists and hospitals. We talked about islands of calm in a day or a
week, pieces of reality that made sense, and we visualized linking them
together with bridges. Lucy told me about sci-fi books she liked and
brought me tapes of her favorite music. Sometimes she brought her pets
along for a visit. "Family therapy," she said.

In and through this everyday conversation, we talked about Lucy's
past, too, but not as a special project, and not about what had been des-
ignated "the trauma." From diaries she had saved, she read aloud to me
the record of her adolescent torments of struggling to establish an identity and find friends who liked her. As I supported Lucy in interactions
with her family, I felt I came to know Lucy's mother quite well, especially
her style of oscillating between needy intrusion and harsh criticism of
Lucy. I came to have a sense of her moody, distant father, too, and even
of the vulnerability mixed in with his abusive, alcoholic rages. Lucy told
me that when she was little, she used to be petrified every night that
someone was going to get killed. She told me how her mother dressed
her up to be her pretty little girl in clothes Lucy hated, and how she
screamed at Lucy when Lucy didn't do her chores right. I heard about the
bullies in Lucy's playground, her childhood pets, and the different houses
she lived in. And sometimes I wondered whether we should be talking
about "the trauma" instead of all of this.

And then, during one of her longer stays in the hospital she had
been using for suicidal emergencies, the staff there decided that Lucy
should, indeed, talk about the trauma. She told me about it after, about
"losing it" and having to be restrained. She had heard herself screaming
ugly words at herself, she said, and in that moment she knew that those
words had been screamed at her—she knew she had been abused—it was
true! After the breakdown, she felt dazed and confused for a while, but
much calmer. Above all, it seemed, she felt vindicated in the eyes of the
hospital staff: she *did* carry horrible stuff inside her; terrible things *had*
really happened to her. Her pain "made sense." She had a right to it.

I didn't understand exactly what had happened to Lucy in hospital,
but I hoped for her sake that it was the breakthrough she longed for. But
sadly, it wasn't. Very soon she was acutely suicidal again, and after three
brief admissions in quick succession, the hospital staff decided to try
another approach. They underlined that part of her diagnosis that read
"borderline," and referred Lucy to a neighboring hospital with a treatment program that reclassified certain "borderlines" as patients with "dissociative identity disorder" and worked with the dissociation. After much

initial fear and suspicion, Lucy began to talk with staff there about the different parts of her that had very different thoughts and feelings, and especially about that small but powerful part who stepped in to take over when she and everybody else was sick of her "whiny self, always in pain, always needing, never getting." That cold, furious part said, "Fuck it. One thing needs to happen here. That whiny self needs to die."

Just learning about these different parts and about the dissociation that kept them apart from each other was a wonderful revelation to Lucy. She came back to me more excited and confident than I had ever seen her. "It's the dissociation—that's the problem! That's always been the problem! None of those hospitals or psychiatrists ever got it—all those years! And it's so obvious! Out of all that treatment, only you got it, only you knew it all along. You've been saying dissociation for years!"

She gave me more credit for understanding what I was doing all those years than I deserved. But it happened that soon after Lucy began her hospital treatment for dissociation, I attended a workshop with Jody Messler Davies, a relational psychoanalyst who specializes in treating survivors of childhood sexual abuse.[3] I came away echoing Lucy: "Yes, it's the dissociation! But not just any kind of dissociation—what matters most in the treatment of abused clients is the *relational* dissociation. All these years, with so many clients, that's the problem I've been trying to understand, trying to engage with! At last somebody is saying it, saying how to put relational dissociation together with relational treatment."

So Lucy and I continue our same style of work together, but now we understand better what we've done. After all the childhood shatterings, when she came to me she was living her life in disconnected pieces. Her previous "trauma therapy" had left her with more difficult and disturbing pieces to deal with. At first all she could bring to me were those disconnected bits and pieces of her experience, keeping her deeply shamed sense of an empty, worthless self far away. But over time those bits of past and present began to hold together, and she began to live in everyday time and space. After two or three years she noticed, "It's like I can feel a past behind me, like it's real, there's continuity." She said, "It's like I can finally be here. But I don't like it. It hurts a lot." What hurt the most was what she described as searing, overwhelming shame. When she came close to feeling it with me, it was more than she could bear.

Through this long process of getting safer and becoming more present, Lucy began to approach more directly the central shattering in her life, the splintering of her personality into fragments of self-with-other systems of interaction, each of which took on a life of its own.

Eventually I, too, had to fight with the brutal, omnipotent killer of Lucy's vulnerability, and I was allowed closer to the terrified, shamed child-self who thought she deserved to be dead. These two fragments of herself—actually two pieces of how Lucy can experience self-with-other—are the most important of Lucy's "parts." But now that we know how they work, we can identify other self-with-other systems that pop up to help her deal with difficulties.

Lucy and her new boyfriend have come in together to talk about the parts of themselves they each have that just react to each other, causing scary, repetitive fights. In spite of the fights and because of the talking, that relationship became quite open and safe. It has also become an extremely important place for Lucy to notice many fragments of self-with-other feelings and link them together into a growing sense of a whole self in relation to others.

The more Lucy experiences herself as a whole, real person operating with a psychological system she recognizes and regulates as best she can, the more her overwhelming shame subsides. Now her shame is tied mostly to specific interpersonal events, and after "running and hiding," she can usually find ways to reframe or repair what happened and then reconnect. She and her boyfriend are talking of getting married. And then, they think, they might move away—away from their toxic families of origin, away to the mountains or the coast, where they can get a fresh start together.

"Leaving you will be hard," Lucy says. But I think she will manage just fine, especially if she finds the support she needs in her new location. She knows how to develop trusting relationships now; she knows how to ask for help and how to use it. I think that this is exactly how our long therapy needs to come to an end: Lucy will leave home, the home where fragments of her being came together as a self. She will leave whole and strong enough to be able to make the new relationships that will support her in her own life in the world. I will wish her well from the bottom of my heart, and whenever she writes to keep me posted on her progress, I'll write a note of acknowledgment and encouragement back.[4]

THE ANTIDOTE TO RELATIONAL DISSOCIATION

Lucy's story illustrates how important it is to keep therapy anchored in the present—because that's where the past is making trouble. Lucy's story also shows, quite graphically, what kind of trouble the past makes. As she and I both said, "It's the dissociation!" If the trouble is dissociation, what's required as its cure or antidote is a containing, holding, and linking kind of remembering. But even more can be said about *relational* remembering in the face of *relational* dissociation. Let me begin with a very brief review of Jody Davies' position.

I went to Davies' workshop knowing she was a relational psychoanalyst. As I had hoped, she proposed a relational model of mind—horizontal, associational, meaning-making—a model in which unintegrated trauma lives outside the sphere of what can make sense. Thus, for the traumatized person, the trauma is truly "nowhere." Davies contrasted this model of mind with a vertical, linear, drive-based model in which trauma is known but is then repressed "somewhere"—into unconscious regions beneath consciousness. She argued that trauma survivors don't repress what they know; it is dissociated from them before they have a chance to know it. As I have done, she spoke of both physiological and psychological dissociation.

For Davies, as for me, personal psychology is all about relational processes. In a relational model, a child's experience becomes a sense of coherent self only within the consistent, affirming, holding presence of responsive others. A relational psychology, then, understands that dissociation happens when those processes that hold a self in being fail. Without important, close others to help contain and soothe a child's hurt and fear, traumatic experience is just too overwhelming for a child to integrate. This experience then becomes dissociated; it goes to "nowhere." But it doesn't disappear. It becomes a dissociated process with a life of its own. Other self-with-other processes emerge as protection against those feelings—like Lucy's killer—and they, too, take on a life of their own outside of what the whole child knows. If a child's entire self-with-other experience is painful, chaotic, and overwhelming, the child's entire system of self-with-other splinters into disconnected parts, each of which maintains isolated, disconnected ways of relating to the world.

But if the core processes of trauma stay alive and powerful in repetitive loops of self-with-other interactions that are isolated from each other, what does that mean for the relational treatment of trauma? This was Davies' new question, galvanizing for me. All good trauma theory emphasizes the importance of a healing therapeutic relationship. The therapist is a knowledgeable, calm expert who can help the survivor manage the intrusive symptoms of post-traumatic stress. She is an empowering witness who embodies compassion and justice. She is a companion along a dark path of mourning who brings personal integrity to the task of facing loss, pain, and evil. All of these ways of being-with are important aspects of a relational treatment of trauma. But how does a therapist be with those repetitive loops of self-with-other interactions that comprise a trauma survivor's fractured sense of self? To find ways to engage in those loops with a client would be to contact the most significant ways in which a trauma survivor's memory constructs her "now." It would be the best, most powerful kind of relational remembering-with, for it would carry the possibility that something about those self-with-other loops could be changed as the therapist and client lived through them together.

Before we go further, let me summarize what I've said so far about a relational "remembering" therapy: such therapy contains a trauma survivor's unintegrated feelings and holds her fragments of life and memory while the survivor slowly reassembles herself. But this is only a first step. To go further, the relational dissociations that keep a survivor's core self disintegrated need something more from a therapist—a lively interest in how the client's self-with-other systems work, and a willingness to find out how those systems work from the inside, that is, from the experience of being the "other" to each fragment of the client's self. Taking this next step requires using two therapeutic techniques of remembering that are the most characteristic of relational therapy. They are (1) remembering by way of exploring recurring relational images or model scenes; and (2) remembering by way of what's often called transference. We'll finish this chapter with an explanation of model scenes, and then we'll spend all of Chapter 5 exploring the complications of transference.

A CONTINUUM OF DISSOCIATION

We're about to discuss how a relational kind of remembering becomes an antidote for dissociation. But first I need to point out that dissociation takes many forms. Your clients don't need to live in a world as fragmented as Lucy's once was in order for you to understand their struggle in terms of dissociation. Once again, I find the idea of a continuum helpful: a continuum of dissociation that mirrors the continuum of relational trauma. At the severe end of the dissociation continuum are trauma survivors like Lucy whose fragments of self-systems have little connection with each other and whose core experience is one of being "gone" or annihilated. In a rare condition known as multiple personality disorder, or a profound dissociative identity disorder, each self-system operates independently, with little or no knowledge or memory of the others. At the other end of the continuum are clients like Megan. Her dissociation is far less severe, but she, too, has split away from herself a certain group of troubling self-with-other experiences, meanings, and feelings. And so the most fundamental principles of relational treatment are the same for both Lucy and Megan: the therapist encourages the client to bring to therapy all the parts of herself that trouble her—problems, symptoms, memories, feelings—and she holds all of that within empathic care and understanding. The therapist also helps the client trace and feel the self-with-other scenarios that cause her pain and shame: critical, powerful aspects of her trouble that she hasn't recognized on her own. With a severely traumatized client, there are many unintegrated bits to hold and a very long process of linking them together. With someone like Megan, there's not as much missing from the center, and not as many discon-nected aspects of self for the therapist to hold. Only part of Megan's relational life was problematic, and so the work of connecting with what was dissociated didn't take nearly as long.

But with both young women, the essential part of the work was to track and to trace how certain troubling self-with-other systems worked. Lucy's most devastating experience was to turn to people for help and have them disbelieve that she was in trouble. Every trip to hospital con-tained the threat that this would happen to her. Even hints of disbelief would flood her with humiliation and rage. Once, when the disbelief was blatant, the "killer" part of herself took over, stalked out coldly from the hospital, took the streetcar home, and with stockpiled pills nearly succeeded in annihilating her "sucky, whiny" self forever.

We came to call the beginnings of this sequence "not being taken seriously," and for a long time it was so explosively shameful that Lucy couldn't remember or tell me the details of how it happened. But after many instances, we began to piece together the crucial interactions. Lucy would say in one way or another, "I'm at the end of my rope. I just want to die. I can't keep myself together and safe any longer."

Then the people on the other side would say in one way or another, "That's not true." They might say, intending to be helpful, that she was stronger than she thought or that she'd felt this way before and come through it. Or they might impatiently insinuate that she was manipulat-ing the system with threats of self-harm. But whatever they intended, to Lucy it all meant the same thing: they did not believe the truth of her experience. She was trying to tell them how it was for her, and they were telling her she was lying.

We would look at exactly what Lucy had said and what she'd hoped to hear in response. We'd contrast the bad times with times when Lucy had felt heard and helped. We'd conclude over and over again that what Lucy needed at these crucial times was that people would believe how annihilated, helpless, and "in pieces" she felt, and that her desperate pain would matter to them enough that they would want to help. Of course, their belief and care would have to be demonstrated in some kind of good-faith action, but once she felt believed with empathy and care, Lucy was able to receive help in whatever form it was available to her.

At the center of Megan's brief work, there was that same tracing of a particular painful sequence of self-with-other interactions and feelings. In her case, though, we did the tracing mostly hypothetically, as she practiced what she might say to her parents and anticipated their responses. She wanted to tell them she needed her own life, her own space, and she felt sure that they would try to keep her in their space, looking after their needs. She wouldn't have been so sure of that without a history of those kinds of interactions behind her, but she didn't need to tell me about the history. Imagining the next important interaction seemed to give her enough contact with how that system worked; it was all the remembering she needed to do.

I didn't try to help Lucy and Megan change how they did their parts of the interactions. That wasn't the point. We were just remembering: making contact with something that was past and present at the same time, something we could be sure was important because not only did it cause such trouble, it was also very hard to know about. What was the point of making contact with it? We could hope for at least two kinds of spontaneous changes. For both Lucy and Megan, important parts of who they were and how they felt were entangled in interactions they couldn't bear to know much about. As they worked through the interactions, they could reclaim those important lost parts of their own experience. This reclamation might stir anger and grief about what happened, but it could also eventually help them feel much more whole, centered, and resilient.

But integration of lost parts of self wasn't the only payoff we could hope for. We could also expect that as we traced and retraced how those interactions worked, they would lose some of their power to repeat themselves automatically. Just sensing how the old loops worked gave Lucy and Megan more freedom to try new interactions. For each of them, their first experiences of a different need-response sequence happened in their relationship with their therapist. But each was able, in her own time, to take her new freedom out to where she needed it in her life.

"MODEL SCENE" MARKERS OF MEMORY/NOW

If, as a relational therapist, you take seriously these two ideas—that there's a continuum of relational trauma and a counterpart continuum of disso-ciation—with most clients you will be on the lookout for signs of repeti-tive interpersonal interactions that are mysteriously powerful in their lives. If you think in self-in-relation terms, you may catch glimpses of certain relational images that, like unposed snapshots, capture lasting self-defin-ing moments between your client and other people. Or you might be interested in looking for signs of "model scenes," an idea recently devel-oped as part of relational psychoanalytic technique.[5] I like noticing model scenes and working with them because they're not just still-shots; they illustrate important sets of feelings with drama, action, and gesture.

The truth of a model scene is like the truth of a powerful scene in a film or novel that catches the essence of a character's complicated exist-ence: Macbeth's dialogue with the dagger; Bogart on the Casablanca tarmac; the moment of Sophie's choice. But your clients' model scenes won't appear to you so artistically framed. In fact, they'll be hard to see at first, if obvious later. I'm thinking of the client, not used to remembering her dreams, who said one day with a laugh, "I had the weirdest little dream. I was trying to run away from home, and my parents were Hitler and Eva Braun. I had to slide like a shadow out the door and not let them see me."

She laughed at first because her parents were hardly Hitler and Eva; they were a well-respected clergyman and his wife. But the more she thought about it, the more she saw that the dream captured critical, hid-den aspects of her life with them: she feared the cruel tyrant her father could sometimes be; she despised her mother's self-abnegating fixation on him; she felt like a prisoner in the walls her parents had built around the family, and she had been trying for a long time and in many small ways to disappear in order to escape. This scene also caught the gist of how, in general, she still feared authority figures, didn't have much re-spect for women, and kept herself invisible for safety's sake.

A dream is only one form a model scene can take. Often a model scene comes as a memory. Here is an interpersonal model scene that captures how one client learned to dissociate from pain—while learning not to need help from her mother: "I've had a bike wreck and cut my knee. It's a deep cut, and it's bleeding a lot. I'm 9 or 10, I think. I get myself home. My knee really hurts, and I'm scared because inside the cut I can see white stuff that looks like bone. When my mom sees all the blood, she freaks out, and all of a sudden, my knee doesn't hurt any-more. I'm totally calm and I calm her down and I tell her it's all right; it's not very bad; I can take care of it myself. So she leaves me alone. And I take care of it." It's no surprise that the client who tells this story has long been able to ignore acute physical and emotional pain even while suffer-ing its effects. Now it's catching up with her. Even now, however, she can't expect any support or compassion from others for what she feels.

Model scenes of family relationships often turn up as mealtime memories, such as: "I'm sitting at the supper table and nobody is saying a word because we waited for supper until my father came home. He came home just a little drunk, and now he's angry because she's angry at him. But nobody says a word about it and we have to be very good. I can't taste my food; I can't even eat it, but I have to. Then my brother spills his milk, and my dad yells at him and sends him to his room, and I feel like crying but I know I can't."

A different model scene captures a different family system: "Every-body talks a lot at the table, and the person with the best argument wins. You've got to be smart and articulate, or you lose and feel dumb. I'm the youngest, so I'm not quick enough; my words get stuck in my throat. So I feel stupid and like I don't belong." If each of these mealtime memories is, indeed, a model scene, we're not surprised that the interpersonal feel-ings caught by these vignettes are still alive and making trouble for the persons remembering the scene. The one who felt like crying but couldn't still freezes at the first sign of conflict. Fearing that her feelings are explo-sive, she contains them tightly. The youngest sibling who couldn't get into the conversation has to work hard, as an adult, to speak up and believe in his own points of view. To remember the past by way of a model scene memory is to know something important about the present.

As we've noted before, a client can remember that present past with-out even thinking back in time. Here-and-now model scenes can help him do that. Often, as a client tells you his stories about everyday things that bother him, you will begin to notice that many of the stories are about the same kinds of feelings, stirred by very similar interpersonal interactions. Any one of those stories could stand for many others like it, and in that sense it's a model scene. It captures an essential tension or dilemma that is often present for your client with others—fearing criti-cism, feeling unknown or misunderstood, resisting authority, or escap-ing needy demands, to name just a few possibilities. Understanding repetitive interactions as model scenes links them to the organizing prin-ciples that construct your client's model scenes and that give them their meanings. When you and your client pay attention to many of his model scenes, past and present—the memories, dreams, interactions, and images that disturb or move him—together you will see how they all tell versions of the same interpersonal stories. These are the stories that, as your client lives them out, keep on making him who he knows himself to be.

Why are model scenes so useful? Because over time they help link up a client's past stories and present stories in patterns that make better sense of many parts of his experience. But first they matter insofar as each one helps him find a link between feeling bad and what happened to make him feel bad. In relational trauma, what happened is often very hard to recognize, for what gets dissociated from conscious awareness are those very self-with-other interactions that make him feel an awful kind of bad.

Why would this be? Because what hurts the most is precisely what happened between your client and that other person. No physical pain lasts like the repeated, inescapable experience of being controlled, rejected, discounted, or humiliated. So your client has tried not to know about those experiences. It's likely the other person wouldn't want him to know about them either. He or she would be happy to help your client pretend none of it happened. Furthermore, those painful experiences are often embedded in quite ordinary events, and that makes them hard to see—until they start turning up as "model scenes." A model scene gives your client the gist of an important interaction between himself and someone else. It shows him, draws him a picture, stages the drama. Then, when he pays attention to how the scene unfolds and to what it seems to mean, his feelings start to come back to him and he starts to make better sense to himself.

The kind of model scene that's most powerful for many clients is the kind that plays out between themselves and their therapists. This kind of model scene is often given the special name "transference," as if it's a phenomenon peculiar to psychotherapy. Actually what's called transference is just one more repetition of a self-with-other interaction that has been painful for a client in many other contexts. Except this time the painful interaction is happening with his therapist! What could be more distressing? This is the very person he has been learning to trust to be on his side, to understand him, and to care about how he feels. A sudden shattering of his new, fragile trust may fill him with such helpless rage and despair that leaving therapy seems like the only way out. Sadly, in some therapy relationships, it is the only way out.

But a relational therapist doesn't lose heart when the therapy relationship becomes fraught with pain. She knows that here is a chance to engage with those dissociated parts of self that the trauma survivor tries so hard to keep under wraps—but can't, really. If the therapist can find ways to understand the pain she has caused and thereby build an understanding relationship with those frightened, angry "parts of self"—that is, with those repetitive loops of self-with-other experience—she will be able to provide her client with the most powerful relational antidote available for relational dissociation. Very often, when a relational therapist is right there to do her part of this difficult transference work, there is a way through it, and then there are significant rewards for making it to the other side. Chapter 5 is all about those very difficult but potentially rewarding passages.

ENDNOTES

1. Judith Lewis Herman, *Trauma and Recovery* (New York: Basic Books, 1992).
2. Herman, *Trauma and Recovery*, 154.
3. Davies' 1999 workshop carried forward ideas she introduced in her first book: Jody Messler Davies and Mary Gail Frawley, *Treating the Adult Survivor of Childhood Sexual Abuse: A Psychoanalytic Perspective* (New York: Basic Books, 1994).
4. Lucy and her boyfriend did, indeed, get married and move to a small coastal town far away, and she does keep me posted on the new life they are making together. Soon after she left, I sent her a draft of this chapter, and she replied by phone and then by letter, pleased to give her permission for me to use her story the way I had written it. Since that time, and with a good support network, she has managed pregnancy, birthing, and mothering an infant. The family of three is doing well. Recently she sent photos and wrote that even when it's hard, she knows that this is the life she has always wanted.
5. Joseph Lichtenberg, Frank Lachmann, and James Fosshage, *Self and Motivational Systems: Toward a Theory of Psychoanalytic Technique* (Hillsdale, NJ: Analytic Press, 1992).

5

THE TERRIBLY HARD PART
OF RELATIONAL
PSYCHOTHERAPY

YOUR WRITER IS IN TROUBLE!

I do want to write this chapter, but I've been stopped in my tracks by an uncanny turn of events. I don't like this situation one bit, but I find myself in one of those difficult passages I've promised to write about: I'm trying to get through a painful model scene with my therapist. It began two chapters ago, and I was hoping it would be over by now. I have no idea how I'll get through it. It crosses my mind that maybe this time I will have to leave therapy. More of me thinks not, reminding myself that I've been through these hard times before and I've come out all right.

That's exactly what this chapter is about—getting through these hard times. But if I don't know whether I'll get through or not, how can I write the chapter? I tell myself just to keep speaking in the same therapist's voice I've been using. From my therapist's chair, I'm always more confident (though never sure) that a client and I can find a way to work through difficult interpersonal feelings. But if I assume that calm, knowing voice now, I'll have to dissociate from large, loud parts of what's going on for me. My writing will be here and I will be elsewhere. How can I perpetrate such falseness in a chapter that's supposed to be about honesty and integration?

So I have decided to begin this chapter from inside my current experience and find out if that can take me to what I need to say to you, my readers. Just now you might be wondering what I, a therapist, am doing in therapy, anyway. Or maybe most therapists, seasoned or novice, understand that it behooves them to do their own therapy work, and I will be preaching to the choir. But in any case, let me make a brief case for therapists being in therapy.

In the first place, since therapists are ordinary humans to whom painful things can happen, we need help as much as anyone else. Second, the job demands large reserves of emotional presence and resilience, and since therapists can't talk about their work at home or with friends, we often bring the trouble stirred up by our work to our own therapy. In a more personal way than a supervisor or consultant does, a therapist attends to our feelings of confusion, frustration, and depletion. And third, most of us therapists take up the work because we know something about emotional pain and psychological dissonance from the inside. Many of us were parentified children in troubled families. Emotional attunement comes easily to us, and we thrive on providing the empathy we once longed to receive. But this means, too, that we live somewhere on the continuum of relational trauma, with a propensity to keep important parts of our self-with-other experience out of our own awareness. Sometimes, for example, providing care can be a very effective way to disavow a need, long-denied, to be cared for. But such disavowals wreak havoc when they keep us from recognizing what motivates our own responses to clients, especially when those responses become part of model scenes clients experience as destructive. Therapy can prevent and undo some of those unconscious entanglements with clients' issues.

And finally, of course, therapists are in therapy because we believe in the process. We therapists who know about feeling bad from the inside are also in the business of helping others feel better. Therefore we are perhaps more optimistic than most people might be about our own chances of being helped to feel better through another course of therapy. We keep trying.

For all of these reasons, I have been in several different rounds of therapy over the course of my career as a therapist. Right now I'm thinking that the only reason good enough to keep me in this current therapy is the hope of feeling better—which is as it should be. I doubt anyone stays with this terribly hard part of relational therapy unless it's to try to accomplish something really worth the risk. I'm still trying for it, it seems. Now I will tell you what's happening as simply as I can.

THE STORY BEHIND THE TROUBLE

Not long ago, after completing the opening chapters of this book, I was beginning to feel quite excited about writing it, and I spoke of my feelings in therapy. My therapist not only empathized with my feelings, he also seemed to think that the book was a valuable project, and that it might make a worthwhile contribution to our shared field of work. He seemed genuinely interested. Made bold (or foolish) by his interest, I brought him a photocopied draft of the first two chapters of the book. He thanked me politely. As I was talking about what it meant to me to give him some of my work, I noted that it was a risk, since I knew he was a busy man. He responded by saying that it would, indeed, be a while before he could get around to reading what I had given him. My heart sank, though I didn't know how far it sank until I had left the session. But then suddenly I knew that above all else, I had to get those chapters back.

I got my chapters back, unread, at the beginning of the next session, and I began to try to talk about what had happened. The components of the model scene, as I had experienced it, weren't complicated. I had dared to hope that my analyst's interest in my work was genuine and that he shared my excitement about it. But in his response I heard no excitement, only polite and wary protection of his boundaries and a subtle indication that my request was a burden. As soon as I heard that, I was filled with shame for having asked. I knew at once that I had asked for far too much; of course, the only time he owed me was the time in session that he was paid for. I had made a terrible and humiliating mistake. It was as if I had been caught asking him to put a childish drawing of mine on his fridge.

I tried to say what had happened to me, but his silent listening felt like a cold, critical void. I ran stuck and fell silent myself. I hated having to talk to him about this; it completed my humiliation. I told him, "Shame is like a burn, a bad burn. And talking about it is like having to strip the dead skin away so that it can heal." I wanted him at least to hear how horrible I felt. I felt flattened and grief-stricken, though I didn't know what I had lost. In the first days after this rupture, I went for long walks, trying to calm myself. Slowly I did grow calmer, and I began to get my feet under me. My equilibrium returned as I was able to think that I didn't need his approval. I didn't need him to share my excitement. My book was an adult project in the real world, and what mattered was to do it well and find a publisher. I would do that. He would never hear about the book again until it was a finished project. Or if it turned out to be a failed project, he would never hear about it again. I could feel myself gathering up my angry humiliation and using it as fuel to keep my project going and thus to keep myself going. Indeed, that was the move I had been making from the very moment when I knew, "I have to get those chapters back."

I can understand that from the outside my feelings look like a huge overreaction to my therapist's expectable, reasonable response to my request. That in itself is embarrassing. But those feelings become more comprehensible if I provide a bit of background that explains why this simple interchange was actually a potent model scene for me.

My father was a theologian in a religious tradition that did not allow women to be leaders or thinkers. This might not have mattered a lot to me, except that as his oldest child, I identified with him and couldn't help but want to follow in his footsteps. Ours was a complicated relationship, because there was also deep trouble in his personal relationships with women, especially the women he loved. And so I tried to find a place with him as a pseudo-son. I learned from him how to hammer a nail, paint a room, drive a mowing tractor, shoot a rifle, and pitch a tent in the rain. I developed, during the years of listening to his preaching, a passion of my own to put words together in ways that would make people think. But I was never invited into my father's study.

In my second year of university, I wrote my first philosophy paper, and I brought it home to him in hopes that he would read it. He never mentioned it again to me. Weeks later I found it lying crumpled behind the couch. As I understand my own history and how it stays with me, that philosophy-paper model scene is itself a condensation of many earlier experiences that convinced me that what I felt and had to say as my own person didn't matter much to my father. What did matter was whatever he wanted me to think, feel, say, and do. He was easily troubled, easily angered, and I learned very young to do whatever I could to keep him happy. I also learned that I should never ask for too much from him—or from anyone. In fact, I shouldn't really ask for anything; I should always just be grateful for what I had been given.

And now, as an adult with that history, I have chosen to be in therapy with a man who is not just my senior but also a psychiatrist trained as an analyst. This puts him well "above" me, for although I work as a psychotherapist, I am a social worker by profession—one of the feminized professions well down in a mental health hierarchy dominated by mostly male psychiatrists. In my professional life, I have lived in the shadow of the tall towers of psychoanalysis, but I have been barred from the castle. Or so it seems sometimes. As an academic, I have written about psychoanalysis, but I remain outside the fraternity, I believe, and always will be outside. And part of that is by choice, because I don't want "them" to own me. I want to think and speak for myself. My complicated interest in psychoanalysis is like tilting at windmills, or so my organizing principles say. I could just as well have tried to be a woman theologian trying to speak my truth in my father's patriarchal religious tradition. (Or I could just as well have tried, as a very small child, to resist his powerful need to control my feelings and construct my being in ways that would mirror him.)

This was the fraught relational context in which I became brave enough to talk to my analyst about my own place in the world of relational psychotherapy. After countless tests of his empathy, including careful repairs of previous misunderstandings and ruptures in our relationship, I was secure enough to risk it. I could dare to say to him that maybe what I had to offer was valuable even if it wasn't psychoanalysis, that maybe my writing could say something that was both quintessentially me, in my own voice, and also useful. I had reason to hope that this particular man/psychiatrist/analyst might see that my ways of thinking and feeling, of being and expressing myself, were worth something just as they were. I wanted my self to matter in his eyes—and in his feelings, I think.

That's how much was riding on my casual request that he read what I had written about the work we had in common. In retrospect I can see that the situation was far too fraught for my needs to be simply met. The situation had to shatter—so that I could experience what it was all about. For a while I thought that if only he had responded with just the right degree of enthusiastic pleasure when I gave him my writing, then all would have been well, even if he hadn't been able to read it for a while. But that response would have just kept the model scene moving, fraughtness intact, toward some other moment when his response would fall short of my hopes. I doubt he could have kept on being "perfect" enough to protect us from the implosion of shame that happens at the heart of the model scene I am reliving with him. That shame is too large a part of my life experience, with too many trip wires running off in every direction. Furthermore, the situation I set up seems, in retrospect, uncannily calculated to bring the old model scene to life between us. The implosion of shame was hardly an accident. I must have known that I would see some hesitation if I asked him to read a long piece of my writing on his own time and right before his holidays. As I have said to him bitterly since, "I knew better."

Readers might well wonder, "Why did you do it then?" First of all, I didn't knowingly choose to do it. I chose my small action, of course, but I didn't see the large picture with its quality of model scene before I chose, or notice the clues that I might be setting myself up for shame. It seems I was compelled to set up that particular old/new scene and risk the shame. Something drew me, an unchosen "why." I think it was a compelling hope, just out of my awareness, that my therapist's positive response to me would wipe out that whole other system of self-with-other feelings and meanings that had been constricting and tormenting me for years. I believe I thought, without really thinking it, "If I set it all up again and he is the exact and perfect opposite of my father, I can at last be free." There's a powerful logic there, and in fact, in very small, imperfect increments worked out over time, that's exactly how relational psychotherapy works.

But this model scene, with all it stands for, is far too powerful and too thoroughly entangled in my personality to destroy with one blow. I can't vaporize the fraughtness; I need to feel it. As I was saying in the last chapter, integration means to reconnect with the core self-with-other events and feelings that are at the heart of relational trauma. And that's a third answer to the question, "Why did you do it?" I guess I needed to reconnect with a part of myself who has been too painfully humiliated to reach out or to be embraced. I'm not sure I want to know her now or that she wants to be known. For in that split-off relational world where she lives, others have no time or space for her. She feels like nothing, a nobody, to them, and then she feels greedy and disgusting for wanting more. That's the core relational truth at the heart of my model scene, though the scene takes the shape of an effort to change that truth and the inevitable failure of that effort.

Other scenes are clustered around that relational truth but further from the center and more protective of it. I could mention winning a prize, when I was 6, for the second highest marks in my British grade one class, and my bewildered surprise at my parents' pleasure. And then the penny dropped: "Oh, *this* is how I can matter!" My father didn't read that philosophy paper of mine, but I finished my philosophy major with honors. I can feel myself doing it again, typing away at this project, looking for a publisher, determined to get it done in spite of my therapist.

The last time I saw him I said, "I'm bigger than whether this therapy turns out okay or not. I can leave it if I have to. It feels really good to say that. My life, my *self*, is bigger than this. You can't destroy me. I will survive. No, I'll do better than survive."

Bravado. But also a way to keep my balance—to keep from falling into that powerful self-with-other fragment of not mattering, that pit of shame. After a lifetime of practice, I do it well. I also know it's only a second-best solution. But it might be all I have, and if so, it's far better than nothing.

I imagine readers wondering, "If you can see all of this so clearly, why aren't you over the shame already? Why do you have to keep playing your game of 'I don't need you'?" To tell the truth, I don't know for sure. I think it's because I feel all alone in this. I wish insight were the cure. I wish that just the repetition, the powerful experience of "old" feelings surging through me, a catharsis of pain and grief, would release me. I wish there was something I could do to change how I feel. Even writing doesn't help.

But although I can't see my way out, I'm not without hope. My hope is that I won't be alone in this forever. I can't feel that it's happening yet, but maybe if I keep on telling my therapist what I feel, I'll begin to know that he's still there. That would help. And maybe if I'm calmer I'll be able to make those brief, careful visits to that unbearably humiliated little girl and find out that we can survive the contact.

But my feelings go back and forth, up and down. Right now I can't shake the conviction that my therapist is against me. Whatever he says is dangerous; his voice makes me angry and afraid that I'll lose my shaky balance.

Yet I still want to keep on hearing from him. I want the danger to wear off. I want to be able to survive that contact, too, especially the part where my unbearably humiliated self is right there before his eyes.

Right now that's what I can't stand. I want to be very far away.

But I keep coming back, because I believe in the slow, patient work of integration. Surely the feelings will become less intense with each visit to the site of shame. Bit by bit, acknowledged and respected, the danger will diminish. My therapist can't be a parent I never had; he can't even complete one perfect gesture to right a wrong done to me. But he will keep offering many small and imperfect, but consistent and intentional moments of understanding, and they will help me find my way back to the security of the relationship.

That's the theory. The problem is that I still can't *feel* that he understands.

But as I've said, I still want to hear from him. I want those moments of understanding again; I miss how they feel. In spite of everything, it must be true that I still trust him, because I'm counting on him to hear, without defenses or explanations, how I hate being with him, how I despise what I feel, and how I wonder whether I can ever trust him again. As the danger wears off, perhaps I'll once again feel his understanding and my trust.

I can say all of this hopefully, but I can't imagine how my next hour of therapy will feel much better.

A WAY THROUGH

In fact, after I had written those words of mixed-up feelings and guarded hope, I spent most of the next session locked in a shamed, angry silence. I had made a terrible mess for myself, it seemed, and nothing I could say would help—yet he still waited for me to speak. By now this felt almost like a taunt to me, a mockery of my helplessness: Surely I could do this analysis properly and find what I needed to say! Clearly I was just nursing a childish tantrum! But I couldn't speak these thoughts; I could only retreat further.

Finally, after six sessions, two before and four after a holiday break, my analyst took the initiative to say, "I think it might help if we went back and talked about what happened." I wondered why he had waited so long to intervene, to say something. But I remembered my angry, scared reactions to any words from him in the very first sessions after the rupture; perhaps he'd just been waiting for time to ease things a bit. I could also imagine that he had been offering his silence as open, nonintrusive acceptance while I was experiencing it as cold disconnection and a taunt.

But by this time I couldn't go directly back to talk about what happened. First I needed to say what was silencing me now: "I feel stupid about not being able to talk because it's like I got myself into this trouble and I should be able to get myself out. But I can't."

He said it made sense to him that I couldn't talk: "It's clear to you, partly because of what your history tells you, but also because of things that have happened between us, that I won't listen to you or understand you."

"Yes," I said. "But it's worse than that. You'll be angry and disgusted, too."

"All the more reason, then, that you can't talk!"

Then I felt safe enough say, "What I can't get over is that picture I have of myself asking you to read stuff I've written. It makes me so ashamed. Because I shouldn't have asked. I was asking you to spend time outside of the time I pay for."

"Well, first of all," he answered, "this relationship isn't limited in that way. It has its own meanings and feelings, and it stirs up new feelings like wanting something. There's nothing wrong with asking for something extra. You just might get it. It was good to ask—a positive step for you."

This did not feel fine at all, even though I knew what he meant. "No, there has to be something very wrong about wanting and asking, because of how I feel afterward. Asking makes me feel that there's something really wrong with me."

"Then there must have been something in my response to your asking that made it go wrong for you," he suggested.

"When you said you wouldn't be able to get around to it for a while, then it seemed that it was a burden and a chore, and I shouldn't have asked."

He noted the irony that in trying to prevent my disappointment about a delay in his reading, he had disappointed me much more deeply. He asked what kind of response would have been more what I needed. I had thought about that. "If only you had been *excited* to get it, like I was *excited* to give it to you—then I don't think it would have mattered how long it took you to read it." But I told him the rest of my thought, too: that the situation was just too fraught and probably had to shatter, sooner or later.

He disagreed about the situation having to shatter. Was he just trying to keep me from still making it my own fault? Someday, in another kind of space, I'll ask him whether my concept of "fraughtness" makes sense to him, whether he doesn't agree that sometimes what's being worked out between two people is so loaded with disowned stuff from the past that it *needs* to "go wrong" and break open—so that the disowned stuff comes clear and new integrations can start to happen.

Now that we were talking, I could tell him how I was using my humiliated anger to fuel both my writing and my determination to get my work published in the real world. "That's a good plan," he said. "But there's just one wrinkle in it. When you come in here, you still feel bad about yourself."

"Exactly!" I thought. "So how *will* I feel better about myself? Not until we work this thing out between us!" That didn't seem impossible anymore, but I still had my doubts. Remembering the intensity of my reactions still made me flinch with shame. His long silence had made the shame worse, and somehow that silence had felt intentionally shaming.

I began the next session by asking him why he had waited so long to suggest that we talk about what happened. I told him my idea of why: that in his mind the best way to do analysis is for the patient (me) to do all the associating. The analyst shouldn't have to help the patient. It would be second-best analytic work if I were to be helped—bailed out of my own mess, as it were. I should be able to get myself out of it. (This isn't what I believe about my own work with clients, but insofar as analysis is some-how different from "ordinary" therapy, perhaps this would be part of the difference: "No being helped!") As I spun out this theory, I could see how it replicated the basic model scene: In the given nature of things, I'm inferior to him (in this case as an ordinary therapist is inferior to an analyst); if he thinks of me, it's with some kind of disgust or derision; and my best efforts won't change what he thinks.

He heard me out and then asked if I'd be interested to know the real reason why he waited so long to suggest that we talk about what had happened. Yes, indeed, I was interested! "I really thought you would never want to go back to it again," he said. "I thought it was so painful, you wouldn't want to touch it."

I was stunned. How could he think that? Didn't he know me better than that? Don't I always try to talk about hard things? As I reminded him at once, in my family of origin nothing can ever be talked about, and that's just horrible. Feelings build, tension mounts, nerves fray, and even after it all goes underground, there's no chance of easy, friendly close-ness. Against that background, for someone just to say, "I wonder if we could talk about what happened," is an amazing relief. How could he not know that? He didn't answer that question, and I'm still puzzled that he thought I wouldn't want to go back and talk about what happened. Maybe he was operating from his own history and organizing principles, and maybe in this respect they're very different from mine. But it seems I didn't need for him to answer that question. Now that his reason for silence and our difference is in the open, it may be puzzling, but it's not a threat. We can move ahead anyway.

Moving ahead, I needed to tell him what was beginning to feel like a secret: that in order to keep writing, I had begun to write the two of us into Chapter 5, and that I might just keep us in the book as good mate-rial. Now it felt that if I didn't talk to him about it, the writing would become a silent third presence in our work together, and I didn't want that. "And if you're very good and ask nicely," I added, "someday I might let you read what I've written about you." I quickly admitted that this was a backward way to draw attention to the biggest unresolved part of the trouble between us. "I'm sure that I will never, ever again ask you to read something that I've written!"

"You'd have to be completely convinced that I was interested and wanted to read it before you could ask."

"That's right," I said. "And I really can't imagine that ever happening."

"But you're playing with the idea," he replied. "With that bit about if I'm good and ask nicely." I had to grant him that, but I still can't imagine asking again.

When I looked about for other unfinished, unresolved bits to talk about, I expected to find my earlier shame about the intensity of my reactions and feelings. But it was gone. Had it vanished once I knew that his silence hadn't been to shame me? All I could know for sure was that in this calmer, more connected self-state, I found myself satisfied (almost proud) of the way I had seen our relational trouble through. "It's like when I play a sport," I said. "I always play hard; I want to do it the best I can. That's how I feel about this therapy: I like that I do it hard. I like that about myself."

Suddenly I had the briefest of visions: a little blue book in my hand and then in my therapist's hand. I knew what it was. "It was my book, all finished, published," I told him. "If it got that far, then you might look at it; then it would be important enough to matter."

"I'd be willing to watch you score goals but not watch you play."

"Right. And you sure wouldn't want to watch me practice!"

He laughed, and in that moment I liked the feeling between us. Then the session was over.

COMMENTS

With detailed transcripts of our conversations, six relational analysts could write six quite different articles about how my therapist and I worked our way through this interpersonal crisis. I'm in no position to make a final statement about what happened. I'm including the story in this chapter because it illustrates some important points I want to make about how to understand and manage those times when relational therapy feels relationally terrible to your client and also, then, to you.

First of all, although I was able to maintain my commitment to my own therapeutic project and to believe that my therapist would stay with it too, my strong, consistent feelings were: "I hate how I feel; I hate what you're doing to me (even if you don't mean to); this relationship is hopeless; I'm bitterly angry, and I want out!" I want you to know that I truly could not see my way through. As a relational therapist, you need to understand that this kind of hopelessness, rage, and despair can be held within a constructive therapeutic process. Those feelings can all be completely true for your client—and yet not the end of things.

If you can hold this knowledge with relative calm, you will provide fundamental safety and security for your client, even as she despairs and rages at you. Your calm confidence in the process of working things out between you will probably help her decide to stay with the process rather than leave it precipitously. Leaving might seem to her like the only way to take care of herself. But at the same time, if she leaves, she might take with her just one more retraumatizing experience of a painful model scene, whereas if she stays, she might experience the benefits of getting to the other side of it. Consciously or unconsciously, she may know that these are the stakes for her.

Sometimes it's helpful to talk directly with your client about the process of working through a repetition of trauma, about what's at stake, and the pros and cons of her staying or leaving. You might tell her that you believe very firmly in the value of this hard work, that you're committed to doing your part of it, and that you really hope she won't have to leave the relationship. You will certainly encourage her to help herself in any way possible—especially by speaking whatever truth she can about her experience, no matter how bitter, angry, confused, contradictory, and despairing it may be.

Second, I want to emphasize that a difficult time like this is only part of a much larger process of relational therapy. I wouldn't have gotten through it—or even dared to get into it—without having spent a long while developing a relatively secure and resilient relationship with my therapist. I expect that the benefits of getting through it will emerge only slowly in our ongoing relationship now that the crisis has passed.

Although working through these kinds of relational ruptures can be a very important part of the larger therapy process, I'm not suggesting that it's the most important or most powerful work to do in therapy. Most relational psychoanalysts, including self psychologists, would say that working through breaks and impasses is crucial if change is to happen in therapy. It seems that feminist self-in-relation theorists would make these repetitions of negative experience secondary to developing healthier, more positive self-with-other patterns in therapy. I lean toward the former position: these negative self-with-other model scenes are invaluable when they play themselves out so strongly because they make plain exactly what's getting in the way of healthier, happier relationship. When they appear, they make possible the conscious integration of previously dissociated feelings and meanings. This process clears the way for developing more positive self-with-other patterns.

But in the end, the point about the therapeutic value of relational ruptures is moot. Nobody, neither client nor therapist, would ever intentionally instigate them. They just happen sometimes. Then, whether a certain client's therapy is rife with relational turmoil or it happens only rarely and quietly, it's crucial to her entire therapy project that she and you find a way to deal with the trouble honestly and thoroughly.

And finally, I want to make very clear that dealing honestly with relational trouble and thereby getting to the other side of a negative model scene doesn't all by itself "fix" anything. I had to impose an arbitrary ending on my own story because it didn't tie itself up neatly; nothing was finished or fixed for good. I'm still convinced that I will never again ask my therapist to read something I have written—at least not on his own time. What about that happy ending, then, where I finally give him my writing, he likes it, and I am never again afraid or ashamed? If I can't have that, what was the point of going through all of that angst?

But something has changed and is changing. I can feel it already, especially in the quality of the connection between my therapist and myself. It's easier, lighter, less weighted and freighted than it was before. What happened? I reconnected (unwillingly!) with a tightly wound bundle of humiliated feelings, and I did so (hating every minute of it!) in the presence of someone who offered steady patience and understanding. I survived to tell the tale. And now it seems that I am not so frightened of my wantings or of my shame. I can talk about wanting and shame much more freely in therapy; it's not such an unspeakable secret. And it's a good bet, I think, that outside of therapy, I won't have to struggle so often to pretend that my wanting isn't there or work so hard to avoid situations where shame might break through. Nothing is "fixed" or finished. But instead, new possibilities open up, new chances to be in the world with more entitlement, ease, and freedom. I'll take that instead of a happy ending.

HOW DO THESE BAD EXPERIENCES
BELONG TO GOOD THERAPY?

It's time, now, to step back a few paces and set my story within a larger context. My telling of it assumes that these relationally hard times belong to good therapy, but I should clarify that they belong only to good *relational* therapy. In some kinds of therapy, relational ruptures cause nothing but trouble. When a mode of therapy carries no mandate to explore and work through the relational dynamics between client and therapist, the work usually stays "cooperative"—played out as a comfortable exchange between the therapist's benign, helpful authority and the client's compliance. In this context, if relational trouble happens, a client probably does well to get out of the therapy. If he stays, he will either bury the trouble, which will sabotage his therapy work, or he'll embark on a struggle to find out whether it's he or his therapist who's doing therapy wrong. That kind of win-lose situation can only replicate a destructive relational model scene for a client, and one which a nonrelational therapy can't turn toward constructive learning.

I'm arguing, in other words, that only a relational perspective makes therapy a safe enough place for working out relational trouble between client and therapist. Let's review the main points of that perspective. First, as a relational therapist, you understand that the bad feelings about himself that a client brings to therapy have their origins in how he experiences himself in relation to others in his life. Second, you expect that as the therapy relationship becomes more significant to your client, these very fears and anxieties will come to life between the two of you. As we saw in the last chapter, a relational therapist hopes to make contact with even the most traumatized, isolated, and destructive parts of a client's self-with-other experience. Third, your therapeutic intention is not to change how your client interacts with others, but rather to help him experience the meanings and feelings of his interactions more directly, and always with a compassionate kind of understanding for his subjective experience and the dilemmas of his life. You know that his lifelong principles of self-protection will soften only in the warmth of compassionate empathy, and that only then, as his organizing principles slowly change from the inside out, will he start to experience new kinds of connections with others.

But it's this compassionate empathy that, in the therapy relationship, also draws your client into more painful dilemmas than he had ever anticipated. As he spends time with you, he begins to glimpse and desire emotional goods he had long ago given up. He begins to enjoy interested, sympathetic attention, he wants to be known and remembered for exactly who he is, and he longs to matter deeply to someone, to be special. At the very same time he is certain that these wants will be denied or turned against him in some way so that he'll end up even more disappointed and humiliated for having wanted. He "knows" this will happen because it's a self-with-other experience that has formed his way of being in the world and one against which he protects himself carefully. As he lives on this knife-edge of anxiety in therapy, he alternates between careful retreat and daring to try for new experience. As I did, he might dare to ask for something he would never have asked for before.

And then sometimes the worst does happen. The doom falls, just as he knew it would, and he finds himself swamped by helpless rage and bleak despair. The shame he's been dodging and masking out in the world has exploded, full force, in this relationship. The self-loathing voices are loud in his ears, and he takes desperate measures to silence them. Why does the worst happen sometimes? Not because the client brings it on himself, but rather, because you, his therapist, are a human being who doesn't always get exactly what's going on between yourself and your client. On certain days, you might be just tired or distracted, or maybe what your client is talking about is hard for you to hear for reasons that have nothing to do with him. But in any case, you fail to pick up his cues that tell you what he needs right now. And because of the intentional intensity of the therapy situation, this "miss" of yours suddenly stands in for all the misses he's known in his life and all they've meant to him about being "too much" or worthless or forgettable.

I'm suggesting, once again, that in the relational therapy situation, there's probably something inevitable about these "misses" and ruptures of understanding that spin you and your client into unwitting replays of painful model scenes. But to say they are inevitable is not to say that they are your client's fault—or your fault. For the client, the inevitability of being misunderstood isn't fundamentally a product of his neediness or sensitivity; nor is the inevitability of your failure to understand him a product of your own unresolved issues. Most fundamentally and simply put, misunderstanding belongs to the humanness of the therapist–client exchange. That's not good and it's not bad; it's just life.

This important point—that "the worst" befalls the two of you together—can sometimes get lost in talk of reactivated model scenes and organizing principles. Such talk can make it seem as though what the client brings to the therapy relationship is what makes it go wrong. But a relational therapist knows that when things go wrong in therapy, something happened in the therapy. The problem isn't just a product of the client's history or relational incapacities; *something happened*. In my story, though I might still suspect (given my tenacious organizing principles) that what happened was that I asked for too much, my therapist insists that "what happened" was set off by his response to my legitimate asking. I was doing fine, he says, feeling stronger, hoping for new things, even daring to ask for them—something like a small child getting her feet under her, learning to walk on her own. But then, as he puts it, he happened to put a chair in my path. When my particular desire and striving met his particular response, what happened was a rupture in our relationship.

In traditional psychoanalytic psychotherapies, it would be important that my therapist examine his response for signs of his own conflicted or overinvolved feelings—that he search for the "countertransference" feelings that motivated his response to me. The point would be to neutralize those feelings and "clear the field" for my feelings. But in a more relational therapy, the point of such self-scrutiny is that he is able to acknowledge, without defensiveness, what happened between us and to stay openly engaged in the relationship. Relational theory changes the shape and meaning of the classic psychoanalytic concepts of "transference" and "countertransference." Explaining how a relational therapist handles these concepts is complicated enough to require a section of its own.

RELATIONAL TAKES ON TRANSFERENCE

It might be said that this chapter is all about working through the effects of a client's transference of negative feelings from her past into the present relationship with her therapist. A relational perspective, however, doesn't match up well with this traditional idea of negative transference. Traditional concepts of transference and countertransference imply psychic messages and influences that client and therapist launch at each other from bastions of isolated individuality. But we have seen how relational theory insists on the "unbearable embeddedness of being." In this relational view, anyone's ongoing sense of self is continually being created by relationships, relationships happening right now and those carried as the generalized principles that make sense of what's happening right now. So when any two people are together, two subjectivities or complex senses of self, with their respective organizing principles, are being elicited and regulated by one another. Each subjectivity is intimately involved in the shape and feel of the relationship and in how each experiences self and other in it.

Therefore, as the relationalist Lewis Aron argues, any analysis of what's going on in therapy must be an analysis of the relationship, not just of one person's contributions to it.[1] Then what was once called the client's resistance to therapy will be seen as her legitimate self-protection against certain aspects of the therapist's personality that she recognizes as threatening to her. "Resistance" comes into being where this particular therapist and client meet. Likewise, her so-called negative transference is an interpersonal event—an integral part of all the ways she and her therapist, with their respective organizing principles, mutually construct and regulate their relationship.[2]

It's possible, then, to see transference and countertransference as the idiosyncratic ways in which a certain client and therapist attempt a relationship as best they can. As Stephen Mitchell puts it, transference is both contextual and constructed: it's the client's response to particular interpersonal circumstances, and it's produced for a particular purpose. Though it may be based on past experience, the prime purpose of transference is to provide the client a point of entry into this relationship. Likewise, countertransference is the (largely unconscious) form through which the therapist tries to reach the client, using her own experience as a way to enter the client's story.[3] With all of this in mind, it's clear that when things go wrong in therapy, it doesn't make sense to explain it in terms of what the client is bringing from her past. It makes far more sense for the therapist to ask, "What just happened? How did I miss you? Where did I misunderstand you? What did you hear in my response to you?"

We might well wonder why relational therapists persist with the language of transference when they use it to describe such normal interpersonal events. It's probably always the case that key concepts in a strong tradition die hard. It's also the case that the language of transference is a kind of symbolic shorthand for the initiated that captures what I have called the intentional intensity of the therapeutic relationship, that particular quality of therapy that makes it both frightening and a powerful agent for change. The relational therapist Donna Orange suggests the word "cotransference" as a way both to honor the intense complexities of the therapeutic relationship and also to emphasize that therapists participate with clients in the intersubjective field or "play space" of the therapy conversation. In that space, she says, the organizing activity of the client and the therapist are two faces of the same complex, ongoing dynamic between them. Neither activity needs to carry the negative connotations associated with both transference and countertransference.[4]

As therapists, we all know that sometimes a complex, ongoing dynamic between client and therapist does become toxic. No discussion of the relationally painful passages of therapy would be complete without an acknowledgment that sometimes even a relational therapy self-destructs. It goes most wrong when not only the client but also the therapist becomes frightened by the intensity of the feelings in the relationship. In traditional terms these failures wouldn't be seen as relational failures; instead, they would be blamed on malignant or psychotic negative transference: clearly the client brought impossible demands and responses to the consulting room. More relationally-minded traditional therapists might admit to a transference–countertransference impasse: they just couldn't get past their own reactions in the face of difficult demands and chaotic storms of feeling. Radically relational theorists suggest that therapy relationships don't need to come to such a bitter standoff. Downward relational spirals can be stopped early. Their argument goes like this:

Client and therapist are always communicating from necessarily different organizations of experience. When this communication is successful, their differences are invisible. However, when either person feels threatened by the other's organizing of their mutual experience, interpersonal protective operations suddenly appear. Feeling ambushed, ignored, or helpless, the therapist may "diagnose" the client's self-protections as resistance, negative transference, or something more fundamentally wrong in the client's psychological makeup. Then at least the therapist knows what's going on! As you might remember from Chapter 4, this was what often happened to Lucy in hospital emergency rooms.

But when a client's feelings are interpreted as a distortion of reality, she has only two choices. She can give in and let her reality be annihilated. Or she can fight back. But by now fighting back can only mean trying to destroy her therapist's belief about what's going on between them, her therapist's reality, which is threatening to annihilate her own reality. This is how the stage is set for a transference–countertransference crisis and a downward spiral toward relational impasse. Neither client nor therapist can afford to give up her desperate attempts to maintain her own organization of experience against the threat posed by the other.

However, things won't disintegrate so badly if the therapist can recognize and respond to the core of experienced, subjective truth in what the client is first trying to say, no matter how that truth comes wrapped in hurt and angry feelings. But to do so, the therapist has to believe that although what's coming at her has roots in the client's painful past experience, it is, nevertheless, not a distortion of reality. It *is* reality—the client's real feelings about something that's actually happening right now in the relationship between the two of them. Even relational therapists prefer to believe that they're not implicated in their client's distress. They feel, "I didn't do anything! I don't deserve this! *I'm* being misunderstood!" And even they can be surprised at how well things turn out if they can put their own truth on hold just long enough to believe the truth that their client is telling them.

HOW DOES A RELATIONAL TAKE ON TRANSFERENCE HELP A CLIENT?

So what does this relational revision of transference, and especially of negative transference, mean for a client in relational therapy? It means, first of all, that when he feels that his therapist has misunderstood, criticized, belittled, or ignored him, he can be sure that his therapist wants to hear about it. He can be confident that he's doing good work when he talks honestly about what he feels in the therapy relationship, and this confidence will help him keep his bearings when the feelings in question are chaotic or hopeless. As his therapist, you want to hear about his experience not in order to make a diagnostic map of his psyche, but because you believe that knowing what happened for him is a first step in understanding and righting what's gone wrong between you.

Just as importantly, this relational reinterpretation of negative transference ensures that it's safe for a client to speak his feelings, his protests, his questions, and his thoughts. "Safe" means that as his therapist you won't blame, shame, or pathologize him for what he feels and says. Instead, you will work with him to find out where the two of you were first at odds, paying special attention to where you missed the cues he gave you about the kind of response or understanding he needed. If relational ruptures are, indeed, the product of "cotransference," or the interaction of your client's and your own relational organizing principles, then whatever is happening cannot be your client's fault, alone. In fact, it can't be anyone's fault, alone. The organizing principles of two people can be so different as to miss each other, scare each other, and set each other off in all kinds of unpredictable ways. But as I said above, that's just life—in relationship.

"But what about how my client's organizing principles come from his past?" you might ask. "Doesn't this focus on what's happening right now deny the power of the past?" Well, as we explored at length in Chapter 4, the present is exactly where the past is alive and powerful; the present is where we can see the past in operation. But you're not finished with your question: "Don't our clients have to make conscious links between what's happening now and their past, their history, so that they can integrate dissociated experience and grieve their losses? Isn't that what you said before? What about your own reconnection to those 'little girl' humiliated feelings?"

These are very good questions—because they push me to find a way out of the either/or dilemmas they set up. It seems to me that the best way out of having to choose between the power of the past and the power of the present or between the value of insight and the value of experience is to talk about the sequence of processes in relational therapy. You might remember that in my own story, I wished very hard that just making contact with my humiliated self would be my cure. But just the breakdown of the dissociative wall, just the reconnection with the old and present pain, could not make me feel better. Reexperiencing trauma, even in the form of negative transference, can't make anyone feel better. Genuine integration and healing happen only when a new experience of relationship allows the old feelings to be understood more gently and thus be laid to a better rest.

That's why relational therapy begins by focusing on the here-and-now therapy relationship and on changes for the better in that relationship: in order to create a space within which integration and insight will eventually find a home. That's why after a client reconnects with traumatic relational experience, relational therapy expends so much time and energy reworking the relational context of that experience. Relational therapy knows that the bumps and grinds of life and the therapy relationship will produce plenty of new/old memories, transferences, feelings, and thoughts to integrate, but unless there's a new relational way to be with it all, nothing will change in how a client can feel and think about herself.

In a nutshell, then, the good news that comes to your client when "negative transference" is reinterpreted as a process of mutual regulation or "cotransference" goes as follows: It's good news that the trouble she thought was only inside her and coming only from her painful past is actually something that's happening right now between her and her therapist. It's even better news that the trouble that's happening right now isn't just her fault, her distortion of reality: the two of you are doing it together, somehow. But the best news of all is that since you're doing it together, you can probably find a way to understand what you're doing and then do it differently together. That's how your client will be able to get to the other side of painful old model scenes with you. That's how the therapy starts to hold open space for new organizing principles to emerge.

In an evolving relational process that sometimes seems to have a life and a mind of its own, relational therapy becomes first a place where a client feels better as she feels understood, then a place where she sometimes feels worse than ever (but finds herself, in the end, still understood), and finally a place where new interpersonal confidence can emerge, along with new insight and self-integration—providing a sturdier, more durable kind of feeling better.

HARD TIMES FROM A THERAPIST'S PERSPECTIVE

At this point, it goes without saying that when negative transference is redefined in this way, it's not just up to the client to take responsibility for her feelings and to own her projections in order to find her way out of a relational dilemma. In fact, there's no way she can find her way out by herself. As her therapist, you have to help her. You must be as engaged as she is in a cooperative process of trying to discover what happened and what could change between you.

This is different, on your part, too, from taking responsibility for what happened. The whole notion of taking responsibility shifts when transference is no longer a matter of "your baggage" and "my baggage," but rather a matter of mutually constructed relational dynamics. Now "taking responsibility" looks not like admitting to fault, or even to "baggage," but like keeping oneself honest, present, and open in the relationship. It's with this sense of response-ability that you can own what you have done in the relationship without feeling defensive and guilty about the effects of your unintentional mistakes and omissions.

In this same spirit, you won't blame your client or her "transference" for what's happening. You won't try to explain it away by talking about your good intentions. In fact, you will do your best to step inside your client's negative experience of you, even wearing, for the time being, the hurtful intentions and feelings she attributes to you, the better to understand how the relationship feels to her. All the while that the two of you are trying to get through this hard time together, you will be especially careful to pay close attention to the details and the movements of her ongoing experience of you.

The therapeutic tasks that I have just described add up to a very tall order. This work is not easy. Depending on the nature of the mutually constructed model scene you and your client are living out together, the following are just some of the ways in which she might be experiencing your presence. Any one of these phrases might capture exactly who you are to a particular client in a given moment.

- You're going to think badly of me for what I'm saying now. No, you *are* thinking badly of me.
- You don't have problems like this; your life is perfect. Next to you, I'm a real loser, and I hate telling you this loser stuff about my life.
- Sure, you understand what I'm saying, but you don't really care.
- If I tell you my secrets, you'll use them against me later. You'll bring them back when I'm vulnerable.
- When you add something to what I say, that means I have to think what you think. You want to take over my thinking.
- You congratulate me, but you're really pushing me away. All that matters is how I perform.
- If I do well, it's really something about you—you're the therapist who made this possible. It's your success, not mine.
- You're feeling sorry for me. That means I'm pathetic. You think I'm pathetic.
- If I believe you care about me, I'll find out differently later and be terribly humiliated for having been gullible. Humiliating me feels good to you.
- If I get close to you in any way, you'll hurt me, use me, in ways I can't even imagine. I don't know what's going to happen, but the threat is real, all the time.
- If I start to count on your understanding and need you, you'll feel like I'm clinging; you'll scrape me off with disgust.

As a therapist, your first natural impulse will be to disagree with any such conviction when you start to recognize it. This isn't what you feel toward your client! This isn't who you are! This just isn't the truth, and furthermore, it feels rotten to be in a relationship shaped by such a truth. Doesn't your client need to hear that you actually feel quite differently from what he or she expects?

Reassuring your clients that you do care for them and accept them does seem like a natural approach to take when emotional convictions as negative as these emerge in therapy. As a relational therapist, however, when such feelings start to surface, you will do something that doesn't seem natural. Rather than protesting and disagreeing with your clients' distressing relational experiences of you (and rather than trying desperately to be such a good therapist that the distress will disappear) you will try to understand how it feels for them to be in those painful self-states and to have such troubling fears and dire expectations of you.

As you do the work in this way, you will have to count on one of the most counterintuitive but reliable principles of relational work with relational problems: There's no way that you can change a client's pervasive negative experience of you directly. None of your reassurances will make any difference. But if you consistently understand that experience from your client's point of view, eventually you become not only the one who is feared and mistrusted, but also the one who understands your client's fear and mistrust. And that's the pivot for change. For your client, to have her negative feelings simply accepted and understood is a very particular and unexpected form of being understood, and it lays a foundation for the eventual development of a different kind of relationship between your client and yourself.

My own story probably illustrates quite well how this kind of work was done with me. But in order to talk further about relational hard times from a therapist's perspective, I won't presume to know my therapist's mind. Instead I will tell you a story drawn from my therapy practice. The relational dynamic is similar here, but this time I'm on the other side of it, with a much better view of what the therapist is feeling and thinking.

A STORY FROM THE THERAPIST'S SIDE OF RELATIONAL TROUBLE

One day a quite fiercely independent, professionally successful, and rather lonely client (I'll call him Dave) was telling me about one of his recent accomplishments. Earlier in the session he had been edging into the possibility of making better interpersonal connections in his life, something I really hoped would happen for him. So I responded to his story of achievement by suggesting that eventually he would be able to feel both accomplished and connected with others; he would be able to "put it all together." Dave went quiet then, but it was close to the end of the session and I didn't know anything was wrong until he came back the next week.

Then he was so agitated that he couldn't even sit down for a while. He told me that after the last session he'd been so angry he'd had to go for a walk, and then he ended up in his own backyard, hurling snowballs at the garage. Dave had no trouble knowing what I had done, and exactly when I did it. My "suggestion" of putting it all together totally undercut the good thing he was trying to tell me; it said that his good thing wasn't good enough, in fact, that it wasn't good at all, because it wasn't up to my standard. "What's the point of telling you something good about myself, if what you're going to do is criticize!" he said. "It's like you're telling me there's something wrong with being proud of myself!—and that's exactly how I feel now. It *is* wrong. There are these voices in my head that keep telling me I'm stupid, I'm childish, so I deserve this. I want to smash something. I want to smash myself."

Obviously Dave had learned in the process of our work together that whatever his feelings were, I wanted to hear about them—especially if they were about what was going on between us. "Negative transference" had just come to rolling boil in that room. Now what would I do? How would I respond?

I'll leave the immediacy of the scene for a moment to compare how different takes on transference would lead me to respond to Dave in different ways. If I worked with a classical definition of negative transference, I might have said to him, "I understand that's what you feel I did to you, and that it's very painful. In fact, I did something quite different, and that lets us know that these powerful, painful feelings are coming from somewhere else, probably from somewhere in your past. I'm wondering if these are familiar feelings, whether you've been here before—perhaps with your mother or your father."

If I worked with a slightly more progressive, interactive view of transference, I might have said, "I can see how my suggestion felt critical to you. That's a very plausible construction of what my words meant. But there were other ways you could have heard me, too. So I wonder why you understood me in that particular, very painful way." In other words, I'd admit that Dave's feelings didn't come from nowhere, but from something I really did. Yet I'd emphasize the power of his past to construct our interaction in this particular way.

In a more interpersonalist mode of working with transference, I might have said, "It's hard for you that out of a whole session, what stays with you is something that feels critical and undercutting. As we've noticed before, all you can do at a time like that is withdraw, taking your anger away with you. But I think something is changing for you, too— you've come back to tell me about it. Maybe now we can get a bigger picture of your options." In this mode, my point is that there's something limiting about Dave's interpersonal style, but it's getting less constrictive. My ongoing task is to engage with him so that I can let him know, without blame, how his style works. Since this kind of learning is driven by immediate, emotional experience, it is potent impetus for Dave to expand his relational repertoire.

But I'm a relational therapist who actually thinks more in terms of organizations of experience than in terms of transference. And so I simply accept the truth of my client's experience. Dave had been feeling expansive and I had punctured his golden bubble with a sly criticism. Now he needed to hear, "Yes, that's what I did to you," as he struggled to cope with the intensity of his reactions. Disturbed and shamed by that intensity, Dave needed to know that his reactions made sense. That's where we had to begin. I knew that.

And yet, after Dave's opening explosion, I found myself trying to explain what I had been intending to do in the previous session, hoping Dave would understand that I had been trying to help, not hurt him. Fortunately he had the gumption and the relational honesty to say to me, "I can't hear that from you right now."

"No, of course you can't," I said, and I brought myself back (sharply) to the work at hand. I wanted to say I was sorry for what I had done, but I knew that an apology wouldn't help either. It would be just one more way for me to try to feel better, to get my goof behind us. What we needed, instead, was to be right in the middle of all the trouble my mistake had caused. First of all I had to hear it, and I had to hear it thoroughly and well.

There were two kinds of trouble—what was between us and what, as a consequence, Dave was suffering on his own. Cut off from supportive connection with me, he kept deriding himself for his own stupidity, and then he would counter this "whiny" self-loathing with what he called a swift kick in the butt: "Forget it. Don't be such a loser. Get on with things." Dave was sleeping poorly, and he spent his days in a funk, trying not to snap at colleagues. As he told me how bad things were, I listened attentively and carefully, encouraging him to say more and hoping that my responses would let him hear and see that I took his distress seriously.

Dave had to tell me forcefully and in detail how horrible he was feeling, and he had to be sure that I got it. That took one session. Only after he knew he'd been heard on that score could he return, in the next session, to the "scene of the crime" in order to try to find out more about what had happened. He was calmer now, and we could go directly to his first experience of my lapse and walk through it slowly, knowing that we were on the right track. Dave said that it had been such a cold, rude shock to him. He had come to trust that I would be on his side, and then I wasn't.

I noted what a risk he had taken, just to tell me that he was feeling good about himself. That was an unguarded, hopeful, open moment. I agreed that I had, indeed "set him up for it" by being a good listener. I had led him to believe that it was safe to be proud of himself with me—and then WHAM! I had delivered a betrayal of that new, tender, fledgling trust. And for all those reasons, this was a serious injury, I said.

As Dave grew more confident that I wouldn't disregard or belittle his experience, he could tell me more. In the third session after the rupture, he mused, "It's like you want me to be good, but not too big for my britches. It's like my being good should make you feel pleased about yourself—'Look what I made happen here!' But it can't be different from what you want. I have to be *your* kind of good. And you want me never, ever, to show you up. You've gotta keep me in my place, keep reminding me who's boss, who really knows things around here."

That's when he made the connection, "Right after I left that bad session, when I was angry, out on the street, I felt like I used to when I'd show something I made to my dad. He always found something not quite right with it, something to improve. And I'd just want to destroy it, crumple it up, smash it."

"I did to you the same sort of thing that your dad did many times— I undercut you in the guise of being helpful."

"Yes! And for some of the same reasons."

"Because I don't want the competition," I ventured (wearing what he was attributing to me). "But it's more complicated than that, isn't it? There's a double message coming from me: 'Grow up, be strong like me. But you'll never do it right.'"

This fit for Dave. But even more important than the accuracy of my understanding was his huge relief to be understood from inside of his own experience. The symptoms that had followed his experience of being badly misunderstood and cut off from me—anger, irritability, anxiety, depression, self-loathing, and sleeplessness—faded rapidly. And then our relationship began to feel much sturdier, more trustworthy and secure, than it had felt before the break.

I understood this as follows: during the repair of the injury, Dave was having two experiences of me at once: the hurtful one, which we worked to understand as fully as possible, and the experience that I was completely committed to understanding him without protecting myself at his expense. This latter experience was now eclipsing the first one. However, Dave will always have a realistic memory of getting hurt by my clumsiness, which might happen again. But we can deal with it if it happens; Dave knows that, too. This is another sign of a more complex, resilient, and differentiated relationship, a relationship being performed differently between us.

FINAL COMMENTS

In summary form, I'd like to note connections between the main points of this chapter and the story I've just told. For Dave and me, this episode was but one part of a long process of relational growth and change. We couldn't have gotten through it without having first developed some reliable mutual rapport, and the outcome of the episode was a subtle but profound strengthening of mutual trust that we can now carry forward. The episode was generated not by Dave's pathology, but by an interaction that went wrong between us. *Something happened.* Drawn by the experience and promise of empathic understanding, Dave took an important relational risk. And then I failed to understand what was going on between us and what he needed from me. His risk and my failure created a compressed version, a "model scene," of a very important aspect of his relational life, and it stirred memories of times in his formative years when he had been misunderstood and undercut in similar ways.

But by itself, Dave's sudden, painful connection with disowned feelings and memories wouldn't have helped him. What he needed was to feel his hurt in a relational context that was radically different from the one where the original hurt had been inflicted. As soon as I realized that Dave was injured, I knew it was critical that I, the very person who had hurt him, do all that I could to understand how he felt and what had happened to him. It was this steady intention to understand him that made this a radically different relational experience for him. When his hurt feelings mattered, they were no longer overwhelming or shameful. He could carry them much more easily. He could explore their history and their meanings. He could let them go, too.

But what about my feelings? Before I end this chapter, I should at least ask the traditional questions about my "countertransference" in this relationship. Why did I respond to Dave's proud sense of accomplishment by suggesting that he could be both accomplished and connected? Probably because I like being with him better when he's "connecting." And my hope (my agenda) for him lies in the direction of a fuller, richer relational life. I think I was disappointed when he fell back on his achievements in order to feel good, and perhaps a bit impatient with him, too. There's also a good chance that I was feeling put in the shade by his professional success, so that my words were, indeed, intended to "keep him in his place," as he suspected.

Now it's a good thing that I know about my tendencies to want certain things for my clients, to be impatient sometimes, and at other times to feel inferior. It's important that I monitor those tendencies so that I don't throw around a lot of impatience and competition in my therapeutic relationships. On the other hand, those tendencies are a part of me. If I interact, eventually they, along with many other parts of me, may emerge. I can't prevent that happening; I can only be ready to deal with the effects of my human fallibility.

A much more dangerous kind of countertransference is the kind that happens right after there's been a sudden rupture in therapy. Who likes to make a mistake? I'm a therapist, making a life's work out of helping and caring; I *hate* to be experienced as an inflictor of pain. It's astounding and disturbing to see an apparently small "miss" become so hugely destructive. How, then, can I escape feeling guilt or anger or despair? How can I avoid defensive responses that pit my own reality and my client's reality against each other? When things go terribly wrong, how can I not worry myself sick or throw up my hands and walk away? These are the crucial "countertransference" questions. I can't escape them, for it's relational therapy that I do. That means I'm really in these relationships—when they go well, but also when they go badly.

I reiterate: for relational therapy, it's not a problem that a therapist's feelings are present and invested in the therapy he or she does. As I've been saying all along, that's what you, as a relational therapist, offer your clients: a real person, willing to be in relationship with them. But it does matter a great deal how you "perform" your feelings in therapeutic relationships, especially once there's trouble. You must know enough about what you're feeling to be able to sort out what to put aside for now and what to use. Whatever you use must be put in the service of the task at hand, which is always to understand the client's experience as fully as possible. You can trust that when you do that, you and your client may have a rocky ride, but you will probably come through the trouble together. You will be trying just to concentrate on doing the best empathic work you can do in this tough situation. That's how you can put aside your guilt or anger for the moment, and if it's still there later, you can talk gently with yourself or with a colleague about it.

This may sound like a convoluted process, but it's not so different in structure from what good parents do. Parents, too, strive to be emotionally present, available, and genuine, and at the same time they contain and manage their feelings in ways they believe will be best for their children. Relational therapy didn't invent the use and management of self for the good of the other. Relational therapists borrow the self-for-other wisdom that good parents, mentors, teachers, and spiritual guides have always counted on, and they turn it to a very particular purpose: using self to counter the effects of their clients' toxic self-with-other experiences.

All of us in therapy, clients and therapists alike, want never again to taste the bitterness of toxic relationship. It's our heartfelt desire not to have to go through rotten times with each other. If we're lucky, it won't happen often. But when it does happen, we have reasons to hope that getting through these hard times honestly and together will be worth the trouble. This chapter has been about those reasons to hope.

ENDNOTES

1. Lewis Aron, *A Meeting of Minds*, 82.
2. Lewis Aron, *A Meeting of Minds*, 127, 77.
3. Stephen Mitchell, *Influence and Autonomy in Psychoanalysis*, 146.
4. Donna Orange, *Emotional Understanding*, 67–68.

6

—•—

THE WONDERFULLY GOOD PART OF RELATIONAL THERAPY

ABOUT ORDINARY (BUT WONDERFUL) GOODNESS

"Wonderfully good"? Isn't that a bit over the top? How does something as undramatic and unassuming as relational talk therapy get to be "wonderfully good"? Well, I'll try to tell you. I mean the words literally, and I'll start with "good." What does it mean to say that life is good? It means different things to different people, but for most of us, it probably begins with an ordinary, everyday sense of well-being. We can welcome a new day when we get up in the morning. Probably we're physically well enough to be comfortable in our bodies and to meet the challenges of the day. We know what we do well and what people like about us. We have a sense of belonging within family, community, workplace, and a network of friends. We're satisfied with some of our accomplishments, and we can look forward to new adventures, chances to try new things. We're finding constructive and productive ways to take our place in the world, creative ways to express ourselves. There's a match between our values and our lives as we live them.

If life is good, most likely our significant relationships are working fairly well. With the people close to us, we can feel known, understood, and loved, and we know that others count on our support and love, too. When there are problems, we can talk about them. When we're hurt, it's safe to be angry. In fact, we can speak about and hear all kinds of feelings

163

in these closer relationships of ours. With this kind of security with others, we feel secure and balanced within ourselves. Disappointments get us down, but we're able to bounce back. Losses hurt, but we're able to share the hurt and let others help us grieve. We can accept our failings and mistakes, and we've learned that laughing at ourselves can help. On the whole, we like ourselves pretty well.

This is the kind of "good" I mean. It's ordinary. Feeling this kind of well-being doesn't depend on accomplishing major achievements or amassing material wealth. People who experience such goodness in their lives aren't stars or heroes or saints. They probably haven't grasped the meaning of the universe, and they can't rise above the hurts, conflicts, and confusions of everyday life. But they are able to be here, okay in themselves and connected with others. All of this is what I mean by goodness. We may not be able to have it all the time, but it's certainly worth desiring.

This unremarkable goodness of ordinary life is often taken for granted by people who enjoy good physical and emotional health. But it's the very kind of well-being that eludes our troubled, anxious, and depressed clients. Now if a client has been in therapy for a while to try to ease the pervasive, insidious bad feelings we began to talk about in Chapter 3, and then she starts to feel this quiet, connected kind of well-being, it will probably come as a surprise to her. She will feel it with a sense of wonder, perhaps even disbelief. Chances are she has never experienced this kind of well-being before—feeling okay in herself and connected with others. Since she never had it before, she didn't know that this kind of feeling was possible. When she came to therapy, all she wanted was relief from feeling bad. She couldn't imagine what "good" would feel like; she didn't even know to hope for it. But with no fireworks or grand illuminations, no sudden breakthroughs or transformations, this wonderful sense of well-being has sneaked up on her and surprised her.

This everyday kind of "wonderfully good" is the opposite of the terribly hard part of relational therapy that we discussed in Chapter 5. The painful feelings of those difficult times may be connected to traumatic model scenes, but they are stirred up by quite ordinary, everyday failures of empathy and understanding. When relationship goes wrong in everyday ways, the pain is no less bad for being ordinary. Likewise, when relationship goes right in ordinary ways, the well-being it brings can be unexpectedly wonderful.

THE CONNECTION BETWEEN HARD TIMES
AND GOOD TIMES IN THERAPY

The hard times of the last chapter and the good times of this chapter are closely connected in relational therapy. Both kinds of experience are set in motion by a therapist's empathy. Your empathy invites a client to be more open, trusting, and vulnerable than would normally be comfortable for her. As we saw in Chapter 2, getting into relational therapy is like stepping into empathy—into the experience of being understood from one's own point of view, from within one's own frame of reference. Your client doesn't have to adjust her thoughts and feelings to your expectations; instead, your main concern is to "get" exactly what she's saying to you, what she means and how she feels. When she is met in this way, she can start to believe in her own perceptions and emotions. She begins to realize she's not crazy or weak or flawed. She starts to feel not so isolated, less angry and sad, and she begins to have some genuine, respectful empathy for her own struggles.

And just because this new relationship makes a client feel better understood and more okay in herself than she usually feels, the relationship becomes more and more important to her. Feeling safer yet, she begins to explore more of her thoughts and feelings; she brings forward more of who she is; she lets herself make contact with experiences and emotions she usually keeps well hidden, even from herself. As she does all of this, she begins to realize that not only does she feel safe in this relationship, she also feels frightened. The risks she is taking scare her. Something tells her that this is going to go wrong, and she'll be disappointed and hurt.

As we saw in the last chapter, sometimes those fears become reality, at least for a while, when the therapist who has been consistently present and understanding suddenly fails to be there or to get it. As we have seen, those breaks are painful and they matter a lot because there's so much riding on the relationship. In this chapter, we will spend more time exploring just what is riding on the relationship. In brief, the therapy relationship offers to understand, respect, and to a certain extent fulfill some of a client's most basic human needs for psychological and emotional well-being.

These are current needs that a client, along with all the rest of us, carries around every day. However, for your client they are complicated and shrouded by doubt because the circumstances of her life haven't helped her get those needs met. In fact, the circumstances of her life have taught her that those needs are to be squelched because they are shameful. And so she doesn't really know that she carries them around every day. She thinks they've gone away. But they've just gone underground. If your client does notice these needs, she probably thinks they're childish, because it was probably back in her childhood that she first made them go away.

Sometimes these very important components of adult emotional and relational life—needs to belong, to matter, to be respected and honored for one's uniqueness, to express and create, to have feelings received, to feel safe and secure—have childlike qualities to them when a client first makes contact with them as an adult. That's because these components haven't had the everyday life-exposure that turns them into their adult forms. But as soon as they are "out," they can turn into their adult forms quite quickly.

However, these ordinary, good needs don't make it into the light of day without trouble. Since they've been squelched for so long, they have a lot of urgency about them, and this urgency heightens your client's fearful anxiety that she'll just be disappointed again. Furthermore, she had very good reason, as a child, to decide that these needs were wrong and should be silenced. These very needs once caused her a lot of confusion. Things scared her and made her sad, and she needed help; she needed someone to understand what life was like for her; she needed to matter, to be seen and to be special. But she didn't get what she needed.

When her environment failed to meet her basic emotional needs, your client turned her hurt, empty wanting into feeling badly about herself. Now, in the principles that organize her psychological life, wanting and needing are tightly linked to feeling badly about herself. In other words, it's not just hard for her to receive the ordinary, everyday goodness that relational therapy promises; it's hard for her even to let herself want it. Since the first session of her therapy, you have tried to meet this client's needs for certain kinds of respect, support, and understanding. And from its very beginnings, the good that relational therapy promises and offers her has been thoroughly entangled in model scenes and organizing principles that tell her that she can't have this goodness, and that wanting it is wrong or stupid.

Although early in therapy your empathy starts to wake up a client's strong self-with-other needs, along with the anxieties that attend them, it takes a while for these new feelings to take recognizable forms and move out of the shadows and into a client's awareness. Then, once she starts to feel both the good and the bad, the promise of even more connection and the fear of wanting it, it's more than she can feel all at once. Her feelings alternate, giving way to each other again and again. It's almost inevitable that after she has felt good for a while—connected, understood, self-respecting—either you will "miss" her in a therapy session or, seemingly of its own accord, her mounting anxiety will break through from the negative side of her experience. Then "wanting" feels impossible, futile, and dangerous to her; she feels disconnected from you and down on herself. Though some of these breaks can be large and distressing, as the last chapter illustrates, most of these misses and worries are relatively small and can be easily talked through in a session or two.

Sometimes these small misses are obvious. I remember a client who was telling me how angry she was with herself that she couldn't tell, in advance, whether a particular man was going to hurt her or not. I knew that since childhood she had been in relationships with some very manipulative men, and I didn't like to hear her holding herself responsible for their deviousness. So I told her, "I know you feel responsible for not being able to 'tell in advance,' but it really isn't your fault when the men in your life are tricky and devious."

She replied, "We've been here before, Pat. You try to tell me something isn't my fault, but that makes me feel powerless."

I was responding out of some sense of the big picture of her life, but in fact, I had missed the emotional point of her story. I answered, "Yes, I see what you're saying. Of course that's how it works. You need to feel like you should be able to tell in advance because that would give you some power in the situation."

It seems that this was the response she needed because she nodded and went right on. She had corrected my "miss," bringing my empathy back to her experience, and now she would think and feel her way through this issue in her own way, with me paying attention to what *she* meant.

Another client, who had to develop very powerful interpersonal radar as a child in a violent family, often asks me toward the end of a session whether her talking has been too much for me, her stories too hard to hear, or too boring. We have often explored what lies behind her question: her longing to be heard and her conviction that others are either too fragile or too disinterested to hear her. Therefore, she doesn't matter and shouldn't be heard. That's what turns up again and again.

But when she asks her questions, it's also important that I scan my own behavior and feelings in order to respond honestly. If I have been a bit distracted by personal worries, or I haven't had a good night's sleep, it's important that I say so, simply and briefly. Because if I don't, she'll still know that something is off between us, and she will take that to mean that something is wrong with her. That's how subtle a "miss" can be.

But in a therapy that's working well, when these inevitable misses and worries happen, talking them through brings your client back to the positive side of wanting and connecting. Each talking through and re-connecting reinforces her belief that this relationship is safe and that it will give her more than she's hoped for before. Just to be able to say "Ouch!" or "I'm worried," or "You're not getting it," is more than she ever thought possible at first.

And then, as she carries on talking about her life, thoughts, and feelings, she will become aware of some new frontier signaled by a new edge of anxiety in the relationship with you. There's something else that she wants from you, perhaps, and she "knows" she can't have it. Or she's sure you're thinking something bad about her. Or there's something she wants to tell you about herself, and she's sure you won't like it or even understand it. Whatever the problem is, it's another chance for her to talk her way through bad feelings and back to good connection. So it goes, over and over, and the cumulative effect is a relationship of more complexity and security, and more possibilities for interesting, good surprises.

TWO DIMENSIONS OF TRANSFERENCE: SELF PSYCHOLOGY

The self psychologists Stolorow and Atwood call this movement between disheartening and encouraging feelings in therapy a shift between two dimensions of transference. They call your client's fears and troubled expectations "repetitive transference"—a repetition of the past. This kind of transference, laid down as psychological organizing principles, turns up over and over again in many guises, and it needs countless counter-repetitions of understanding just how it feels. These repetitions of understanding, along with other kinds of understanding and support, add up to good relational feelings that self psychologists call "selfobject transference." According to Stolorow and Atwood, these painful and helpful relational feelings, this "repetitive transference" and "selfobject transference," are not two separate kinds of transference, but rather two different dimensions of one complex transference that develops and changes over time between client and therapist.[1]

Chapter 5 was all about what self psychology calls repetitive transference. In this chapter, because we're trying to understand how therapy contributes to experiences of emotional well-being, we'll spend time with what self psychology calls selfobject transference. (You might remember that "selfobject experience" refers to the client's ongoing or internalized experience of the therapist's supportive presence.) Self psychologists such as Stolorow and Atwood believe that as a client comes to understand how the repetitive transference plays out between himself and his therapist, he will come to understand how his psychological organizing principles make sense of his interpersonal experience for him. This is the most significant aspect of his "unconscious" for him to investigate in therapy.[2] But while he is doing this, and also in the quiet, comfortable spaces between bouts of this uncomfortable repetitive transference work, something ultimately more important is happening for him. His shaky, insecure, fragmented self is being strengthened through the selfobject transference.

Some self psychologists prefer to drop the word "transference" and just speak of a client's selfobject needs and his selfobject experiences. Not only do these needs deserve respect and understanding as he begins to feel and express them in therapy, they also deserve to be met as well as they can be within the limits of the therapy situation. Howard Bacal calls this therapeutic stance "optimal responsiveness,"[3] and he and Kenneth Newman list the following examples of how therapists provide selfobject experiences: by "attunement to affective states; validation of subjective experience—including temporary identification with the 'rightness' of the child's or patient's perceptions; affect containment, tension regulation, and soothing; sustaining and organizing or restoring a weakened sense of self disrupted by selfobject failure; and recognition of uniqueness and creative potential."[4] These are all moment-to-moment ways in which a therapist might try to provide optimal responses to clients' needs to have certain selfobject experiences in particular moments.

GOOD EXPERIENCE
AS "SELFOBJECT TRANSFERENCE"

Simply put, a selfobject experience is a self-with-other experience that feels supportive, enlivening, comfortable, freeing, and life-enhancing. The experience of the other's being with you is so "just right" that you hardly notice it. Think of how you feel most yourself with a close friend, how good in yourself that kind of being-with can make you feel. And think of the prototype of that experience—a secure, happy, confident infant, toddler, or young child, who doesn't realize that her happiness and security is being created for her by the others around her on a daily basis, and even moment by moment. Her selfobject surroundings allow her just to be—to explore, do, feel, relate, grow, and develop.

Sadly, some children don't receive much of this concentrated attention to their needs, and some receive some kinds of it and not other kinds—for example, lots of safety and protection, but not much admiration for the child's accomplishments, or lots of pride, but little companionship or understanding. If a client has such gaps in his relational experience, they may lead to what self psychologists call deficits in his self experience. A large part of his therapy can be a repair of those deficits, which will give him a second chance to develop a cohesive, competent self in secure relationship with others. The therapist provides the selfobject experiences the client uses for such repair. In order for the repair to "take," the therapy relationship has to have significant intensity, an intensity summed up in the word "transference." When there is enough intensity, the selfobject dimension of the therapy relationship can put into motion major changes in what a client expects and experiences in the rest of his life.

Heinz Kohut, the father of self psychology, identified three major forms of selfobject transference. In idealizing transference, the client needs to feel connected with and protected by someone good, strong, and wise, someone he can trust, idealize, and hope to emulate. A mirroring transference is structured by the client's need to be noticed, accepted, and affirmed in his strengths, ambitions, and creativity. He needs someone to admire and smile, to back up his dreams and plans. An alter ego or twinship transference focuses on an essential alikeness between client and therapist. "Being like" is an important kind of belonging; it counters feelings of being alone and alien in the world.[5]

In a textbook on self psychology written after Kohut's death, a close colleague, Ernest Wolf, identified three more important needs that are met in what he calls a self-sustaining selfobject ambience. In a merger transference, the client needs the therapist to be exactly and finely attuned to her experience. Any difference is perceived as a threat. Quite different needs lead to an adversarial transference, which gives the client a chance to assert difference toward someone who will take a firm opposite stand but who will also continue to be supportive, responsive, and affirming of the client's self. Wolf also notes the client's need to feel her own efficacy in the relationship. In particular, she needs to know that she has an impact on the therapist and can evoke the kinds of responses that will help her.[6]

To this list of selfobject needs and transferences, Stolorow and Atwood add what they call self-delineating selfobject transference. This transference takes shape with those clients whose caregivers gave them so little early experience of validating attunement that they have been able to put together only a sketchy sense of self. They have a shaky hold on their own perceptions and opinions, which are easily usurped by the opinions of others. Their affects are real to them as bodily sensations, even as powerfully felt emotional storms, but they cannot put these feelings into words or symbols to make sense of them. In the therapy relationship, a client with this kind of amorphous or chaotic self-experience will depend on the therapist's responses to help him delineate the shapes and feelings of his own experience until he begins to have a durable sense of being present as a valid, feeling, experiencing self in his own right.[7]

WHAT DOES A SELFOBJECT TRANSFERENCE MEAN FOR YOUR CLIENT?

The language of selfobject transference captures some important aspects of the everyday goodness a client can experience in the relationship with his therapist, and that's what I want to talk about here. The most basic kind of goodness, or well-being, is a client's confidence that his existence is real and valid, that his feelings make sense, that his thoughts can withstand others' differences of opinion, and that his unique self is present, recognizable, and durable over time. If he is one of those survivors of relational trauma who has lived with many kinds of dissociation, he has struggled hard to know, "I am here and I am me."

In the chapter on trauma, we saw how important it was for you, as this client's therapist, to attend carefully to all the many scattered details of his experience, becoming, for a while, a container of pieces too painful or too chaotic for him to manage. Through your here-and-now attention to all of his thoughts and feelings, he can begin to experience the shape, feel, and reality of a self at the center of his fragmented experience. In time, he becomes able to integrate that experience, past and present, into a reliable sense of "This is the road I've traveled to be here. This is who I am now." In the language of self psychology, his selfobject experiences with you have helped him delineate a self.

If that's where your client is coming from, getting here in one piece (self-delineation) is just the beginning of the good experiences possible for him; there's much more that he missed out on. For those clients who are not so fragmented, those who have some clear sense of self but don't like that self very much, there's probably also a wealth of positive relationship they missed out on. Let me describe what else your clients may be missing, most likely first of all missing it from parent figures.

A client may be missing somebody who can just be close whenever he needs her to be there. He wants someone to wrap her caring around him, someone to understand him and help calm and soothe whatever trouble he's feeling. And even when he's not in trouble, he wants the reassurance of knowing that she's there, ready to listen.

Another client may be missing somebody who can be strong for her in ways she's not, somebody capable and wise. So if something difficult turns up, she won't be on her own with it; she can look to him for help to figure out what to do. She can count on him to back her up, lending her his power and insight so that she feels strong and capable herself.

A client might need someone who sees exactly what's good about him and who smiles at him about that. It's a kind of approval and admiration with no strings attached, so he can take it in: "Yes, that's me. I am good at that. I can shine. It's good to shine, to perform and be the best I can. He sees me and he likes what he sees. He smiles and he's proud to know me. And I'm happy to be able to be myself, accomplishing this!"

Or a client might be desperate for a best friend, a soulmate, someone who sees the world just like he does, who knows just how it is because it's a lot the same for her. He can see himself in her, so he must be okay. He wants someone who shares his interests; someone who can work with him on a project that means a lot to both of them. When he's alongside her, he belongs in the world.

A client might be missing somebody who's glad to hear the strong things she has to say, who enjoys taking her on. Her anger and her edges are fine with him, because he likes how she wants to change things and make things happen. He likes it when she pushes against his ideas, and he enjoys pushing back. This client wants someone who can play hard, as hard as she likes to play, and someone who's not a bit scared of the bumps. Then she can be as assertive as she wants to be—and safe, too, with him.

Underneath all of these different and particular ways that clients long for some "he" or "she" to respond to them, there runs their common hope that somehow they will be able to make the response happen, that they can do whatever it takes to get what they need from the other.

These are selfobject transferences in the language of everyday wanting. In their simple forms, they can sound like childishness exposed. Perhaps that's why it's so hard for clients to admit to themselves and to you that these are, indeed, the experiences that they crave. Perhaps that's why it can be hard for you to respond comfortably as clients find some of these needs met with you. The truth, however, is that all of these desires, in various forms, belong not only to healthy infant and child experience, but also to healthy adult relational experience.

Or maybe you're comfortable with the idea of meeting some of these basic relational needs in therapy, but what bothers you is calling them "transference." In my opinion, it doesn't matter if you put the name "idealizing transference" on your client's deepening trust in you or "mirroring transference" on how much it helps him when you smile at his success. What matters is that your client is having those experiences—and, yes, it's important not to chill that warm personal reality with a cold technical term.

But the "transference" idea might turn out to be useful to both you and your client in the end. There's a complication about how this good relational experience works in therapy. It's not clear whether good selfobject experiences, all by themselves, can accomplish the work of "healing" or change for a client. It might seem so. I'd suggest, however, that even when it seems that our kindness cures, what's helping most is the influence of those new selfobject experiences on the client's organizing principles. What's helping him is a change in how many parts of his relational experience can be processed, or a change in his self-structure, as some self psychologists would say.

Now it's true that clients don't have to be able to see or understand those changes to profit from them. On the other hand, self-understanding usually speeds up and strengthens the processes of change. Here's where the idea of transference can be helpful in the therapy. Referring to it allows both you and your client to step back just a bit from your relationship to understand more clearly what's happening. Together you can acknowledge that your client is feeling better not just because you are a nice person, but because of specific new kinds of interactions taking place between you, interactions that have very particular and powerful meanings in the context of the client's life and history.

Probably therapy works best when new experience in relational therapy is accompanied by a client's significant new insights about how his own self-with-other system works. The insights are important, and perhaps even more important is the client's experience of connecting with you in an engaged and cooperative way as the two of you work on what's going on between you and what's going on for him. A client doesn't have to struggle to remember the learning that happens in an experiential relational therapy. It goes to his psychological bones. But it's also possible, and very useful in such a therapy, for a client to know a lot about what has happened, and to claim it, cognitively, as his own.

Such experiences of self-reflection and self-understanding add context and depth to a client's experiences of getting relational needs met. "Transference" is one of those concepts that can help him with his process of self-reflection. The word reminds both you and him of the intentional work you're doing together: you're allowing deep, important needs to emerge in the therapy relationship, along with all the conflict and trouble they may cause him. In the midst of these complex, powerful experiences, you're working together to find words and meanings for them, until your client comes to understand more fully: "So this is how my self-with-other system works!"

OTHER DEVELOPMENTAL STORIES

Self psychology says that therapy should be a sustaining selfobject milieu for your clients. Through selfobject experience their subjective selves can become delineated and cohesive, they can be supported in their ambitions and affirmed in their values, and they can develop into respectful, self-respecting members of the human community. But self psychology's story of how a self develops is a speculative one worked out from therapists' transference experiences with adult clients. There are other interesting stories about the power of relationship in human development that begin with infant and child studies. I'll briefly look at some of them because they, too, support the idea that a relational therapy can bring some healing to developmental damage clients have suffered, and thus help them experience a new sense of well-being in the world.

Attachment Theory

Mary Ainsworth and John Bowlby have identified and documented three main patterns of attachment between infants and caregivers.[8] A caregiver's consistent availability and sensitive responses to a child's communications lead to *secure attachment* and the child's confident ability to venture out and explore. In *anxious resistant attachment*, the child doesn't know for sure that the caregiver will be available and responsive—sometimes she is, but sometimes she is absent or threatens abandonment. The child tends to worry about separations, cling, and be anxious about exploring the world. When an inconsistent caregiver also rebuffs the child's advances, an *anxious avoidant attachment* is set in motion. Eventually this child avoids contact in order to hide her needs. Often a self-sufficient, competent veneer masks this child's pervasive anxiety and anger.

After the first two or three years of a child's life, Bowlby says, these patterns become habitual, or "working models" of how all interactions work. A securely attached child will update her working models as she grows because of the free communication between herself and her parents. She can move on to more mature forms of secure attachment as a base for more mature forms of confidence and exploration. Since an insecurely attached child lives in a less communicative, responsive environment, her working models of other and self are likely to persist unchanged, first with her original caregivers, and then with others, even when they treat her quite differently than her original caregivers did.

"Working models of parent and self" are similar to what I have called self-with-other organizing principles. Bowlby holds out the hope that although change becomes more difficult as we age, there are always chances that our working models of attachment can be influenced for the better. When working models of self-with-other aren't held too tightly, life experience can continue to alter them to match new relational life situations. But the more anxious and insecure a working model is, the more likely it is to be quite rigidly repetitive of early experience. Here therapy can help, Bowlby says.

Therapy becomes a new attachment in which a client's working model of attachment can be subverted, if ever so slowly. How can this happen? In healthy parent–child relationships, working models change through what Bowlby describes as free-flowing, warmly personal conversation, laced with feeling. This is the kind of conversation relational therapy works toward. In the beginning stages of therapy, a client may be quite afraid to bring much of herself forward. But each time she does, there isn't the disinterest or rejection she anticipates. Slowly she finds she can speak more freely of herself and her feelings. Even difficult times of misunderstanding eventually prove the reliability of this new model of attachment. New security gives the client a base for new explorations and undertakings. And all the while, this new working model of relationship is becoming more exportable to other relationships in the rest of her life.

Attachment theory offers this picture of the developmental repair therapy can make possible for clients. It suggests that a secure base will allow them to explore life with more confidence. But beyond that, the "goods" are all in the negative: clients won't feel so anxious, angry, or depressed. For a more positive description of the "goods" of healthy development and redevelopment, we'll look briefly at the work of Daniel Stern and Joseph Lichtenberg, work often linked with relational psychoanalytic theory.

Daniel Stern

Stern describes four different kinds of relatedness that emerge in sequence between an infant and her parents and that then carry on into the child's adult life: emergent relatedness, core relatedness, intersubjective relatedness, and verbal relatedness.[9] Each kind of relatedness develops as an intricate matching of cues and responses between parent and child; each requires an infant constitutionally able to give and respond to cues, and a parent who can do the same, offering nonintrusive, interested, consistent and relatively accurate attunement to the child's signals.

Emergent relatedness is the self-with-other system within which an infant sorts and cross-matches perceptions and stimuli to make patterned sense of the world, especially of her social world. This emergent domain of relatedness and of self carries on into adulthood as capacities to learn, to manage stimulation and anxiety, and to make contact with others.

Core relatedness is the relationship between the infant's energy and excitement patterns and her parents' responses to them. Through responses rich with matching and complimentary energy, parents provide a reliable context in which an infant can experience core senses of self such as agency, affectivity, coherence, and continuity. More importantly, she comes to experience a balanced well-being in that core sense of self, an equilibrium that depends on her parents' interactive presence with her. Later in life, the domain of core relatedness has to do with how well a person can use various relationships to maintain a cohesive, balanced, resilient sense of core self.

In intersubjective relatedness the focus of the infant–parent relationship moves to the sharing of subjective experience. In interactions between two selves, parent and child, meanings and feelings are communicated and understood. Affective attunement makes this sharing possible. Parents' capacities to attune and to empathize determine, in large part, what kinds of affective experiences can be safely included in the child's sense of self, and they influence the feeling tones of the child's self-states. Throughout life, the domain of intersubjective relatedness is the "place" for the giving and receiving of empathy and understanding and thus for maintaining self-esteem and comfortable self-states.

For Stern, verbal relatedness is the beginning of the possibility of false relatedness, for a child can be spoken to and taught to speak in ways that deny what the child's body and emotions tell her is really happening. Everything that is not included in this social world of language becomes either "private" or "disavowed" or "not-me" experience, according to Stern. In adulthood, these experiences that lie outside of what's socially sanctioned often generate feelings of inauthenticity, anxiety, and alienation. But if one can share the private experiences and integrate the disavowed and "not-me" experiences of one's life, verbal relatedness can become a domain in which one is known and affirmed as contradictory and imperfect, but also as a unique and valuable self. It's clear that this could be a job for therapy. In Stern's scheme, however, the therapy relationship is able to touch and shape each kind of adult relatedness, not just verbal relatedness.

In Stern's terms, a client's secure therapy relationship can sometimes take the form of emergent relatedness, helping him make better contact with the world and turn some of his life's chaos into patterns he can manage. As core relatedness, a client's being with his therapist will support the dynamic balance of his core senses of self—his emotions, will, and agency, and who he feels himself to be in space and time. In the domain of intersubjective relatedness, emotional attunement and empathy will broaden and deepen a client's sense of who he is "inside" and invite him into the positive feelings of interpersonal sharing and connection. And as verbal relatedness, therapy makes space for conversations that bridge the gap between who the client knows himself to be and the social self he believes he must present to the world.

Lichtenberg and Motivational Systems

Joseph Lichtenberg proposes a theory of structured motivation (instead of a theory of structured self) as a way to explain the behavior of infants observed in their natural surroundings and also the behavior and feel-

ings of adults in therapy. He says that human motivation is best concep-
tualized as a series of systems designed to promote the fulfillment and
regulation of basic needs, which he sorts into five categories: (1) the need
for psychic regulation of physiological requirements (for food, warmth,
and sleep, for example), (2) the need for attachment and affiliation, (3)
the need for exploration and assertion, (4) the need to react with aversion, either fight or flight, when in danger, and (5) the need for sensual
and sexual enjoyment.[10]

Exchanges between parent and child give each motivational system
its robustness, contours, limits, and feeling-tones. The parent's feelings
are a powerful regulator of the child's experience of his own motivations.
If, for example, a caregiver responds to exploration with encouragement,
the child will explore more confidently and his exploratory system will be
strengthened. If the responses to a child's attachment strivings are warm,
reaching out to others feels good to him, not shameful. If there is a blank
in caretaker response when it comes to a child's sensuality and sexuality,
he will be limited in this area of self-knowledge and self-expression.

Parent–child interactions that are loaded with a lot of feeling become clustered together in what Lichtenberg calls model scenes. In therapy
with adults, as we have seen, model scenes turn up as stories, dreams,
and memories that represent emotionally loaded formative experiences
from infancy, childhood, adolescence, and earlier adulthood.[11] In
Lichtenberg's scheme, the model scenes that emerge in a client's therapy
will be linked to the ways in which caregivers responded to his basic
needs, which in turn shaped the motivational systems through which he
continues to try to stifle or take care of those needs.

Sometimes the therapy process can show a client new ways to take
care of those needs: the therapy room may become a place for a special
kind of relaxed well-being; in your presence, a client can explore previously forbidden areas of feeling and new ways of being with another person; a client may learn to assert himself in therapy, and to fight back or
withdraw in useful self-protection if you inadvertently hurt him. The client will not only be having these new experiences, he will be talking
about how his motivational systems work for him both in and out of
therapy. Talking about them when they're "hot," that is, when he's embroiled in a model scene in which he is working to get the best outcome
he thinks he can have, has significant power to change how his motivational systems work for him, especially when that kind of talking is embedded in ongoing self-reflection within a supportive selfobject
relationship.

The Boston Process of Change Study Group

In 1995 a group of infant and child clinicians and researchers, practicing psychoanalysts, and analytic theorists (including Daniel Stern) came to-gether in Boston to study the question of how change takes place in psy-chotherapy. From the beginning, they intended to develop a model of change that would be based on infant research and that would explain the "something more than insight" that produces change in therapy. Thus their work attends more to questions about dyadic process than to ques-tions about the structure of self or of motivation. The group explores the interactive, mutual, non-linear processes that organize an infant's emo-tional states and also his sense of how to do things with intimate others, a kind of knowledge that the group calls "implicit relational knowing." Then they make links between these processes and processes of change in therapy.[12]

Clients bring implicit relational knowing to the therapeutic rela-tionship, the Boston Group says, a knowing that profoundly affects the quality of their relational lives inside and outside of therapy. Therapists, of course, bring to their work their own implicit knowledge about rela-tional procedure. Over time, then, a client and therapist will find them-selves within a way of "getting along" influenced by both partners' implicit relational knowledge. How can this lead to change for a client? Here the connection is made to infant development.

Just as a parent can provide a mental/emotional context for expanded and more complex states of shared consciousness with a child, so a thera-pist can engage with a client in ways that produce for both of them an expanded sense of how they can be in this relationship. A client's states of consciousness can be expanded into more coherent and complex states in collaboration with a self-organizing system that is already more coher-ent and complex. In other words, the therapist brings to the relationship ways of interacting and of exploring interaction that the client wouldn't have known about. At the same time the client is bringing challenges into the relational system that require the therapist to expand his own repertoire of understanding and response. As the client–therapist rela-tionship expands, new forms of agency and shared experience become available within it. These new patterns of organization can also be put into operation in other relationships.

The Boston Group believes that changes in such implicit relational knowing are what produce the important changes in therapy that can't be attributed to insight. Such changes come about through unplanned

events in therapy. In an improvisational mode of talking and being together, at unpremeditated times, what the group calls "now moments"
happen between client and therapist. These are the moments when something new could emerge that would change what both client and therapist know about the possibilities of relating to one another. If now
moments are handled in a therapeutic way that fosters a "specific moment of meeting," the relationship does change (if ever so slightly), and
the implicit knowledge of each partner is altered by the new and different intersubjective context between them. They then return to "moving
along" in therapy, a process consisting of many small matches–mismatches,
ruptures, and repairs that put the new shape of implicit knowing into
play—until another "now moment" offers new possibilities for expanding
their shared and individual consciousness.

THE LIMITS OF A SELF-FOR-OTHER
PERSPECTIVE IN THERAPY

The genius of all of these therapies that connect adult health to infant
development is that they recognize that "health" or "good experience"
isn't what's left over when conflicts are worked through in therapy. They
see therapy as more than treating disease or dysfunction so that clients
can return to "normal." For these therapies, psychological health or emotional well-being is itself an interpersonal creation. They know what effective parents, teachers, mentors, and coaches know: it takes artful,
intentional, caring activity to provide the interactive contexts that sustain many different kinds of good learning experiences for those who
count on you to help them develop.

However, self-for-other relational therapy needs the check and balance of a self-with-other perspective. Seeing the therapist as only the provider of experience that repairs developmental deficits, strengthens new
self-structures, and facilitates expanded kinds of relational knowing would
seriously limit a relational perspective. In the first place, the assumption
that the therapist uses empathy just to know what the client needs and
how to meet those needs shifts the therapist away from the mutuality of
empathic exchange with the client. In such "knowing," the therapist takes
the position of an expert who observes and acts from outside the immediacy of the client–therapist interactions. Too many of those moments of
knowing add up to the therapist's exit from mutual, reciprocal relation-

ship. Too much focus on providing what clients need blocks a therapist's ability to be a real other person engaged with her clients.

Therapies that script the therapist as just a provider subtly patronize a client. All the while, however, she knows that she is an adult in therapy. If she has thought about her history in this way, she has probably recognized that her organizing principles for attachment, achievement, and taking care of herself are thoroughly woven into her adult personality. They make her who she is now, and she can't go back in time and undo them, no matter how well her therapist might meet her needs. Furthermore, she doesn't want to find herself feeling like a perpetual victim of her own history.

This client needs a therapist who is as present *with* her, here and now, as she is a provider of empathy *for* her. A self-with-other focus offers therapy in which it's very clear that a client is not a regressed child or a victim, but rather an active explorer of the intensities of how relationship works for her right now and how it could be different. In such therapy, she will do this exploring *with* you, her therapist, and you will be challenged to explore your own experience, too, and to devise no subtle escapes from the immediacy of the relationship.

In this mode, relational therapy gives a client the chance to experience her unfulfilled neediness as desires that are completely appropriate in a here-and-now adult relationship. Her problem is that these desires have been twisted into opaque, dense impossibilities by powerful anxiety. Her anxiety comes from the past ("I mustn't want, mustn't ask; if she says *no*, that means I'm disgusting"). But the point of her therapy is not that this "she" (you, her therapist) will say *yes* in order to meet her need, but that your client will have the chance, here and now, to experience and to think about both her legitimate adult desires for connection and the longstanding anxieties that turn them into trouble. It's useful for her to understand those longstanding anxieties in terms of her own history, but liberation comes as she finds the courage to accept her adult desires and to act on them in new ways.[13]

THE "GOODS" A SELF-WITH-OTHER PERSPECTIVE OFFERS

With its developmental and intersubjective emphases, self psychology is both a self-for-other and a self-with-other therapy. Relational psychoanalysis also contains both themes, but it puts a stronger emphasis on the current, mutual dance of self with other. Aron and Mitchell describe positive outcomes in therapy not as a self becoming stronger and more cohesive, enjoying enhanced capacities to self-right and self-reflect, nor as changes in organizing principles or in motivational or self-structures. Instead, they speak of meanings that client and therapist negotiate about what's happening between them, and of the larger, related meanings that these two partners in therapy co-construct and that turn out to be pragmatically useful narratives of the client's life experience.[14] "Pragmatically useful" means that therapy has generated a sense of self and relationships that a client feels to be important, meaningful, and "authentic," that is, deeply his own.[15]

If a client's life is stuck because old constraints keep foreclosing possibilities for new experiences, one could say, as Mitchell puts it, that his life is stuck because of a failure of imagination. His therapy relationship is where new things can happen to prime his imagination, things invented neither by you nor by him, but brought to birth by what happens and what might happen next between you.[16] These new things might feel good or they might not; what matters is that they will feel meaningful and authentic to him, and that they will be windows for his imagination and pathways to further important movement—the opposite of his habit of shuttered, constricting stuckness.

This more philosophical version of relational psychoanalysis doesn't focus on ameliorating life's agonies with care and understanding. It invites a client to embrace the inevitable clashes, impossibilities, and tragedies inherent in human life. It resonates with an existential sense of the contradictions and conundrums of everyday experience, which at best become creative dialectic tensions to live out with courage and imagination. In this view, the meanings that a client makes of his life experience are not only constructed in relationship with others (especially his therapist), they are also dialogical meanings, that is, though they belong to him, they are also shareable with others in the human community. Engaging in such dialogical relationship is part of a client's movement beyond the limits of victim and dominator positions in social relations. A relational therapy enhances his ability to become, instead, a player engaged mutually with others, enjoying the meeting of minds.[17]

Jessica Benjamin, a feminist relational psychoanalyst, has put forward a definition of intersubjectivity that highlights self-*with*-other. She begins with the feminist insistence that psychoanalytic discourse treat women as full subjects, not just as love/hate objects for male subjects, and she goes on to argue that all relationships should be "intersubjective," that is, products of negotiations between persons who mutually recognize one another as subjects. Benjamin is saying that intersubjectivity is something more than the situation created when two or more subjectivities share a field of existence. (This is the field theory of intersubjectivity developed by self psychological intersubjectivists like Stolorow, Atwood, and Orange.) Benjamin reserves the term intersubjectivity for the mutual recognition that can be negotiated between any two subjects, including infant and parent. In this kind of intersubjectivity, neither subject exists for the other. In moments and modes of intersubjectivity, each partner is engaged in mutual and reciprocal processes of asserting self and recognizing the other's self-assertion.

Benjamin highlights the necessary instability of such intersubjectivity as it makes space for aggression, competition, and the inevitable breakdowns and repairs of recognition that happen in the course of a relationship. The demands of empathy become conflictual when empathy must run two ways. Domination of one person by the other is always a possibility. But relational analysis is doing its best work, Benjamin proposes, when it helps its analysands develop the capacity for achieving and sustaining the "intersubjectivity" of two-way recognition. The other side of this work is helping analysands develop capacities to contain and work with what happens when intersubjectivity breaks down: with the internal tensions generated by clashes of wills and frustrated aggression, and with fantasies of reversals and reprisals.[18]

The women of the Stone Center also speak to the ideal of mutuality in relationship. In part, they do so by ascribing to women innate capacities for empathy and recognition, while linking aggression to masculinity and patriarchy. Their version of relational therapy is based on a developmental model in which the development and exercise of women's ways of connection become the paradigm for all healthy human development and psychology. Like the other relational therapies we have considered, this self-in-relation model is also a psychodynamic therapy. It depends on emotionally "connecting" relational experiences between client and therapist to generate insight about relational patterns. These relational patterns are condensed in transference feelings and old relational images. Stone Center theory maintains that this combination of experiencing connection and developing insight will produce change in clients' current relationships and in their well-being. In other words, some of the goods of this therapy are like the goods of the other developmentally oriented relational therapies we've discussed.[19]

The Stone Center theorists, however, strive to locate movement and change within the therapy relationship itself, which they characterize as mutual, as Aron and Benjamin do. "Self-in-relation" is the primary human reality, they say, within which we might have fantasies about our autonomy and independence, but they are only fantasies. Therapy can't be a fully mutual relationship, insofar as a therapist must put the client's subjective experience at the center of the therapy and speak of her own experience only as it might be helpful to the client. However, within this context, there can be real connection, mutual respect, emotional availability, and openness to change on both sides of the relationship. These experiences of mutuality often deepen and grow with the therapy.[20] Thus, as other mutually empathic relationships do, the therapy relationship produces for both partners what Miller and Stiver call the five components of empowerment: "zest," action, knowledge, worth, and a desire for more connection—five powerful, in-relation "goods."

Zest in-relation is the opposite of isolated depression. It's the vitality and energy one feels in moments of mutual connection, whether those moments be filled with sadness, fear, anger, or joy. Those moments of mutual connection are themselves moments of mutual action in which each person affects the other. When a person knows she has a powerful or meaningful effect on someone, she feels all the more empowered to take further action and to believe it will be effective. A therapy relationship that's working well will stir such energy in both you and your client. Furthermore, sharing within mutual relationship produces a lot of new knowledge for the sharers. In the therapeutic relationship, you and your client learn about her as you speak. From your responses to her, she learns important things about you; and you are both constantly gaining new knowledge about how the relationship works for you.

There's also something about being responded to, having someone engage with her feelings and stay with her process, that makes your client feel worthwhile. In mutual relationships between peers, both participants feel like they matter more in the world when they have mattered to each other in their interchange. When therapy works well, you'll feel that your presence there has been important. What matters more in therapy, of course, is that your client's sense of worthiness increases as she feels your honest and interested engagement with her.

And finally, these "goods" of zest, empowerment, knowledge, and worth stir within both of you a desire for more connection. Your client's relational life improves as she acts on this desire with you, with her partner in an intimate relationship, with friends, and even with people beyond her circle of close connection. All of these positive outcomes of therapy flow from what goes on between you and your client. None of these "goods" can be abstracted from the relationship and turned into purely personal gains. They exist for your client because she is a self-in-relation and while she is a self-in-relation.

It's interesting that although interpersonalist, dialectical, and feminist versions of relational therapy differ in their expressions of philosophy, politics, and ethics, they agree on this point: The well-being or the "goods" that therapy produces are primarily self-with-other phenomena, even though they emerge in the context of a therapy that is clearly for the client.

WHAT IF YOUR CLIENT FALLS IN LOVE WITH YOU (OR YOU FALL IN LOVE WITH YOUR CLIENT)?

As you read about all these benefits of intimate connection in therapy, the thought might cross your mind: Don't these positive feelings in an intense interpersonal relationship increase the chances that some kind of falling in love might happen here? I know of no studies that address this question, but the answer to it may well be yes. Falling in love happens in all kinds of therapy, and maybe it happens especially in relational therapy, where a client learns to bring herself more fully and deeply into connection than she ever has done before. As you listen to her, you are consistently warm, attentive, and responsive. She shares the longings of her heart and the troubles of her soul with you, and you are there for her week after week. In this situation, a certain kind of falling in love is almost inevitable—she will develop a heightened awareness of your ways of being and speaking, intense feelings of various kinds when the two of you are together, and many thoughts and fantasies about you when you're apart. Some of those feelings, thoughts, and fantasies may be sexual. That's natural, too.

As we know from our everyday adult lives, it's natural that feelings of emotional intimacy lead to desires for physical and sexual intimacy. We also know that having those feelings and acting on them are two very different things. So it is in therapy. But there are some special considerations around the issue of falling in love in therapy. First of all, although a client's loving and sexual feelings are fine and often helpful in therapy, under no conditions is it fine or helpful for you to respond to those feelings with a romantic or sexual interest of your own. It may be the case that you feel loving and sexual toward her, but if you act on those feelings, you are taking advantage of your client's vulnerability in the relationship—a clear breach of your ethical responsibility to her. So says every code of professional ethics for psychotherapists.

That being said, let's return to how it might be helpful for your client to fall in love with you, and to how you might manage that situation in her best interests (whether or not your own feelings are involved). Falling in love is just one more variety of the kinds of intensity that make relational therapy work. It can be described as a particular kind of transference, often called "erotic transference." Like the other varieties of transference we've talked about, it has a negative, repetitive dimension, which might be your client's fear that her love will be coldly rejected or, on the other hand, that her love will be snatched greedily and then twisted to abuse her. In the positive, helpful dimension of erotic transference, her experience of having her love treated respectfully can lead to new depths of self-respect and stronger capacities for safe, mutual connections with others.

So although falling in love is not to be acted out in therapy, if it happens, it's best for your client not to hide it from you. All the thoughts and feelings your client has about her relationship with you are important, and her loving and sexual feelings are certainly no exception. It's your responsibility not to become entangled, either positively or negatively, in her feelings, but to listen to them carefully in order to understand her world and her feelings more fully and deeply. In short, it's your job to receive her loving feelings, and all the conflicts around them, with the same empathy you bring to anything else she talks about.

So if your client falls in love with you and is terribly anxious and ashamed about the situation, you can reassure her that this is a natural thing to happen, quite common in therapy, and therefore nothing to be ashamed of. And then you will help her find ways to talk about her feelings with you. That's how you can help her turn her feelings of love and attraction into something positive for her growth beyond therapy and her relationship with you. If she takes the risk of talking about her feelings, she (and you) will probably be surprised how easy it turns out to be, and how simply okay it is to let these feelings be part of who she is right now in this relationship.

(Please note: if you find yourself having strong, persistent romantic and erotic fantasies about a client, whether or not the client has expressed loving and sexual feelings toward you, you must get yourself to a supervisor you trust, and try to understand the meaning of your feelings—not only in the context of the therapy, but also in the context of your own personal life. As a relational therapist, you will have been trained to enter into emotional intimacy that you don't mistake for falling in love. If you're making that mistake now and feeling the pull to cross a professional ethical boundary, chances are that something is wrong or missing in your personal intimate relationships.)

WHAT ABOUT DEPENDENCY?

The good feelings of therapy can also give rise to another kind of fear, fear of dependency. We've come up against realistic, authentic forms of this fear elsewhere in this book. Clients who were never able to count on their parents to support them, for example, will fear starting to count on you, because they expect that you will only disappoint them in the end. As we've seen, these repetitive fears need to be treated with repetitive, gentle understanding. But there's another kind of "fear of dependency" I'd like to address now, and it's not really a fear, it's a judgment.

Sometimes clients are advised by well-meaning friends and loved ones not to rely too much on a therapist for comfort, support, advice, and help in daily living. Such reliance, they're told, will not diminish with time. It's a dependency trap induced by therapists to line their pockets or feed their egos. Sadly, as in any profession, there are some therapists who are poorly trained, less than competent, or even unscrupulous, and some of them do manipulate their clients into long-term dependent relationships. But people who are deeply suspicious of dependency don't usually discriminate between good and poor therapy. To them, it's all suspect.

Behind such suspicions stand certain cultural assumptions: dependence is the opposite of independence; in optimal development, one grows out of dependency and into autonomy; dependency on others is a less healthy situation than autonomous independence from others. All of the relational therapies we've looked at take issue with those assumptions. The core project of the Stone Center theorists is to turn these assumptions upside-down. They argue that dependence is not the opposite of independence, for the two kinds of being-with are completely entwined in social relationships. Being able to count on others is what gives any one of us self-confidence and the power to move forward. Wishing or pretending to grow out of the human condition of interdependency, like denying one's own vulnerability and emotions, is a recipe for relational and psychological disaster.[21]

The Stone Center models healthy development on healthy mother–daughter relationships in which a daughter, under less social pressure than her brother to become "autonomously" separate from their parents, differentiates *within* the relationship with her mother. As both she and her mother develop and continue to adapt to development in the other, their relationship offers more complexity, fluidity, and choices to both of them. As they take the risks of expressing a full range of feeling with each other and negotiate changes in what they each want from the relationship, both mother and daughter feel more emotionally "real," vital, and purposeful in relationship. This authenticity-in-relationship is the counterpart of their differentiation-in-relationship, and both of these kinds of connection belong to a vision of maturity for both men and women that has nothing to do with an isolated, freestanding autonomy.[22]

And finally, the Stone Center says, dependency on others isn't unhealthy; it's just a fact of interpersonal life that sometimes you have to count on others to help you cope with things you don't have the experience, time, or skill to manage as well for yourself. Other times you are the lender of help, expertise, and support. The "helping" themes and moments of relationships become unhealthy only when one person needs to keep another person subservient or powerless in the relationship. Otherwise, dependency is normal and growth promoting. In Stiver's words, dependency allows you to experience yourself "*as being enhanced and empowered through the very process of counting on others for help.*"[23]

The Stone Center theorists would tell your client that it's not just all right for her to count on you for your responsive understanding, it's the only way to grow. Emotional self-differentiation and self-authenticity simply don't happen outside of this kind of empathic connection. Self psychology, too, refuses to see normal psychological development as movement from dependence to autonomy. That movement, says Kohut, is impossible. Instead, healthy growth and development is a story of changes in the relationships between yourself and the others you have relied on, and continue to rely on, in your life.[24] Thus, in both of these developmental models of relational therapy, as you get stronger (in relationship or in your self), you continue to need others, but you need them in different ways. You find new ways—outside of therapy, too—to enter and to enjoy empathic, enlivening, mutual relationships.

When a relational therapy emphasizes self-*for*-other, "what's wrong" has to do with failures in a client's environment, and as his therapist you provide a healthy relational environment that can alter his whole experience of relationship, self, and life. It can take some time for this strengthening of his self (-in-relation) to take root and grow. But he is steadily growing not out of dependency, but into modes of dependency that are more and more reciprocal and fluid, more empowering and useful to him in his life. He is slowly making his peace with how much he needs to depend on others for his everyday happiness and success. When this gets settled, he'll be able to recognize how much he has to offer, too, in healthy interdependent relationships.

When relational therapy emphasizes self-*with*-other, it seems at first glance less vulnerable to a dependency critique. In this mode, the therapist is less a provider of good experience than a partner in a challenging project. But the client can still become deeply embroiled in this powerful relationship that brings to life his most painful ways of being in the world. Something looks like dependency after all, but it's his deep investment in the project and the time it takes for the two of you to work yourselves into a better way of being together. Therapy has to be long enough and intense enough to get through to his repetitive destructive ways of being. In such therapy, he gets caught in relational impossibilities—but he starts to see them for what they are. Each "aha!" makes a crack in the rigidity of his repetitions, and it sets some imagination loose in the relationship. Although a client may come to count on this relationship for an intense kind of engagement he's known nowhere else, the word for this intense, shared adventure of discovery is hardly "dependency"!

All the different versions of relational psychotherapy we've looked at offer clients double protection against being drawn into a kind of dependency that would belittle or control them. First, each of these therapies acknowledges up front that this kind of therapy is all about relationship. When you agree to engage in a therapeutic relationship with a client, you are fully aware of the power she is choosing to invest in you and of the responsibilities that go along with that power. Her "dependency," such as it is, is voluntary, and she enters into it for reasons that both of you respect. This project will require that you will continue to respect the many relational powers that will be awakened in your work together, and that you find ways to keep trusting each other's good-faith commitment to the work. This is the relational frame or structure of the work you hope to do, and it is your client's first protection against unhealthy dependency in therapy.

There's a second protection against disempowering dependency in relational therapy, and it happens throughout the therapy process: relational therapies put the dynamics of the therapy relationship on the table and keep them there. The client is always encouraged to talk about whatever she feels is going on between herself and her therapist. There are no strings attached to that encouragement, no unspoken but particular rules about what she must say in order to keep the relationship safe and her therapist happy with her. Since there's nothing about the therapeutic relationship that can't be noticed and questioned, if your client is feeling at all trapped or belittled or dependent—that's exactly what she needs to talk about! As her therapist, you can prime the pump for such talking and you can respond to it receptively. Then your client can find her way back to active partnership in everything that's going on.

"I ALMOST SMILED AT YOU TODAY!"
(A STORY ABOUT ORDINARY GOODNESS)

To end this chapter on what ordinary goodness in therapy can be, I'd like to tell a story about a surprising little "good" that sneaked up on a client of mine. Though apparently small, this moment of (almost?) well-being turns out to illustrate almost every account of well-being that, in this chapter, we've seen relational therapies put forward.

"Kim" came in one day and sat silently for a few moments, as she often did. Then she said quietly, her eyes on the floor, "I almost smiled at you today when I was coming in the door." I was puzzled, because during the course of our sessions she had smiled at me before. Yet what she was saying seemed very important. What did it mean to her? What was going on between us that she almost smiled at me (and then she didn't)? By this time, we'd been in therapy together for more than three years. I thought she'd tell me all she could about what was happening. She did, and as she did, I also knew enough about her history and our history together to have the following ideas about the goodness or the well-being that was emerging here.

Thinking like a self psychologist, I had learned over the years that one of the selfobject experiences Kim needed most from me was evidence that I paid very close attention to her, evidence like responsive facial expressions, understanding sounds, and short sentences that summed up what I was getting. Any blankness or extended silence on my part meant to her that I was disinterested or not even there with her. And that, in turn, meant to her that she was utterly worthless. However, when she could feel my interest, she felt well-being: a sense of connection with her inner thoughts and feelings and a sense of mattering both to me and to herself.

The particular selfobject relationship that so far had come most to life between us was the one Kohut would have called "alter ego" or "twinship." Her ways of seeking connection with me asked me to relate to her as a fellow human being with experiences that were in some important ways essentially like hers. She longed to experience herself as "normal," as "belonging," and less like an alien on earth. As our connection grew around various kinds of alikeness, Kim felt less like an outsider in her own life. It wasn't surprising, then, that she could smile more easily with me.

But Kim was telling me that at stake here wasn't just any kind of smiling, it was *smiling as she came in the door*. That made me think in more particular ways about her attachment history. I knew that she had experienced both of her parents as distant and disinterested, which explained to me her need that I be so reassuringly present. They also never shared what went on inside them, what moved them or mattered to them. This deprived Kim of experiences of being like them in important ways, of belonging to the same social and emotional world they did, and it also generated the intensity of her search for meaningful likeness with me. But what in her history made it dangerous to smile as she came in the door?

In Bowlby's terms, her working model of attachment was insecure and avoidant. She had experienced not only detachment from both parents, but also rejections and rebuffs of her advances. As she mused on this, she said, "Well, my dad had those paranoid tendencies, so from him it was like, 'What do you want from me?' And my mom was so self-conscious, it was like wanting to know her was just going to expose her somehow. My wanting to connect just scared them both, I guess. It still does!"

An insecure avoidant pattern was clear in stories Kim told about everyday events that troubled her: how she'd sometimes cross the street not to have to say "Hi" to a colleague; how the more she liked and admired certain people, the more she avoided them, for it became impossible to imagine making contact that would feel good to her, not shaming. With me she was always pleasant and respectful, and social smiling was part of that package. But I also felt that she held back, expecting very little in return, fearing to offer too much or to want too much.

In this context, I could understand that smiling at me to greet me would be an enormous risk to take. As Kim explained, "Then it would be just me in your face, saying, 'Here I am! Smile back! Or *something!*' It seems like way too much to ask. I'll be in trouble for sure." The trouble she anticipated, I thought, would be that sting of an aloof rebuff, a nonresponse, and the sickening slide into shame that would follow, a sequence she knew well in her bones, if not in her conscious mind. But on the other hand, after more than three years of my consistent, attentive responsiveness, something was getting through to that insecure, avoidant working model of attachment. She'd had the *impulse* to smile. She was telling me about it! She was thinking about it from every angle.

In terms of Stern's domain of core relatedness, Kim needed to find out whether I would match my energy to hers, or whether preoccupation with my own needs or my own depression would leave her stranded with her "up," interactive strivings, and then disorganized and alone with a struggle to regain her equilibrium. In the domain of intersubjective relatedness, the question would be more about whether we could share the feelings and meanings of our inner worlds. Would she see in my eyes and in my face pleasure about our connection, anticipation of taking it further and deeper into knowing each other? Or would she see "Stay away from me!"—her father's paranoid fear of being taken over and used or her mother's fear of exposure?

"I almost smiled at you today!" was a moment full of goodness because new RIGs, new sequences of interactions and possible interactions, were jostling for space with those old RIGs. Our interactive core relatedness might have already helped Kim experience a self of more lively, balanced presence and energy; our intersubjective relatedness might have helped Kim experience the value of her inner world and the goodness of her unique thoughts and feelings. Furthermore, this unsettling process of RIGs jostling for space was becoming a story that helped Kim reflect deeply about the patterns and meanings of her everyday experience.

In Kim's moment of almost smiling, attachment–affiliation was the motivational system most actively in operation. Despite the rebuffs she suffered as a child, her parents must have provided enough affective response to her early needs for closeness to activate that system well. The good news is that her urge to smile and make friendly contact has survived, in spite of the forces that regularly squelch the urge. As she came through my door, whatever happened—something she saw in my face or manner combined with other model scenes of rejection—activated a secondary motivational system, aversion. To protect herself from rebuff and shame, she withdrew from the source of threat. The ability to self-protect is also good. But the "higher," therapeutic good about all of this, according to a motivational systems version of therapy, is Kim's new ability to notice it all, talk about it, and thus move beyond unconscious, destructive repetitions of what's harmful to her in the present.

The moment of almost smiling was a "now moment" between us,

and in this instance it was Kim who began to turn it into a moment of meeting by telling me about it. As we shared together the meanings and feelings of an almost-smile between us, something shifted in how we each knew each other, and we could hope that Kim's sense of the possibilities of relationship, her "implicit relational knowing," might have been deepened and expanded through that meeting.

So far all of our descriptions and explanations of the goodness inherent in Kim's "I almost smiled at you today!" are goods that accrue to Kim: stronger, more cohesive self-structure, a better working model of attachment, RIGs that better support Kim's equilibrium and vitality, the retooling of aspects of her motivational systems, the expansion of her implicit relational knowledge, and, through all of this, new capacities to reflect on how her self-with-other systems work for her, reflection that stimulates further changes in how those systems work. What about those explanations of goodness that try to keep the "goods" located in the relationship?

Well, in Stone Center terms, there was "zest" between us when Kim spoke of almost smiling. Our fruitful dilemmas—What am I doing to inhibit her smiling? Will she be able to smile? How will I respond? What will we do then?—exist in the form of reciprocal actions we each desire and fear. As we work our way through the meanings of our dilemmas, there's lots of new knowledge to be had; as we better understand each other and ourselves in relation, we feel more secure and worthy; and we find ourselves wanting to pursue this, wanting more mutual authenticity and meaningful connection. Our relationship has grown to this point; the mutuality of our experience has deepened with the therapy, and as it continues to deepen, we can expect more well-being within the relationship.

From a more interpersonalist perspective, "I almost smiled at you!" was a flash of imagination, a thought unthinkable before, something new between Kim and myself after a long time of the same old thing going on between us. We may never know how our work together released that impulse into Kim's awareness, but now that it's between us, many "small" things are changing. Now, instead of just being sure that her advances will be trouble, Kim wonders, "What if my smiling at you means something else to you, something I'd never expect, something I don't even know about?" Possibilities expand, with new fears and new excitement, for both of us. I wonder, "Will she ever actually smile at me? Or is talking about it 'smiling' enough? What would it be like to feel her smile and respond to it? Where might we go then?"

Kim says, "My smiling at friends feels different now. It means different." She doesn't know what it means, exactly. She doesn't know where this "smiling" (more reaching out to others with more expectation of friendly response) will take her in the world. We don't know where reciprocal smiling might take us. In a sense, we haven't even done it yet! But we can feel between us the satisfaction of something old and stuck giving way to something much more warm, alive, and moving even when we just talk about what smiling (and not smiling) means. Making this meaning together feels good. "We-ness" feels sturdier; giving and receiving works better; mutual enjoyment and mutual vulnerability have become more possible between us.

Does this growth in the relationship, or this intense mutuality of the relationship, mean that Kim is dependent on me in an unhealthy way? The same day that Kim told me, "I almost smiled at you," she said later in the hour, "I bumped into a friend on the street. I saw her coming and I didn't duck away. Instead I said, 'Hi, Donna! How *are* you?' I said her name; I spoke first, with *enthusiasm*! I felt like I meant it. It felt good." In the following session, as we kept talking about the meanings of smiling a greeting, Kim listed all the ways she had been putting herself forward a bit more in her life. "It's all about expecting that when I put myself out there, sort of in their faces, they won't find me a bother or a burden," she explained. "It's finding out I'm not a bother or a burden; I can be enjoyed." And then she got scared. "But I'm not sure about that. What if I'm wrong? That's the risk I take if I smile at you. So I don't. Not yet."

I believe that if Kim were dependent on me in an unhealthy way, the supportive aspect of our relationship wouldn't help her expand her strength, interpersonal security, vitality, and sense of self-worth in connection with others. "Support" would keep her weak, scared, and small. But that's not what's happening. Instead, Kim finds herself trying out new ways of being in the world at the very same time that she's trying them out with me. In a situation of unhealthy dependency, Kim and I would duck away from challenging, disturbing questions about what's going on between us in order to hold on to a relatively comfortable, repetitive status quo. However, that's not what we're doing. Instead, even now, we know better than to impose nice "closure" on this almost-smiling episode. What we get out of this doesn't depend on whether we smile at each other exactly "right" in the end. What matters is the change that gets put in motion when we stay true to the question, "What's going on between us?" Unlike the closed loop of dead-end dependency, this kind of therapeutic relationship sets in motion interactions that move outward, opening up relationships and the selves who live them. It asks questions that don't have endings.

Therapies, however, do have endings. And beyond the endings waits the final proof of this "goodness" pudding: Does the well-being last when the therapy is over? That's a question for the next (and last) chapter of this book.

ENDNOTES

1. Stolorow and Atwood, *Contexts of Being*, 82–83.
2. Stolorow and Atwood, *Contexts of Being*, 34.
3. Bacal, Ed., *Optimal Responsiveness*.
4. Howard Bacal and Kenneth Newman, *Theories of Object Relations: Bridges to Self Psychology* (New York: Columbia University Press, 1990), 229.
5. Kohut, *How Does Analysis Cure?*, 192–194.
6. Wolf, *Treating the Self*, 124–126.
7. Stolorow and Atwood, *Contexts of Being*, 34–35.
8. Mary Ainsworth, *Patterns of Attachment: A Psychological Study of the Strange Situation* (Hillsdale, NJ: Lawrence Erlbaum Associates, 1978), and John Bowlby, *A Secure Base: Parent–Child Attachment and Healthy Human Development* (New York: Basic Books, 1988), especially Lecture 7, "The Role of Attachment in Personality Development," 119–136.
9. These four domains of relatedness and their connection to clinical issues are summarized in Stern's *The Interpersonal World of the Infant*, Chapter 9, "The 'Observed Infant' as Seen with a Clinical Eye," 185–230.
10. Lichtenberg, *Psychoanalysis and Motivation*.
11. Lichtenberg, Lachmann, and Fosshage, *Self and Motivational Systems*. In this sequel to Lichtenberg's earlier work, the authors develop a mode of therapeutic work that is based on working with model scenes that have been developed around certain patterns of needs and responses within certain motivational systems.
12. The Boston Group (Nadia Bruschweiler-Stern, Alexandra M. Harrison, Karlen Lyons-Ruth, Alexander C. Morgan, Jeremy P. Nahum, Louis Sander, Daniel Stern, and Edward Z. Tronick) presented a first edition of their study-in-process to a conference in Finland in 1996. Those papers are collected in a special issue of the *Infant Mental Health Journal*, 19(3), 1998.
13. See Stephen Mitchell, *Relational Concepts in Psychoanalysis: An Integration* (Cambridge, MA: Harvard University Press, 1988), Chapter 5, "The Metaphor of the Baby," 127–172.
14. Aron, *A Meeting of Minds*, 262–263.
15. Stephen Mitchell, *Hope and Dread in Psychoanalysis* (New York: Basic Books, 1993), 37.
16. Mitchell, *Hope and Dread*, 222–224.
17. Aron, *A Meeting of Minds*, 150–154.

18. Jessica Benjamin, *The Bonds of Love* and *Like Subjects, Love Objects*, especially "Recognition and Destruction: An Outline of Intersubjectivity," 27–48.
19. Miller and Stiver, *The Healing Connection*, 121–147.
20. Judith Jordan, "The Meaning of Mutuality," in Judith Jordan et al., *Women's Growth in Connection*, 95.
21. See Irene Stiver, "The Meanings of Dependency in Female–Male Relationships," in Jordan et al., *Women's Growth in Connection*, 143–161.
22. Janet Surrey, "The Self-in-Relation: A Theory of Women's Development," in Jordan et al., *Women's Growth in Connection*, 59–61.
23. Stiver, "The Meanings of Dependency," 160, italics in text.
24. Kohut, *How Does Analysis Cure?*, 52, 208.

7

—·—

ENDING AND GOING ON

When a person is about to end something that's been important to her—some schooling, a long road trip, a job she's loved and hated, a difficult relationship, a therapy—before she goes on to other things, it's important that she looks back over the terrain she's traversed in order to fix in her mind a sense of the whole experience. Where has she been? What has it meant? What has she accomplished?

We could undertake that same sort of review as we approach the end of these chapters about relational therapy. They've been structured along the lines of how a therapy might develop. We began where every-body begins therapy: wondering whether a particular kind of therapy, in this case, relational therapy, might be helpful. I laid out a brief, simple answer to the question, "What does relational therapy have to offer?" The answer held within it hints of much more to be said, along with the suggestion that the experience of relational therapy can't ever be cap-tured entirely in words.

But before moving into exploring the experience of relational therapy, I explained where this therapy fits among other therapies. To clarify what I meant by a therapy that's all about "self-with-other in action," I talked about what relational therapy isn't: it's not a medical model of therapy, not a rationalistic or an individualistic model. In those terms, I devel-oped contrasts between other therapies and relational therapy that would bring the relational model into sharper focus. Then I introduced several relational schools of therapy, schools that would give me concepts and words for all my further forays into describing the experience of rela-tional therapy. I noted differences between these schools, but I tried to draw them together into a comprehensive picture of what's unique about the philosophy and practice of relational psychotherapy.

And then, as is the case in any therapy, it was time to step into the experience, beginning with the moment the client contacts you by phone. I talked about what makes the start-up of therapy feel as safe and comfortable as possible for your clients: clarity about the boundaries, the ethical principles, and the mutual expectations of doing this kind of work. But the ambience and soul of relational work is empathy, I said, as I tried to put words to its complex and subtle workings. What helps your clients most is their experience of your empathy—and how that experience can develop into their feeling known, accompanied, and cared for. I suggested that this change, this movement from aloneness to connection, can have a powerful impact on many kinds of psychological suffering, and that therefore relational "empathy work" can move competently across a wide range of pain and trouble.

What *is* the trouble for your clients? All they know is that they feel bad. Where does their "feeling bad" come from? I said that it's not likely to be coming from something simply outside of them, nor from something simply inside them, but that it probably comes from that place that produces all their feelings and self-images, that boundary place where from-the-outside input and from-the-inside organizing patterns come together to create meaning. Different relational theories describe this place of making self-with-other meanings and what goes wrong for your clients there. Each theoretical system accounts for how the oppression, disconnection, violation, neglect, and misunderstanding that come at your clients from the outside seem to take residence within them.

This movement from outside to inside brings up the question of the relationship between past and present in your clients' personal psychology and emotional well-being. The notion of "psychological trauma" suggests that your clients' painful histories will keep reverberating within their present-day lives. As I discussed trauma and dissociation, I suggested that in relational therapy, you will be especially alert to the relational dimensions of the trauma your clients have suffered, ready to remember with them all the many aspects of how it was for them to be with the dangerous, frightening, and confusing people they might have lived with every day, earlier in their lives.

The point of this shared remembering is not the reconstruction of history, I said, but rather the gathering up of a client's broken, scattered bits of self so that they may be reintegrated, with grief and love, into a "self" who can be here relatively centered and whole. I reiterated that access to the past is always through the present, and especially through "model scenes"—dreams, memories, and interpersonal sequences that all enact the same group of self-with-other organizing principles. Relational therapy sees what's often called "transference" as the most powerful kind of model scene, I said, and I promised to devote an entire chapter to the difficulties of working through negative model scenes.

And then what happened in our conversation mirrored in an uncanny way what often happens in this next phase of therapy: I got stuck. There was no way out except—maybe—to stay honest and keep talking. That's how it is in these terribly hard parts of relational therapy, at times like this when your client feels let down, shamed, betrayed, and misunderstood by the very therapist she has come to rely on. When the doom she expects has befallen her (even when she knows it's an old/new model scene), she truly cannot see her way back to reconnection and trust. But then we saw how such a crisis can be resolved when you attend with careful, patient, nondefensive understanding to your client's truth, precisely as that truth is felt and spoken.

Our journey moved on from crisis to denouement, from the "terribly hard" to the "wonderfully good" part of relational therapy, a transition that happens more easily in a text on relational therapy than it does in therapy itself. But although progress is made along circuitous routes and in fits and starts, each impasse broken, each crisis resolved, and each new mutual understanding achieved brings with it a quiet kind of well-being that your client may never have expected. The good feelings sneak up on her and slowly build into the quite wonderful, everyday goodness of being able to be here, okay in herself and connected to others. The rest of the chapter explored the various ways relational therapies account for this sense of well-being—from stories of selfobject needs met, to stories of attachment and development patterns reworked, to stories of imagination rekindled, to stories of "zestful" connection fostered.

The question came up: "What about falling in love in relational therapy?" I said that for a client, falling in love with you shouldn't be considered a problem; in fact, exploring her experience of loving and of having that love simply received could be very important to her healing and growth. On the other hand, I advised, if you notice any inclinations in yourself to cross a boundary of professional ethics with a client, run, don't walk, to your nearest supervisor and find out what's going on with you.

The next question was: "Could all this goodness be just the product of unhealthy dependency?" I answered: "No." Dependency is not by definition unhealthy; a truly unhealthy dependency can't produce well-being; and relational therapies, with their constant honest scrutiny of what goes on in the therapy relationship, have strong built-in protections against the misuse of that relationship. And then I ended that chapter on goodness with a story remarkable not for its massive breakthrough, nor for its grand illumination, but for its sneaky, quiet, unfinished self-with-other goodness: "I almost smiled at you today."

Now we've come to the last of these chapters, which is about the ending of therapy. Clearly, this chapter is a phase and a process, too. And that's just like the ending of therapy. You and your client don't just end therapy one day. You begin to end, and then later you finish ending. What is it that you do during all this ending?

LETTING THE STORY TELL ITSELF OUT

First of all you and your client realize that the story of her therapy is approaching its own natural end. Despite their different political stances and languages, all of the relational therapies suggest that the therapy story, played out with many disguises and reversals, has one basic plot: What's making your client feel bad will move from her life, from her history of subjugation, disconnection, and violation, from her interpersonal conflicts and debilitating symptoms, right into the relationship with you, her therapist.

There her story (her self-with-other history) will be transformed into a new two-person story, structured and powered by all the major relational themes of her life, but played out in a different way. The difference is inescapable, for you are a new and different person and no two relational stories can be the same. But the difference is also intentional, and the most important intentional difference is that both you and your client pay careful attention to what's going on. It's this attention that makes this story therapy and that also makes it a story full of meaning, not a series of random, unrelated events.

The story begins to end as the very conflicts that have made it a coherent and powerful story begin to find resolution. By resolution, I don't mean solutions or a cure. I mean the kind of resolution that belongs to a story well told: meaning emerges from chaos. Horrible events, painful recurring themes, lasting damage—none of this can be erased.

But a tragedy well-understood and well-told moves us with its meaning. Within it, we matter. And when we matter, when there is meaning for us, something changes. The change may be as hard to name as what happens within us as a last series of chords brings to an end the complex themes and variations of a powerful piece of music, but we know, we feel, that all that matters most in this story has been aired, and there is resolution.

It's not easy to end when there's always something more to add, lots of epilogue material. Yet it's epilogue to a story you and your client both know now. The story you both know takes somewhat different forms for different clients. For one client, the story has been all about finding someone trustworthy who could help her with the delicate gathering and slow reassembling of scattered fragments of herself. The story moved from lonely, baffling, chaotic pain to meaningful grief shared with someone who witnessed and understood. In the caring presence of another, she has found her own presence. The wholeness she feels lets you both know that her story is whole now, too, finished enough so that she can move on into a life that belongs to her and into relationships where she can know and be known, love and be loved.

Another client has unpacked most of her story by going through painful troubles in her relationship with you. Hoping for goodness while dreading doom was a subtle, neverending torture for her. She bore the havoc and despair wreaked by your misses and mistakes, sometimes mounting bitter retaliatory strikes, sometimes hunkering down, waiting for something to set her free. Every time she was surprised that your persistent, patient empathy could set the relationship free, eventually, and with every release both of you could feel the story deepening, making more powerful sense. You both know that this story is coming to resolution now because her desperate hopes have quieted into confidence that you are on her side even when you goof, and you no longer seem to have such deadly power to hurt her. In fact, she says that you look a lot like a normal, everyday person to her now, someone with your own troubles, joys, and challenges, someone whose life she doesn't know at all, but whose person she knows very well. For you've been through the wars together and come out the other side.

A third client has come to know her story through finding in you someone who could understand her and be there with her in simple ways she never thought possible. Your strength supported her, your smile brightened her accomplishments, and your everyday humanness made her feel human too. But this new attachment threw into stark relief the deprivation she came from. Taking in this goodness meant knowing how barren life has been for her and grieving the loss of what she has never had. The story of her therapy has become this tapestry of bright against dark. You and she know that the story is ending not only because the tapestry is rich, complex, and complete, but because she knows she can take it home with her. That is to say, the many things you have been for her all belong to her now. Whenever she wants to, she can look at the tapestry you wove together; she can think about it or wrap it around herself for strength, courage, and comfort.

Another client's story has been all about moving from a lonely, disempowered, disconnected place, a prison cell of "safety," toward the risks and rewards of connection. Connection with your empathy made emotional space for him to connect more lovingly with himself and it gave him the strength to seek and to find empowering, enlivening new connections with others. This plot works to shape a good, strong story, too. In fact, all of these are good plots for transformational relational stories, and some clients' stories borrow something from all of them.

As a relational therapist you know that it really doesn't matter how a client's story tells itself to you and your client. What matters is that you've both been paying attention, looking for meaning, and you haven't been disappointed. A story has indeed unfolded. There's a trajectory, a beginning, middle, and an end. Whether it tells itself in terms of fragmentated, dissociated experience reintegrated, transferences resolved, deficits filled, or relational strategies transformed, what matters is that your client now has meanings for what was wrong in his life, words for how you both held that wrongness and worked it out between you, and words for how it's not so wrong anymore.

Above all, in whatever way any client's story is told, it's a story that could have unfolded only in this relationship. With nobody to live it out with him, there would have been no story at all; and the story has taken this particular form because he has lived it out with you, a unique, particular person. The meanings of his extended interaction with you have been created by two worlds of subjectivity, two different, unique ways of organizing experience and relationship. And so your therapy is a first and last edition of this story, a one-of-a-kind creation never to be replicated. The shape of your joint story is not the shape of your client's "stuff." It's the shape of how his stuff met and clashed and melded with your stuff, and how the two of you sorted out the meanings of all of that.

As a relational therapist, you bring into every therapy relationship not only your convictions about how therapy works and your capacities for empathy, understanding, and insight, but also the strengths, gifts,

needs, and quirks of your personality. If this therapy has been meaningful and powerful for a client, it's because you have been there with him as
a person.

And it is this particular person to whom your client will now, soon,
say good-bye.

SAYING GOOD-BYE

Saying good-bye hurts. Grief hurts. But to be allowed to say good-bye
with gratitude and love as well as with sadness and loss is a privilege. Not
long ago, thousands of Canadians lined up for the privilege of taking a
few brief moments to stand before the casket of Pierre Trudeau and say
good-bye. Many more across the country signed books of condolences—
finding words to express what Trudeau meant to them, paying heartfelt
respects, saying meaningful farewells. Thousands of Canadians wept with
Justin Trudeau when he ended his father's eulogy with the words, "He
has kept his promises and earned his sleep. Je t'aime, papa."

And some of those who wept went to their therapy later that week
and wept again, suddenly and profoundly aware of their longing to be
able to say "Je t'aime, papa," and knowing that they would never be able
to say that kind of good-bye to a parent.

During that week, a colleague and I sat musing about what seems to
be a powerful human longing for a clean, deep, uncomplicated grief for
someone loved and honored. We don't want to lose such a person; the
loss causes us pain. But we need the grief, it seems. We move toward it.
Why? Because feeling grief is a way to make loss more than just absence
and emptiness; it's a way to let loss strengthen us. We grieve in order to
be able to take the memory of a loved one with us and to let it keep on
teaching us who we are.

We hear our clients saying, "I will never be able to grieve my father
or mother like that. When they die, I will be grieving for the relationship
I never had, the love I will never share with them." What are our clients
telling us? They seem to be saying that they, too, need and want a clean,
deep, remembering, strengthening kind of grief. To be robbed of such
grief is another grievous loss.

"Do you think that what we want is a grief that ends instead of grief
that never ends?" my colleague asked. "I mean, maybe grieving for what
you never had means that the grief can never really end."

I had been trying to write this chapter, and I disagreed. I said, "I think that when you don't know what you're missing and what's hurting you, then that pain never ends. But when you start to know what it is that you never had and you'll never have, then it becomes a *something*. It becomes not just nameless pain but a *something* you can truly grieve, and then that grief can come to an end, sometime, too." I thought to myself, "Somewhere in this conversation there's the essence of what I think it means for a client to say good-bye to her therapist when a deep and meaningful therapy is complete."

I think that when therapy has gone well and it's time to finish, saying goodbye will evoke both of those kinds of grief for a client, grief for what she never had, and grief for what she's losing. In this therapy in which she has reflected at length on all the major relationships and themes in her life, she already will have grieved for what she never had. The nameless pain of wanting will have become a something for her. She does know what she missed, which would have remained a mystery if she hadn't felt some of that missed goodness with you, her therapist. Over the course of this therapy, you have been the embodiment of many different aspects of what she never had and what she can't go back and have now. She has worked her way through those longings and losses one by one.

But a final good-bye will stir those feelings again, for it means she's giving up the last vestiges of hope that you might give her what she needs in order to change the story of her life and erase her pain. Leaving therapy faces her once again with the fact that her own story is the only story she'll ever have. Although she can be grateful that this is at least something to grieve now, and that therefore the grief will end, every time she does this kind of grieving, it just hurts. There's nothing good to carry away from it except a deeper knowing that she can bear being present in her own skin and in her own life.

But there's also a second kind of grief for your client as she ends therapy, grief for something she *has* had and is losing. If therapy has gone well and it's time to finish, she will be saying good-bye to someone who has become a very important part of her life. Your interest and care have been genuine. In certain ways, you know her more deeply than anyone else does, and she knows a great deal about your presence and being, too. The two of you have felt many feelings together, from fear to pain to joy, and you've worked hard to be honest with each other. In this relationship she's learned more about herself than she ever thought possible, not because you have acted as a teacher, but because you have been willing to engage and respond as a full participant in her process of self-discovery.

Now she will be losing contact with you, giving up the regular experience of being together.

That's what she's losing, and it's something like losing a loved one in whose presence she always felt loved and valued. She will miss your presence. The thought of life without you feels lonely and sad. But if, with your encouragement, she allows herself to move toward these feelings, to feel, for perhaps the first time in her life, a clean, deep, uncomplicated grief about losing someone she loves and respects, she will find herself strengthened. She will probably find words for some of what you have meant to her. Perhaps she'll speak those words directly to you. The two of you will reminisce about the hard times and high points you both remember, and you'll acknowledge the good work you've done together. You will help her realize that keeping herself open to memories and feelings about ending will make her loss more than just absence and emptiness. It will help fill the emptiness with a living, moving, many-faceted image of your relationship to carry with her, a vital memory that will keep on helping her know who she is.

As in so much of the rest of your client's therapy, what you do together is for her well-being, and yet, as you participate in your mutual process, you can't help but be moved, challenged, and strengthened yourself. So it goes with a good ending. There's grief in it for you, too, and sharing memories and feelings about ending will be as good for you as for your client.

WHAT WILL STAY WITH YOUR CLIENT AFTER THERAPY?

Memory is now and now is memory. If this is true about the effects of trauma in our lives, it is also true about the effects of love, care, and understanding. In other words, not only will you stay with your client as a remembered voice of compassionate understanding and as reliable presence backing her up, not only will she have clear, lasting images of how it felt to be with you, she will also carry with her many effects of your relationship that will never cross her conscious mind.

If memory is now and now is memory, that is, if memories are filed on account of their interpersonal emotional potency and according to their emotional meanings, and if, although this whole filing system remains mostly out of her awareness, it's constantly making sense of all of a client's current experiences of self and self-with-other, you can be sure that the potent emotional experiences of your therapy with her will have infiltrated her whole meaning-making system. She won't have to remember those important experiences, for they will be in her psychological bones, in her RIGs, in her organizing principles. Their effects will have already sneaked up on her as goodness that she never, of course, could have expected.

We've already talked a lot about the different forms such goodness takes: how she has absorbed your supportive and admirable qualities so that she feels whole, self-aware, and strong in a flexible, resilient sort of way; how she has developed new, more secure forms of being attached to others and new "model scenes" for speaking and finding what she needs; how she has found herself reconnected with others in ways that empower and enliven her; how she has discovered possibilities for meaning-making and creative self-expression that she could not have imagined before. Each of these kinds of goodness is an ongoing process, not a finished accomplishment or cure. As I've said many times, relational therapy is all about self-with-other in action; each of these forms of goodness comes down to a radically revised sense of how a client can be her self, which also means, simultaneously and inescapably, how she can do or "perform" herself in relationship with others.

So the relational answer to this question, "What stays with a client when therapy is over?" changes the terms of the question. The answer isn't a matter of particular insights or skills she'll have after therapy is over; it's about changes in the ways she can be and feel herself with others. These changes won't be something she has learned and will need to recall. They will be systemic, organic, and self-perpetuating. Her life will probably be much the same, but the way she walks it and feels it will be significantly different.

But what about all the old stuff in those old files? Has it been dumped? What about those powerful model scenes that for years have been telling your client who she is and what's possible for her? What about those strategies she has used for so long to make a semblance of connection while protecting herself from inevitable violation? Do the changes I'm talking about mean that she has been able to replace her destructive old interpersonal software with a completely new version? Sadly, no. The old stuff never goes away. It can't be dumped or erased. The changes I'm talking about mean that the old stuff gets relativized; now (to play with the metaphor) your client's system has the capacity to run more than one program. Most important, now she can notice when the program being run is causing problems, and often just noticing gives her access to another possibility. Or to put it another way, the old model scenes aren't the only truth about life anymore. They haven't been simply replaced by another truth, but they are now vulnerable to her new knowledge of alternative self-with-other truths that she has experienced from the inside out.

The different relational theories we've looked at would express this state of affairs in different ways. Self psychology would say that ongoing empathic processes between your client and others are necessary forever. It's always possible, under stress, for her to fall back into the oldest, most painful and fragmenting ways of experiencing self-with-other. However, because of your client's good therapy, she has been able to make different kinds of relationships with others, and it is this different, here-and-now experience of "selfobject support" that helps pull her out of the old places.

In the Stone Center story, the effects of your client's disconnected, lonely past have been overridden by the empowerment and zest of genuine connection. But her old doubts and anxieties will still lurk in the shadows, to emerge when things go wrong. Here again it's essential for her not to deny the old but to bring it into the presence of the new, into a newly supportive circle of social relationships. In this new place of being connected, your client's old relational images don't disappear, but she finds herself in different relation to them. The empathy she lives with now has softened the edges of the old images and loosened their grip, even when they still bother her. And staying in good connection with others helps her stay with a new set of relational images, one that does her far more good on a daily basis.

Relational psychoanalysis doesn't promise to help your client wipe out the old or invent something brand-new either. Instead, it helps her grasp and exercise her freedom to make new meanings out of old experiences, once their patterns have come to life in the give and take of the therapy relationship. It's a freedom she discovers in cooperative engagement with you, her therapist, and this nonhierarchical, creative endeavor of mutual recognition becomes a paradigm for living a life more open to others, and more open to possibilities, imagination, and creative self-expression. Of course it's always possible that she will find herself once again shunted off into a repetitive loop of stultifying interpersonal patterns. But having broken free once, now she will know how to try to find out what's going on; she knows how to talk it out, act it out, pay attention, and push on it—until something gives.

What stays with your client after the ending of an effective rela-

tional therapy? In short, *she* does—a "she" who has experienced significant changes in how she can be in the world. These changes will be present
with her in her daily performance of self-with-other and her daily experience of self.

RELATIONAL CHANGES CARRY ON . . . AND ON

If at the close of therapy, a client has changed in how he can perform and
experience himself with others, these changes will start to show themselves in all of the important relationships of his life. He will have noticed some changes long before therapy is over. Noticing change will have
been an important part of understanding how things were before the
change and then envisioning new possibilities.

One of the things that happens in the process of relational therapy,
in any of its models, is that a client's capacity for conversation with another person and for understanding another person is improved. He learns
from you not only how to be listened to, but also how to listen. He picks
up how to "make sense" with someone else, mutually. He learns how to
tolerate differences and talk about them. He has found out, by making
his way through difficult model scenes with you, that it can pay to stay in
connection and work on "what's happening" even when his desire to
quit and run away is strong.

All of this pays off most in his most significant relationships. He
can't expect his partner or his best friend to listen to him with your kind
of one-way sustained attention and unflagging empathy. That wouldn't
be an equal partnership or a mutual friendship. But it often happens
that once he knows from talking with you that he's worth listening to, he
starts to open up and talk a little more with his significant others. Since
he's less afraid he'll be discounted, he's less defensive and prickly at the
first sign of misunderstanding. Often this creates more space for his partner or friend to understand him. Furthermore, the good feeling of having been understood by you becomes a kind of settledness within him, a
space where he has time to listen to another's worries. He knows now
what he's giving when he gives undivided attention and the most accurate empathy he can find within himself.

When two people in an important relationship talk openly with
each other, each focusing on understanding the other's meanings and
feelings, the relationship can break free of the fears and expectations
each person has brought to it from the past. This commitment to having

empathy for each other's experience (which isn't the same as commit-ment to agree with each other) can carry a couple through very difficult times of conflicting wants and bitter frustrations. As they keep talking, as they each keep saying where they stand and what they think and feel, and as they each keep listening to the other with the intention of understand-ing and finding a way through together, they are bringing something new into being, a relationship that in its own way can be as powerful as a therapeutic relationship to change how both participants can be a self and a self-in-relation.

If your client is a parent, coming to understand his own childhood and the relationships between himself and his parents will have a pro-found effect on his relationships with his children. A study by attach-ment theorist Mary Main suggests that parents who have come to terms, in thought and feeling, with their own histories of insecure attachment are far less likely to repeat the behaviors that would replicate insecure attachment for their children.[1] In short, your client's understanding of his childhood relationships can free him to be himself with his children, rather than an unconscious copy of his parents.

If there's anything your client has learned in therapy about his own child-self, it's about the importance of empathy. He knows he could have survived everything that happened to him far better—he might even have thrived despite major losses and frustrations—if only someone had taken the time to pay attention to his reality and his feelings. Now that his empathy for his own child-self has opened up his empathy for his children's experience, and now that he's come to know with you how paying atten-tion is done, he can relax and just be there with his very small children. With his older children, he can enter the world of school, friends, hob-bies, and sports with his care and affirmation, but without having to make things right for them. He can approach his adolescents with confi-dence, knowing that he can both honor their privacy and offer them an important listening ear.

If his parents are alive and if he has brothers and sisters, he'll prob-ably find himself hoping that his relationships with them can change, too. He has realized that he learned disconnected forms of relationship at home. Since he has spent therapy time dealing with painful relational images and model scenes from the past, they have lost a lot of their power to disturb him. It makes some sense for him to think that if he could connect better with his parents and siblings now, he would be able to shake off more of the effects of those bad old disconnections. And it's true that if a client's family, despite its "dysfunction," still has some healthy flexibility, some open-ended, self-reflective humor about itself, and some capacity to foster talking about hard things, a client may be richly rewarded for his efforts to reconnect with family. He might be able to find his way toward mutual adult relationships not only with his siblings but also with his parents, and all of that would indeed do him a world of good.

However, the forces for sameness and against change are powerful in most families, and the more damaged, frightened, angry, and defensive the family members are, the more tightly they will cling to the ways they have always used to protect themselves. There were reasons your client could never connect much with his family before, and those reasons probably haven't gone away. He may possess an expanded repertoire of relational organizing principles—but they may not. As a colleague once said to me about her efforts to communicate with the isolated, fragmented people in her family: "I've just realized that I'm doing all the right things—but with the wrong people."

It can be difficult for a client to accept that these people whom he always wanted to know and love might be the wrong people for him to try to be close to now. But mixed in with his disappointment and grief, there can still be an important difference in how he can be with them: He can knowingly choose to give up the struggle to connect "for real." He can find that mix of closeness and distance that works best both to protect him from further hurt and also to express his compassion for their isolation and his respect for the complex persons that they are. It's sad, but also good, he finds, not to need them to be different anymore.

Your client's differentiation of a self in relation to his family has not been an easy process. They haven't helped it along much by changing *with* him. And yet even in these difficult family-of-origin relationships, his movement hasn't been toward "autonomy," toward being cut loose. It's been toward knowing how to be this son and brother in this family, this self with this particular history and heritage, and also this self who doesn't have to replicate the pain of previous generations.

Your client's capacities to be a differentiated self-in-relation and to connect where connection is possible will serve him well in all of life, not just in close social and familial relationships. In relational theory, healthy self-with-other experience is the ground out of which all other competent, generative, creative capacities grow. Self psychology tells us that selfobject needs, when met, develop into confident ambition, a commitment to ideals and community, and the capacity to feel and express empathy for others and to provide, in turn, for their growth and security.

Relational psychoanalysis leans toward a vision of existential authenticity, but that dream is grounded by the relationality of its vision: authenticity as what kind of response to the other, in responsible relationship
with whom? Acknowledging his indebtedness to Benjamin's feminist
theory on this point, Lewis Aron says that one of the major goals of
relational psychoanalysis is that analysands achieve the ability to participate, in all of life, in relationships of nondominating mutual recognition.[2]

Stone Center theorists insist, of course, that individual relationships
of mutuality are the ground for all healthy, mutually respectful and empowering social relations. On the global scene as well as on the interpersonal scene, what matters is not how individuals develop autonomy, but
rather, how individuals open themselves to mutually empowering relationships that extend outward in networks of respect and empowerment.
Stone Center theorists hope to raise the profile of the relationships that
foster such growth, and in so doing, to redefine public visions and goals.
They believe that women in particular, because of their relational strengths,
need to provide the leadership to move all of our societal structures away
from systems based on violence and coercion and toward systems based
on mutual connection and empowerment.

In summary, and put briefly, this relational therapy is not primarily
a journey inward. From the moments of "diagnosis" (what's wrong?), to
the therapist's intention to be-with as fully and deeply as possible, to the
kinds of goodness that flow from this connection, relational therapy is
always moving away from the fantasy of individual self-sufficiency and
toward the realities of human interdependence. Relational therapy offers
no recipe for transcendence, no escape from the realities of history, culture, conflict, and oppression, no exit to a better life, no rising above
pain. It offers only a better chance of being linked with others in this life,
of knowing the joys of kindness, respect, and love, and of trusting that
whatever befalls us, we don't have to be alone.

And now we have come to the end of our final chapter. As I said
earlier, ending is a phase, a conversation of its own. But it isn't a long
phase. So it goes in therapy. When all the ending is over, when you've
reminisced and summed things up, when your client has spoken her gratitude and you have spoken your appreciation of her, and when you have
attended to regrets and good-byes, there's nothing more to do but to let
your client go on her way, ready and able to live the changes that therapy
has set in motion. She is still the same person, living the life she's always
had, and yet you can both hope that her life can be profoundly (if quietly)

different now—just because she's finally more present, more comfortable and secure in herself, and more deeply connected with the people in her life who are on this journey with her.

What you can do now is wish her "Bon voyage!"—and remember her.

I wish you a good journey, too, as you undertake the challenging, difficult, and yet profoundly satisfying work of relational psychotherapy. May you find community that supports your continued development as a person and as a therapist.

ENDNOTES

1. Mary Main, "Recent Studies in Attachment: Overview with Selected Implications for Clinical Social Work," in *Attachment Theory: Social, Developmental, and Clinical Perspectives*, Eds. S. Goldberg, R. Muir, and J. Kerr (Hillsdale, NJ: Analytic Press, 1995), 407–474.
2. Aron, *A Meeting of Minds*, 148–154.

REFERENCES

Ainsworth, M. (1978). *Patterns of attachment: A psychological study of the strange situation.* Hillsdale, NJ: Lawrence Erlbaum.

Altman, Neil. (1995). *The analyst in the inner city: Race, class, and culture through a psychoanalytic lens.* Hillsdale, NJ: Analytic Press.

Aron, L. (1996). *A meeting of minds: Mutuality in psychoanalysis.* Hillsdale, NJ: Analytic Press.

Atwood, G., & Stolorow, R. (1984). *Structures of subjectivity: Explorations in psychoanalytic phenomenology.* Hillsdale, NJ: Analytic Press.

Bacal, H. (Ed.). (1998). *Optimal responsiveness: How therapists heal their patients.* Northvale, NJ: Jason Aronson.

Bacal, H., & Newman, K. (1990). *Theories of object relations: Bridges to self psychology.* New York: Columbia University Press.

Beebe, B., Jaffe, J., Lachmann, F., Feldstein, S., Crown, C., & Jasnow, M. (2000). Systems models in development and psychoanalysis: The case of vocal rhythm coordination and attachment. *Infant Mental Health Journal, 21*(1–2), 99–122.

Benjamin, J. (1988). *The bonds of love: Psychoanalysis, feminism, and the problem of domination.* New York: Pantheon.

Benjamin, J. (1995). *Like subjects, love objects: Essays on recognition and sexual difference.* New Haven and London: Yale University Press.

Boston Process of Change Study Group. (1998). (Nadia Bruschweiler-Stern, Alexandra M. Harrison, Karlen Lyons-Ruth, Alexander C. Morgan, Jeremy P. Nahum, Louis Sander, Daniel Stern, & Edward Z. Tronick). Special issue of *Infant Mental Health Journal, 19*(3).

Bowlby, J. (1988). *A secure base: Parent–child attachment and healthy human development.* New York: Basic Books.

Brandchaft, B. (1994). To free the spirit from its cell. In R. Stolorow, G. Atwood, & B. Brandchaft (Eds.), *The intersubjective perspective* (pp. 57–76). Northvale, NJ: Jason Aronson.

Bromberg, P. M. (1998). *Standing in the spaces: Clinical process, trauma and dissociation.* Hillsdale, NJ: Analytic Press.

Brown, L. (1994). *Subversive dialogues: Theory in feminist therapy.* New York: Basic Books.

Chesler, P. (1972). *Women and madness.* New York: Doubleday.

213

Davies, J. M., & Frawley, M. G. (1994). *Treating the adult survivor of childhood sexual abuse: A psychoanalytic perspective.* New York: Basic Books.

Ehrenberg, D. B. (1992). *The intimate edge: Extending the reach of psychoanalytic interaction.* New York: W.W. Norton.

Freud, S. (1953–1966). *The standard edition of the complete psychological works of Sigmund Freud* (James Strachey, Trans.). London: Hogarth Press.

Herman, J. L. (1992). *Trauma and recovery.* New York: Basic Books.

Jordan, J. V., Kaplan, A. G., Miller, J. B., Stiver, I. P., & Surrey, J. L. (1991). *Women's growth in connection: Writings from the Stone Center.* New York: Guilford Press.

Jordan, J. (1991). Empathy and self boundaries. In J. Jordan et al. (Eds.), *Women's growth in connection: Writings from the Stone Center* (pp. 67–80). New York: Guilford Press.

Jordan, J. (1991). The meaning of mutuality. In J. Jordan et al. (Eds.), *Women's growth in connection: Writings from the Stone Center* (pp. 81–96). New York: Guilford Press.

Jung, C., & von Franz, M. L. (Eds.). (1964). *Man and his symbols.* New York: Doubleday.

Kohut, H. (1984). *How does analysis cure?* Chicago: University of Chicago Press.

Lichtenberg, J. (1989). *Psychoanalysis and motivation.* Hillsdale, NJ: Analytic Press.

Lichtenberg, J., Lachmann, F., & Fosshage, J. (1992). *Self and motivational systems: Toward a theory of psychoanalytic technique.* Hillsdale, NJ: Analytic Press.

Lyons-Ruth, K. (1998). Implicit relational knowing: Its role in development and psychoanalytic treatment. *Infant Mental Health Journal, 19*(3), 282–289.

Main, M. (1995). Recent studies in attachment: Overview with selected implications for clinical social work. In S. Goldberg, R. Muir, & J. Kerr (Eds.), *Attachment theory: Social, developmental, and clinical perspectives* (pp. 407–474). Hillsdale, NJ: Analytic Press.

McNamee, S., & Gergen, K. J. (Eds.). (1992). *Therapy as social construction.* Newbury Park, CA: Sage.

Miller, J. B., & Stiver, I. P. (1997). *The healing connection: How women form relationships in therapy and in life.* Boston: Beacon.

Mitchell, S. A. (1988). *Relational concepts in psychoanalysis: An integration.* Cambridge, MA: Harvard University Press.

Mitchell, S. A. (1993). *Hope and dread in psychoanalysis.* New York: Basic Books.

Mitchell, S. A. (1997). *Influence and autonomy in psychoanalysis.* Hillsdale, NJ: Analytic Press.

Mitchell, S. A. (2000). *Relationality: From attachment to intersubjectivity.* Hillsdale, NJ: Analytic Press.

Orange, D. M. (1995). *Emotional understanding: Studies in psychoanalytic epistemology.* New York: Guilford Press.

Pérez Foster, R., Moskowitz, M., & Javier, R. A. (Eds.). (1996). *Reaching across boundaries of culture and class: Widening the scope of psychotherapy.* Northvale, NJ: Jason Aronson.

Renik, O. (1966). The perils of neutrality. *Psychoanalytic Quarterly, 65,* 495–517.

Rogers, C. (1942). *Counseling and psychotherapy.* Boston: Houghton Mifflin.

Rogers, C. (1961). *On becoming a person.* Boston: Houghton Mifflin.

Stern, D. (1985). *The interpersonal world of the infant: A view from psychoanalysis and developmental psychology.* New York: Basic Books.

Stiver, I. (1991). The meanings of dependency in female–male relationships. In J. Jordan et al. (Eds.), *Women's growth in connection: Writings from the Stone Center* (pp. 143–161). New York: Guilford Press.

Stolorow, R. D., & Atwood, G. E. (1992). *Contexts of being: The intersubjective foundations of psychological life*. Hillsdale, NJ: Analytic Press.

Stolorow, R. D., Atwood, G. E., & Brandchaft, B. (Eds.). (1994). *The intersubjective perspective*. Northvale, NJ: Jason Aronson.

Sullivan, H. S. (1953). *The interpersonal theory of psychiatry*. New York: W.W. Norton.

Surrey, J. (1991). The self-in-relation: A theory of women's development. In J. Jordan et al. (Eds.), *Women's growth in connection: Writings from the Stone Center* (pp. 59-61). New York: Guilford Press.

White, M., & Epston, D. (1990). *Narrative means to therapeutic ends*. New York: W.W. Norton.

Wolf, E. (1988). *Treating the self: Elements of clinical self psychology*. New York: Guilford Press.

INDEX